To
my five daughters-in-law
Hilary, Natasha, Gaby,
Claude and Mioko

SHAKESPEARE
DOMESTICATED

Shakespeare Domesticated

The eighteenth-century editions

Colin Franklin

Scolar Press

Published by
SCOLAR PRESS
Gower House
Croft Road
Aldershot
Hants GU11 3HR
England

Gower Publishing Company
Old Post Road
Brookfield
Vermont 05036
USA

British Library Cataloguing in Publication Data
Franklin, Colin
    Shakespeare domesticated : the eighteenth century editions.
    1. Drama in English. Shakespeare, William, 1564–1616 –
    critical studies
    I. Title
    822.33

    ISBN 0–85967–834–2 C ∪

Library of Congress Cataloging-in-Publication Data
Franklin, Colin.
    Shakespeare domesticated : the eighteenth century editions / Colin
Franklin
        p. cm.   60 03621974
    Includes index.
    ISBN 0–85967–834–2
    1. Shakespeare, William, 1564–1616 – Criticism and interpretation –
History – 18th century. 2. Shakespeare, William, 1564–1616 –
Editors. 3. Editing – History – 18th century. I. Title.
PR2968.F7 1991
822.3′3–dc20   90–28251
                CIP

Printed and bound in Great Britain by
Billing and Sons Limited, Worcester.

Contents

Illustrations

List of Plates

Acknowledgements

I am especially grateful to Sheila Markham for finding learned articles I would otherwise have missed; to Harriet Hawkins, Fellow of Linacre College Oxford, for her critical reading of the typescript; to Carolyn Clark for patiently creating and correcting it from my hand-writing. Laura McGeary's detailed editorial suggestions were extremely useful. David McKitterick made available Edward Capell's manuscripts in the Wren Library at Trinity College Cambridge, Elizabeth Neimyer provided a memorable visit to 18th-century editions at the Folger Library, the London Library has given courteous help. Jean-Paul Getty allowed me to borrow for months a rare assembly of engravings (in a precious binding) and Bill Fletcher generously lent his set of Rowe's edition on large paper. My wife Charlotte has as ever shared and guided my pleasures in the subject.

Note

In keeping with the style of the 18th century, all variant spellings of Shakespeare's name have been retained.

1 Introduction

Shakespeare criticism has swerved and swung between sensitivity and science; both concepts were born in the 18th century. His earliest editors and critics were poets, or gentlemen of taste, or professional scholars. None of the editions came direct from either university, no faculty of English existed; Oxford happened to publish the least academic of them all, but several fellows of colleges on occasion helped and advised. In this most accessible subject anyone could join the debate, and did, and has ever since.

Eighteenth-century editions of Shakespeare form a valid subject, limited, complete. This book is concerned with the succession of Collected Works, sometimes including the Poems, sometimes not, and their editors. Through most decades since the late 16th century there had been small-format pamphlet editions of single plays, generally known as the quartos, commonly for use by actors; in 1709 what publishers call a library edition appeared for the first time, six pleasant octavo volumes for home reading, each play illustrated by an engraving. This new kind of Shakespeare publication grew through the century, with ample debate among the editors; its proper conclusion was not in the year 1800, but with the 21-volume variorum edition of 1821.

It would be wrong to declare that there were no editors of Shakespeare before 1709; the first collected edition appearing in 1623 seven years after he died provided formidable problems for the two who prepared it, his actor colleagues Heminge and Condell, in choosing which words to print, and which plays to include, for they had decisions to take among a confusion of author's manuscript, production manuscript (prompt copy), published quartos of greater and less authority, and oral tradition. The result, to which the world owes vast debt, left legions of difficulties as to sense, printers' errors,

1

compositors' errors, and matters of choice; every scope remained for a more analytic kind of editing together with the need, a century later, to unravel obscurities by wide reading which discovered comparable usage among contemporary writers.

The clearest and most recent detective work upon the 1623 'First Folio' is to be found in Gary Taylor's introduction to the new Oxford Shakespeare. His essay in the Textual Companion to that edition has comments relevant to 18th-century editors in their two approaches, analysis and sensitivity:

> Earlier editors devoted their labours almost exclusively to problems of emendation, with scant regard to the circumstances of transmission; modern textual critics have, for the most part, simply reversed the prejudice.
> Bibliography aspires to the status of a science; at the least it can claim to be an archaeology of texts. Emendation is, by contrast, all too obviously an art – an art for which the despised poet-editors of the eighteenth century might have been rather better equipped, in some respects, than their sophisticated academic twentieth-century successors. Perhaps for this reason, the twentieth century has produced little fruitful discussion of the theory and practice of emendation in Shakespeare's text.

Nobody would now keep every phrase of the First Folio, as in different ways each word of the 1611 Bible might yet be defended, but the view of emendation has completely changed. Taylor ends his essay with disarming diffidence:

> A successful work of scholarship stimulates the very research which will make it obsolete, and, with our own task now behind us, we look forward to our future obsolescence.

– not in the same spirit as Warburton's claim on the title page of his edition from 1747:

> The Genuine Text (collated with all the former Editions, and then corrected and emended) is here settled: Being restored from the *Blunders* of the first two Editors, and the *Interpolations* of the two Last.

Emendation and interpretation absorbed the 18th-century editors, who found every sort of worry in the texts they received. Greek and Latin poets, philosophers, theologians shrouded with critical apparatus were familiar presences in any library, but no English author had been examined in this way before, every line and phrase teased and combed for meaning; Shakespeare as classic author induced the birth of English literary criticism. Emendation reckoned necessary now as then became a science by means of analysis and comparison while sensitivity or taste made decisions between alternative readings. Three computers enabled the modern Oxford editors to be much more precise about Shakespeare's part and Fletcher's in writing *Henry the Eighth*, than was possible for Johnson, who could only conclude as any reader may, that 'the genius of Shakespeare comes in and goes out with Catherine'.

As it was common for an editor to use the most recent text, if only to oppose and replace it, several traditions occur through the century. Theobald, Warburton and Hanmer all used Pope; Johnson's edition, changed and challenged in detail, remained with his name attached for 50 years after its first appearance; Malone, admired now as most dependable among them all, dominated the end of the period; only Capell, with a different version based on early quartos, produced no followers.

From Samuel Johnson to Gordon Craig it has sometimes been said that Shakespeare is better enjoyed in one's own chair at home than from a theatre seat, and in the whole history of Shakespearean *book* production none holds more charm, caught between two worlds, than these 18th-century editions. Before them, the four heavy folios; after, editorial dictation and selection. Among the editors from Rowe to Malone, as their subject developed within manageable scope, one may yet be present at a living debate. From different approaches they worked towards comprehension of a subject which had not become monolithic. Their notes, if one bothers to read them, form a running discourse of suggestion and dispute, civilized argument through more than ten decades, conversational rivalry of such evenings as Boswell recorded. Modern notes are likely to focus upon technical justification for variant readings.

Visually the books represent their time, which looks better than when William Morris viewed it a century ago; sometimes rising above, seldom falling below, occasionally reaching for the heights. The fact is that an ordinary page of type on hand-made paper from the 18th century, before those industrial inventions which produced millions of fox-marked books on machine-made chemical paper, gives pleasure enough without ornament or art; the average volumes of Rowe, Theobald, Johnson and Malone please us now. Boydell's large folios from the 1790s are unbeatable for typographic excellence. Warburton's edition looks wretched, each in its fastidious way provides that peace which the world seldom gives.

There is no correct text of Shakespeare, every version being more or less corrupt; the editors tried to get it right and we shall not be corrupted by reading the volumes they produced. The more scrupulous observed their promises to confine new suggestions or emendations to footnotes, where reasons for every proposed change were given; Pope and Hanmer showed less scruple in this. Nobody risks his experience of Shakespeare by reading an 18th-century edition.

Even if the number of volumes grew from six to 21, from Rowe in 1709 to the variorum editions of 1803, 1813 and 1821, they kept their domesticity; these were for reading at home, not removed (as of course the 'New Variorum' is) for scholarship. Johnson's robust advice about notes comes towards the end of his Preface:

> Notes are often necessary, but they are necessary evils. Let him, that is yet unacquainted with the powers of Shakespeare, and who desires to feel the highest pleasure that the drama can give, read every play from the first scene to the last, with utter negligence of all his commentators. When his fancy is once on the wing, let it not stoop at correction or explanation. When his attention is strongly engaged, let it disdain alike to turn aside to the name of Theobald or of Pope. Let him read on through brightness and obscurity, through integrity and corruption; let him preserve his comprehension of the dialogue and his interest in the fable. And when the pleasures of novelty have ceased, let him attempt exactness, and read the commentators.

But the pleasures of novelty can extend to the informal art of 18th-century exegesis, those footnote debates where they knew that they trespassed beyond the proper borders of reticence. Steevens wrote in his 1793 Advertisement that 'they whose remarks are longest, and who seek the most frequent opportunities of introducing their names at the bottom of our author's page, are not, on that account, the most estimable critics'. Replete with self-knowledge, nobody's notes longer than his own, it was a temptation difficult to resist. He also foresaw that this ever-lengthening footnote game could not forever continue in domestic editions, that such faults of excess 'within half a century, (when the present race of voluminous critics is extinct) cannot fail to be remedied by a judicious and frugal selection from the labours of us all'. He was right, but judicious and frugal selections are no substitute for their presence, dead or living, the 18th-century critics assembled in debate.

Theobald in his footnotes often quoted whole paragraphs of Warburton, from their correspondence, sometimes with tacit acceptance but ready at others to explain why he chose to differ. It was the start of footnote dispute, the seed of a variorum edition. Pope had printed Rowe's *Life*, changing it here and there to a version which was often followed through the 18th century. Theobald used Rowe within his own Preface, and saw no reason to print Pope's Preface. It became common practice after Johnson to print the whole succession of Prefaces, with other essays and researches.

These habits were possible in the prevailing law of copyright. An editor received payment for his edition, by which was meant his text and apparatus; the custom of royalties for copies sold had not yet begun. There seems to have been no breach of authors' copyright[*] in quoting at length other prefaces, long paragraphs of notes and interpretation, and any sort of critical essay; an editor expected the courtesy of quotation if only as prelude to debate. A famous fuss began in the 1780s when Malone refused to reprint, in his own edition, his criticism of notes by Steevens which had appeared – together with Steevens's notes – in Isaac Reed's edition. Malone felt he must keep the freedom to change his mind; Steevens wanted them there for the record, so that he could continue the controversy. This disagreement interrupted a friendship and brought Steevens back to work on Shakespeare for his long edition of 1793. Footnote debate assumed the character of correspondence in a journal. Present-day law allows quotation of 'short passages for the purpose of criticism', a far cry from the leisured practice of publisher and editor in the mid-18th century. I have the right to quote some witty sentence from the latest Oxford editors, if I wish, as for instance: 'Editing might therefore be provisionally defined as a total waste of time which periodically reconstructs our image of the past'. If I chose to print the whole essay without permission (which would not be given) all sorts of trouble and retribution would follow.

H. L. Ford in 1935[1] wrote that 'for those of antiquarian taste without the means of a Midas, there are the first octavo or smaller editions of the sets, and the many issues of the separately published plays printed in the early part of the eighteenth century still available', and that 'there is a charm attached to these early examples that one may seek for in vain elsewhere'. Both his points, charm and availability, remain true half a century later. Ford stopped in mid-18th century. This book will in no way stand comparison with his; I have not given collations, this is not a bibliography; but as neither charm nor availability ends at 1749 I take the natural conclusion to be 1821, stretching it occasionally to include the first editions edited by Singer (1826) and by Knight (1838–43). For anything approaching a complete list of sets of Shakespeare across this period, one refers and defers to Jaggard's standard *Shakespeare Bibliography*, printed at Stratford in 1911. I am concerned with about 20 among them which deserve separate attention because they were indeed new editions (new editors, or the familiar names returning to present new material) or because of their engravings and woodcuts and, occasionally, the typography.

The Fourth Folio, 1685, was a reprint without editorial innovation,

---

[*] A 14-year rule was of benefit to publishers but not authors.
[1] *Shakespeare 1700–1749*, Oxford University Press

21 years after the Third Folio,[*] which came 32 years after the Second. Rowe's enchanting illustrated six-volume octavos appeared 24 years after the Fourth Folio; these and their successors through the length of this book remain by great good luck relatively neglected. A gulf exists, as when Ford wrote, but inflated by time and taste, between the last Folio and first octavo, first illustrated, first edited set; inexplicable except by such quirks of collecting as divide books printed in 1499 (incunabula) from others in 1501.

I should confess, at risk of irritation, that over a remarkably short span of months and with memorable pleasure it was not difficult to assemble the collection I was seeking; thus it has been possible to enjoy an 18th-century experience of reading and writing at home. My chief sources are those editions, a few 18th-century critics, and the 17 volumes of Nichols' *Literary Anecdotes* and *Literary History*, 1812 and 1817.

---

[*] Different impressions of the third folio were issued in 1663 and 1664.

2 The Editions

Good printing is quickly recognized; less easy to analyse, from Pynson to Virginia Woolf, is the charm of its poverty, the failure to rise to an occasion, when under-emphasis in books as in manners becomes more attractive than overstatement. Both occurred in 18th-century Shakespeares. A hundred years later the head of an Oxford College praised his friend's home-printing as having the 'tasteful Tudor touch'.[1] Shakespeare's poems, published in his lifetime, had just that: verses in small type between thick bands of printers' ornament repeated page to page in *The Passionate Pilgrim*, 1599; more matter and less art in the larger type used by Richard Field six years earlier for *Venus and Adonis*, and in 1594 for *Lucrece*. *Shake-Speares Sonnets Never before Imprinted*, 1609, a poor unimaginative performance, suggests decline had set in. For such a major effort as the 1611 Bible all stops were pulled out; folio bibles and Prayer Books through the 17th century exhibited large type and crude decoration; bound sumptuously, as they often were, these stand as handsome monuments. Nobody could claim as much for the Shakespeare folios, or any literary work from the English 17th century, among which few are more wretched to view and handle than first editions of *Paradise Lost*.

I had written 'to view and read', but that would not be true, for a printer's understatement – even his incompetence – may possess stronger appeal than proportion, design and impression. There is a touching moment in *All's Well that Ends Well* when Bertram, exposed defeated and deflated says 'Simply the thing I am shall make

---

[1] Warren of Magdalen, to Daniel of Worcester

7

me live'. The attraction of all these early examples is survival as simply the things they were.

The First Folio, a noble labour of organization, showed English printing at its low ebb and the other three were imitations: poor type unevenly inked, within blundering efforts towards rules and borders. Decorative bands and triangles before each play, and after where space allowed, could not redeem it. Margins were minimal. Without suggesting one might ever prefer a reproduction to the real thing, Horace Hart's Oxford facsimile, 1902, on good paper with margins beyond the old page, becomes almost a fine book to use.

A better period for English printing opened with the new century; Clarendon's *History of the Rebellion*, produced at Oxford between 1702 and 1704, is often mentioned as evidence. No publisher flew higher than Tonson in such fine folios as his edition of Prior's *Poems on Several Occasions* (1718) with its clear large type, powerfully impressed decorations and illustrations, on strong paper. England, after 60 and 70 years, was taking more than a hint from the Imprimerie Royale. His edition of Caesar's *Commentaries* (1712) was upon an even more splendid scale. A new kind of publisher, friend of Pope, member and secretary of the Kit-Kat Club, Jacob Tonson called the shop to which he moved in 1710 *Shakespear's-Head*, hanging above the entrance a portrait which survives. Early in his career he had, to quote David Daiches who phrased it carefully, 'bought the rights of the folio text of Shakespeare from the publishers of the Fourth Folio'. There cannot have been in the history of literature a more wonderful acquisition; so it is curious that Tonson, whose imagination ranged freely, never undertook an edition of Shakespeare comparable with other folios by which he is remembered. Magnificence, for better or worse, came upon Shakespeare from Boydell in the 1790s.

Except for Boydell, who lived at the start of a fine-book era, visually these 18th-century editions were free of bombast; the two which showed some tendency that way (Pope's and Hanmer's) are reckoned textually the worst.

ROWE

Tonson published the first modern edition of Shakespeare's plays in 1709, edited by Nicolas Rowe, a playwright who became Poet Laureate in 1714. Nobody has been very complimentary[2] about those six octavo volumes from that day to this; his 'attempts as an editor were so trifling, as not to require the least notice', wrote Benjamin Victor to Garrick. Rowe and Tonson deserved a better epitaph for their innovation, modestly produced in modern spelling, illustrated with engravings, introducing act and scene divisions where these had been neglected. From 1709 to 1725, if you wanted the latest edition of Shakespeare in one form or another you bought Rowe.

It was twice printed in 1709; they count as first and second editions, word-for-word the same; a few minimal rearrangements of type, an upside-down initial letter, were analysed by Ford in his Oxford book. The printer would not have been so rich in equipment as to have kept type standing for such a long work against possible reprint; it was all set up again in the same year. Page numbers continued from volume to volume, an example not followed in other editions, scene five of the fifth act of *Locrine* ending on page 3324. This remains a very attractive reading edition, witness to Tonson's first intention in planning it. To that extent and for its innovations Jaggard the bibliographer's comment is true: 'In importance and interest, this edition ranks second perhaps to the editio princeps', placing it above the Second, Third and Fourth Folios. That Tonson remembered the existence of book collectors was shown by the issue of a few copies on large paper.

Margins of normal copies were not generous. A thick band of printer's flowers or rectangular ornament appears above the opening of each play, and a simple triangular arrangement or vignette was used on each title page – conventional treatment. Jaggard gives a formidable list of firsts: 'first manual text, the first to present a biography of the poet, the first to bear an editor's name, the first to possess illustrations, and the first of the endless army of editions in octavo'. His last seems to repeat his first point, and it could be argued that Heminge and Condell were editorial names. Rowe's general title reads simply '*The Works of Mr. William Shakespear; in Six Volumes.* Adorn'd with Cuts. Revis'd and Corrected, with an Account of the Life and Writings of the Author. By N. Rowe, Esq;' with Jacob Tonson's name and his address 'within *Grays-Inn* Gate, next *Grays-*

---

[2] Johnson went out of his way to be kind

THE

WORKS

O F

Mr. *William Shakespear*;

I N

SIX VOLUMES.

ADORN'D with CUTS.

Revis'd and Corrected, with an Account of
the Life and Writings of the Author.
By *N. ROWE*, Efq;

L O N D O N:

Printed for *Jacob Tonfon*, within *Grays-Inn*
Gate, next *Grays-Inn* Lane. MDCCIX.

1 Title page of Rowe, 1709. [Actual height of *type* $6\frac{1}{4}$ inches]

Inn Lane', just before Tonson moved to Shakespear's Head by Drury Lane.

As Tonson had bought copyright in the Fourth Folio plays, not the poems, Pope's enemy Curll issued a volume of the poems, calling it 'Volume the Seventh'. It was almost uniform with the others though the type was different and editorial apparatus more extensive, 'With Critical Remarks on his Plays, &c. to which is Prefix'd an ESSAY on the Art, Rise and Progress of the STAGE in *Greece, Rome* and *England*'. That essay, in part a vigorous reply to passages in Rowe's *Life* though tacked on to the volume which pretended to be Rowe's seventh, opened a controversy which absorbed later editors.

Publishers and editors were always doubtful as to whether they should include Shakespeare's poems in his collected works or not. Rowe's editions had them as an additional semi-piratical volume, though in the last (mentioned below) they entered fully. Pope's seventh volume had the same status as the seventh of 1709, but the poems did not reappear as part of a collected edition before Malone's supplementary volume (1780) to the Johnson and Steevens edition of 1778.[3] In his Advertisement for the larger edition of 1793 Steevens wrote: 'We have not reprinted the Sonnets, &c. of Shakespeare, because the strongest act of Parliament that could be framed, would fail to compel readers into their service'. It is not astonishing that they had no place even in the 21-volume variorum for which Steevens was nominally responsible, in 1803 and 1813, but they appeared in volume 20 of Malone's 1821 variorum; not again in any version of substance before Knight.

The several title pages of Rowe's duodecimo edition 1714, in eight and nine volumes, are described in detail by Ford. The third title page, for separate issue of the same sheets, had Tonson and Curll together among the publishers for this version in nine volumes, for which the general title page read:

> The Works of Mr. William Shakespear, in Nine Volumes: With his Life, by N. Rowe Esq; Adorn'd with Cuts. To the last Volume is prefix'd, I. An Essay on the Art, Rise, and Progress of the Stage, in Greece, Rome, and England. II. Observations upon the most Sublime Passages in this Author. III. A Glossary explaining the Antiquated Words made use of throughout his Works.

It advanced from the 1709 edition in planting several roots of critical discussion, which thrived and spread through the century. These pleasant and readable books in small format were supposed by Ford to have been taken for common or garden use, domestic rather than

---

[3] Bell's edition of 1773–4, of no textual authority, included a volume of the poems

library sets. Jaggard called this 'the first stage edition, being produced for sale at the theatres, and for disposal to pedlars who distributed the plays in rural districts', without evidence for his romantic and Autolycan statement. They were page-numbered volume by volume, rather than first to last as in 1709, but not play by play. Most of the 1714 illustrations were similar to those used in 1709, engraved for the smaller format, left to right (see Chapter 6, Illustration). From size, ease of borrowing or numbers printed, the nine volumes from 1714 seem harder to find than the seven from 1709–10.

POPE

Rowe died in 1718; Tonson chose Pope, who was finishing his version of the *Iliad*, for the next edition. The six handsome quartos, so different from Rowe's little books, printed and ready in 1723 but not issued until 1725, suggest an imaginative approach to publishing – but Pope had the habit of quarto and folio; these compare with the Homers. If one were to seek firsts everywhere, I suppose this was the first modern *un*illustrated edition. They were handsomely produced, in the manner of Pope first editions, on good paper with attractive initials and woodcut decoration. It was also the first royal quarto Shakespeare.

Jaggard gives a half-truth, always repeated, 'Volume one is dated 1725; the other five 1723'. It is a point of slight interest. Each volume of plays had the 1723 title page, but Pope kept Tonson waiting for his Preface – also for the complex curious Indexes at the end of volume six. The general title page, in two colours, was dated 1725. Though there is no trace of offset through all the plays, in my copy every leaf of the Preface, Rowe's *Life* and the list of subscribers – the separately numbered prelims – has suffered from offset; but this is not true of the British Library or Folger copies. In haste to get copies bound and out, early sets were pressed before the ink on the prelims dried. The Tonson dynasty, martyrs to editors, faced a similar problem with Samuel Johnson.

'The Seventh Volume' (the poems) had nothing to do with Pope or Tonson; 'The Whole Revis'd and Corrected, with a Preface, By Dr. Sewell', stands to this set as Gildon's extra volume to the Rowe editions before Tonson arranged in 1714 to include it.

MEASURE *for* MEASURE.

ACT I. SCENE I.

A PALACE.

Enter Duke, Efcalus, *and Lords.*

DUKE.

SCALUS.

 Efcal. My lord.

 Duke. Of Government, the properties t' unfold,
Would feem in me t' affect fpeech and difcourfe.
Since I am [a] not to know, that your own fcience
Exceeds, in that, the lifts of all advice
My ftrength can give you: then no more remains;
Put that to your fufficiency, as your worth is able,
And let them work. The nature of our people,
Our city's inftitutions, and the terms
Of common juftice, y'are as pregnant in,
As art and practice hath enriched any
That we remember. There is our commiffion,
From which we would not have you warp. Call hither,
I fay, bid come before us *Angelo:*
What figure of us think you he will bear?
For you muft know, we have with fpecial foul
Elected him our abfence to fupply;

 VOL. I.   T t   Lent

 [a] *put to know.*

2 A page from Pope, 1723. [Actual height of *type area* 9 inches]

THEOBALD 1733

The Works of Shakespeare: in Seven Volumes. Theobald's first edition followed his famous controversy with Pope and detailed correspondence with Pope's friend Warburton. 'Collated with the Oldest Copies, and Corrected; with Notes Explanatory, and Critical' the general title declared, and though Rowe and Pope used similar wording, Theobald's claim was justified. Nobody will ever agree as to the correctness of corrections, but he had done the work.

'The plates are accepted,' one reads in Jaggard, 'together with those in Rowe's 1709 edition, as the earliest authentic pictures of the contemporary dress of the characters.' Jaggard may have examined a grangerized copy, for there were no illustrations except the portrait.

Tonson was present among a syndicate of six publishers. This octavo edition returned to the style of Rowe's (1709), using better paper and decent type. With Theobald's focus on exposition, clarity replaced the mild luxury of Pope's quartos and Rowe's illustrations. This was the first edition with what must then have seemed very ample footnotes. Minor woodcut ornament completed the routine of that day.

Theobald's long Preface included much of Rowe's *Life.* The title of his Table at the end of volume seven showed the new kind of editor at work, a collector working from his own library: 'A Table of the several Editions of Shakespeare's Plays, Collected by the Editor'. This was his absorption, not merely a job commissioned. It is not trespassing too deep to mention here that he divided the editions into three categories of which the last is 'Editions of no Authority'; there he placed Rowe and Pope, and that ends his work except for the Erratum note, a Freudian slip:

> In the Title of the above *Table,* instead of *Collected* by the Editor, read, *Collated* by &c.

Choose which you prefer: it stood corrected in his second edition but Theobald possessed a notable collection.

THEOBALD 1740

Theobald's second edition differed more from 1733 than Rowe's 1714 edition had varied from that of 1709. A memorable series of illustrations appeared here for the first time, one for each play. His Preface and the notes, by which Theobald is best remembered, were both reduced for smaller format, and the custom of printing other men's Prefaces had not yet started. Warburton appeared in the notes, many of which came almost verbatim from their long correspondence, and at the end of volume eight Pope's complex 'Index of the Characters, Sentiments, Similes, Speeches and Descriptions in Shakespeare' was repeated. Difficult to use, generally unhelpful, through the whole period Glossaries and Beauties proliferated. Theobald 1740 was not well printed but the engravings make it an attractive edition.

TONSON 1734

A duodecimo edition, included in this list because it was the first set of the plays issued separately for performance, each with title page illustration, and new page-numbering. The whole assembly may be found bound in seven volumes, including what Malone called the 'doubtful' plays, in no particular order. The first volume included a portrait, and Rowe's *Life* conveniently filled a 12-leaf section followed by the doubtful *Life and Death of Thomas Cromwell* as part of the collation. *Cromwell* in this binding preceded *Hamlet* 'As it is now Acted by his Majesty's Servants'. The plays must have been prepared for (or commissioned by) the Drury Lane company of actors, in opposition to a very similar edition published by Walker with whom Tonson carried on a price war. Tonson won, perhaps without much profit in the victory; Walker's plays are less often found. At the start or end of Tonson's the public was warned, in a style still familiar, against Walker's piracy. This 'Advertisement' was always above the name W. Chetwood, 'Prompter to His Majesty's Company of Comedians at the Theatre-Royal in Drury-Lane'.

> Whereas, R. Walker, with his Accomplices have printed and publish'd several of Shakespear's Plays; and to screen their Innumerable Errors, advertise, That they are Printed as they are Acted, and industriously report, that the said Plays are printed from Copies made use of at the Theatres; I therefore declare, in Justice to the Proprietors, whose Right is basely invaded, as well as in Defence of my self, That no Person ever had, directly or indirectly from me, any such Copy or Copies; neither wou'd I be accessory on any Account in imposing on the Publick such Useless, Pirated, and Maim'd Editions, as are publish'd by the said R. Walker.

It is hard to know what was useless or maimed in Walker's editions, which look the same as Tonson's. These little books have some charm, with their vignettes and engravings, but no editorial apparatus.

WHEREAS *R. Walker*, and his Accomplices have printed and publifhed feveral of *Shake-fpear*'s Plays, and, to fcreen their innumerable Errors, advertize, that they are printed as they are acted; and induftrioufly report, that the faid Plays are printed from Copies made ufe of at the Theatres. I therefore declare, in Juftice to the Proprietors, whofe Right is bafely invaded, as well as in Defence of my felf, that no Perfon ever had, directly, or indirectly, from me any fuch Copy or Copies; neither would I be acceffary, on any Account, to the impofing on the Publick fuch ufelefs, pirated and maimed Editions, as are publifhed by the faid *R. Walker.*

W. Chetwood.

Prompter to his Majefty's Company of Commedians at the Theatre Royal *in* Drury-Lane.

3   Tonson establishing himself against Walker, 1734. [Actual height of *type* $4\frac{1}{4}$ inches]

HANMER 1744

This well-produced quarto edition in six volumes, a little taller than Pope's, was 'Carefully Revised and Corrected by the former Editions, and Adorned with Sculptures designed and executed by the best hands'. Published by Oxford, subsidized by the editor who lived in retirement after a spell as Speaker of the House of Commons, for the first time Tonson's copyright claim was ignored. Hanmer printed Rowe's *Life*, his own Preface and Pope's, but not Theobald's. Pope's Indexes were not included but at the end is a brief Glossary, just 12 pages for all Shakespeare's plays. There are few footnotes. Hanmer is remembered among the last of the amateurs, 'who published a very pompous edition, with his name as the Editor, and without a *fee!*'[4], 'pompously printed with cuts', in Warburton's phrase. It does not now look pompous, but an attractive production comparable with Pope's (for size and print) or with Bentley's royal quarto edition of *Paradise Lost*, which Tonson had published. Hanmer stands alone as 'the Oxford editor', a phrase used with or without irony by Johnson and others in quoting him.

---

[4] Benjamin Victor to Garrick, 1771

T H E

W O R K S

O F

SHAKESPEAR.

I N

SIX VOLUMES.

Carefully REVISED and CORRECTED by the former EDITIONS, and ADORNED with SCULPTURES defigned and executed by the beft hands.

——— *Nil ortum tale.* ———   Hor.

O X F O R D: Printed at the THEATRE, MDCCXLIV.

4   Hanmer's title page, 1744 [Actual height of *type* 9⅛ inches]

HANMER 1745 (The 'Anonymous' Edition) & 1747

The 1745 octavo edition in six volumes, published by Tonson in partnership, was a reply to what he regarded as Oxford's breach of copyright. Giles Dawson[5] argues that Warburton edited it; Arthur Sherbo[6] disagrees, concluding that he merely 'gave the editor or editors notice of some emendations which he wished to claim for himself, and then had nothing else to do with the edition'. It seems impossible, his own edition almost ready, that Warburton would have prepared this new version of Hanmer's. One innovation was described in an 'Advertisement from the Booksellers': a device used in these volumes would identify emendations, a matter ignored by Hanmer, 'and place the discarded Readings at the bottom of the Page, as also to point out the Emendations made by Mr. *Theobald*, Mr. *Warburton*, and Dr. *Thirlby*, in Mr. *Theobald's* Edition, which are used by this Editor'. So Tonson issued the work to assert his rights against Oxford, but Warburton must have urged the need for such editorial attentions rather than bring before the world again something which struck him as deplorable.

This very curious note has the air of a diplomatic communiqué agreed after frank and open discussion. Warburton, standing his ground, drafted a careful form of words and insisted it be used without alteration. So far from acting as editor, his draft became a condition for publication; the man responsible for their next edition, they had reason to avoid Warburton's tantrums. It was a remarkable passage to have printed, eloquently expressing a publisher's problem with his difficult author in 1745:

As to the other Emendations and Notes of Mr. *Warburton* which are for the most part marked likewise in this Edition, we are only commission'd to say thus much; "*That be desires the Publick* would suspend their Opinion of his Conjectures 'till they see how they can be supported: For he holds it as ridiculous to alter the Text of an Author without Reasons assigned, as it was dishonourable to publish those Alterations without leave obtained. When he asks this Indulgence for himself, if the Publick will give it too to the Honourable Editor, he will not complain; as having no objection why his too should not occupy the Place they have usurped, until they be shewn to be arbitrary, groundless, mistaken, and violating not only the Sense of the Author, but all the Rules and Canons of true Criticism: Not that the Violation of these Rules ought to be any more objected to the Editor, than the Violation of the Rules of Poetry to his Author, as both professedly wrote without any."

---

[5] *Studies in Bibliography*, II (1949–50)
[6] *Journal of English and Germanic Philology*, Vol. 51, 1952

ADVERTISEMENT

FROM THE

BOOKSELLERS.

T H I S Edition is exactly copied from that lately printed in *Quarto* at *Oxford*; but the Editor of that not having thought proper to point out the Alterations he has made from the former Copies, we were advised to mark thofe Paffages in the Text thus, ' ` and place the difcarded Readings at the bottom of the Page, as alfo to point out the Emendations made by Mr. *Theobald*, Mr. *Warburton*, and Dr. *Thirlby*, in Mr. *Theobald*'s Edition, which are ufed by this Editor. The changes in the difpofition of the Lines for the Regulation of the Metre are too numerous to be taken particular notice of. As to the other Emendations and Notes of Mr. *Warburton*, which are for the moft part marked likewife in this Edition, we are only commiffion'd to fay thus much; *" That he defires the Publick would fufpend their " Opinion of his Conjectures 'till they fee how they " can be fupported: For he holds it as ridiculous to*

A 2

" alter

5   Attributions established in the 'Anonymous' edition, 1745. [Actual height of *type area* $6\frac{9}{16}$ inches]

Thus the publishers were forced by Warburton to commend their book to the public by castigating its editor's judgement as arbitrary, groundless and mistaken, and the man himself as ignorant of the rules of true criticism. It is a surprising document in the history of advertising.

Hanmer's Shakespeare always sold well. Two years later a Tonson partnership issued it again, this time in nine duodecimo volumes and without the paraphernalia or the Advertisement of 1745. They are charming little books,[7] appearing at the same moment as Warburton's. In the Folger Library is an interleaved set used by Dodd for his *Beauties of Shakespeare*, with Dodd's notes.

---

[7] *Not* illustrated, though Jaggard says it was, with engravings from Theobald's 1740 edition. He must have seen a graingerized copy, the plates cropped; they were too large to fit

WARBURTON 1747

Warburton, Pope's literary executor, had on his title page the phrase 'By Mr. Pope and Mr. Warburton', so this edition may be known as Pope and Warburton, as later editions during Johnson's lifetime and after his death were called Johnson and Steevens. Theobald and Hanmer also used Pope's as the version from which to differ in their own. Warburton, not much admired now, produced the second critical edition and in it attacked Theobald's, the first. After his own entertaining Preface he printed Pope's but no other, and Rowe's *Life:* notes grew higher up the page, with three editors to quote and question. The final volume included Pope's complicated Index. Serious academic analysis, no illustrations except for the portrait, began with the first Theobald edition and continued here. These eight volumes did not rise above the average of their day in printing or paper; Warburton's crotchety edition is visually dull. He kept and added to Pope's system in emphasizing the fine passages or Beauties.

THE

WORKS

OF

SHAKESPEAR

IN EIGHT VOLUMES.

The Genuine Text (collated with all the former
Editions, and then corrected and emended)
is here settled :

Being restored from the *Blunders* of the first Editors,
and the *Interpolations* of the two Last :

WITH

A Comment and Notes, Critical and Explanatory.

By Mr. POPE *and Mr.* WARBURTON.

——Quorum omnium Interpretes, ut Grammatici, Poetarum
proxime ad eorum, quos interpretantur, divinationem vi-
dentur accedere.   *Cic. de Divin.*

ΉΤΩΝ ΛΟΓΩΝ ΚΡΙΣΙΣ ΠΟΛΛΗΣ ΕΣΤΙ ΠΕΙΡΑΣ
ΤΕΛΕΥΤΑΙΟΝ ΕΠΙΓΕΝΝΗΜΑ.   *Long. de Sublim.*

LONDON:

Printed for *J.* and *P. Knapton, S. Birt, T. Longman* and
T. Shewell, H. Lintott, C. Hitch, J. Brindley, J. and *R. Tonson* and *S. Draper, R. Wellington, E. New,* and *B. Dod.*

MDCCXLVII.

---

6   Warburton's aggressive title page, 1747. [Actual height of *type*
6½ inches]

JOHNSON 1765

In mid-century, editions of Shakespeare appeared quite often, must commonly have been available in bookshops, but Johnson's was the next critical version attempting a correct text despite the large claim on Warburton's title page that 'the Genuine Text ... is here settled'. Johnson among many other achievements unsettled Warburton. His eight volumes appeared twice in 1765; one difference distinguishing the first issue is an un-numbered Preface, for Johnson wrote this last and kept the printer waiting as Pope had. The Tonsons headed a syndicate of 12 publishers. A modestly phrased general title steered away from controversy: 'The Plays of William Shakespeare, in Eight Volumes, with the Corrections and Illustrations of Various Commentators; to which are added Notes by Sam. Johnson'. This is sometimes called the first variorum edition because many or most previous notes were reprinted in it, making almost a full page on the many occasions when Johnson opposed Warburton who opposed Theobald. The discourse grew; also Johnson chose to reproduce the prefaces of Pope, Theobald, Hanmer and Warburton after his own long Preface. Rowe's *Life* appeared again, and for the first time Shakespeare's Will. The Appendix of additional notes, a result of suggestions after the plays had circulated in print but before publication, was un-numbered in both 1765 issues. Thicker paper was used for the earlier issue. Johnson added his general reflections after each play, usually brief but occasionally (as after *The Merchant of Venice*) of essay length. This edition was the focal point for them all, opening a textual tradition which endured through Malone and beyond. Unadorned, as was Warburton's edition, it was more clearly printed on better material. It could be fascinating (or boring, and has surely been done) to note each small change from the first to the second issue of Johnson 1765. The final paragraph of volume one, for instance, gives evidence for different setting in the labour-intensive 18th-century composing room.

THE
PLAYS

O F

WILLIAM SHAKESPEARE,

IN EIGHT VOLUMES,

WITH THE

CORRECTIONS and ILLUSTRATIONS

O F

Various COMMENTATORS;

To which are added

NOTES by SAM. JOHNSON.

———————————————

LONDON:
Printed for J. and R. Tonson, C. Corbet, H. Woodfall,
J. Rivington, R. Baldwin, L. Hawes, Clark and
Collins, W. Johnston, T. Caslon, T. Lownds,
and the Executors of B. Dodd.
M,DCC,LXV.

7   Johnson's title page, first edition, first issue, 1765. [Actual height
of *type* $6\frac{5}{16}$ inches]

CAPELL 1767–8

The design of his ten octavo volumes reflects the originality of Edward Capell's text, printed for Tonson by Dryden Leach 'who may be styled,' wrote Nichols, 'the father of *Fine Printing* in this Country'.[8] The wide margins of these charming books gave them the appearance of large-paper copies; small type, though it sometimes showed through, was elegantly used. Capell kept his notes for quarto volumes published later in the cause of completion and perfection, rather oddly expressed, 'of making his future present more perfect, and as worthy of their acceptance as his abilities will let him'. He admitted also

> that a very great part of the world, amongst whom is the editor himself, profess much dislike to this paginary intermixture of text and comment; in works meerly of entertainment, and written in the language of the country; as also – that he, the editor, does not possess the secret of dealing out notes by measure, and distributing them among his volumes so nicely that the equality of their bulk shall not be broke in upon the thickness of a sheet of paper . . .

The father of fine printing in this country was not always clever in distributing the equality of bulk either, hyphenating 'thinks' as thinks in lines which followed that passage and printing the title of a new scene on the bottom line of a page which opened the next; and the truth of Capell's embarrassment is manifest in one note of the *Introduction* which occupies 11 lines at the foot of nine successive pages.

This neat edition is not illustrated except for the small portrait below the editor's 74-page essay.

---

[8] *Literary Anecdotes*, II, p. 453

Mr WILLIAM SHAKESPEARE

his

COMEDIES, HISTORIES, and TRAGEDIES,

set out by himself in quarto,
or by the Players his Fellows in folio,
and now faithfully republish'd from those
Editions
in ten Volumes octavo; with an
INTRODUCTION:

Whereunto will be added, in some other Volumes,
NOTES, critical and explanatory, and a Body of
VARIOUS READINGS
entire.

Qui genus humanum ingenio superavit, et omneis
Præstinxit, stellas exortus uti æthereus Sol.
                         LUCR. *Lib.* 3. *l.* 1056.

LONDON:
Printed by DRYDEN LEACH,
for J. *and* R. TONSON *in the Strand.*

8   Edward Capell's title page, 1767. [Actual height of *type* $4\frac{1}{2}$ inches]

THE STRATFORD SHAKESPEARE, 1768

These nine duodecimo volumes are sufficiently attractive and curious to earn their place in the story. Bibliographically Jaggard was enthusiastic about a minor first: 'An edition of unusual interest. It was produced at the suggestion of David Garrick, for sale at the great Stratford jubilee of 1769, and is the first Warwickshire edition of its deathless native'. The 'portrait by an unknown artist, specially engraved for this edition' has no mention in Gaskell's thorough collation[9] and does not exist in my copy. Typographically the edition has interest as the first major responsibility of Robert Martin at Baskerville's press and with his types, in a period when the great man himself suffered the first of several phases of depression after financial failure of his major work, the Cambridge Bible. Baskerville had tried, through Benjamin Franklin, to sell his whole works and plant to France; that endeavour also failed (the atmosphere must have been extremely discouraging for Martin, his workshop manager meanwhile) but he returned to life and power and thought, printing the quarto series of classics after this semi-breakdown. Martin's Shakespeare with Baskerville's types, printed in Birmingham for the Stratford celebrations, an elegant and uncommon work recognizably in Baskerville's style, makes it doubly strange to remember that Nichols called Dryden Leach, who produced Capell's Shakespeare at about the same time, 'father of English fine printing'.

In 1768 those volumes produced upon the initiative of Garrick were 'from Mr. Pope's Edition'. Johnson's had been published three years before; perhaps it was too soon to use that, but copyright in an edition remained obscure. They did not observe Pope's quirks of taste – the Porter in *Macbeth* was not relegated to footnote italic. It was really another issue of Warburton's Pope, the commonly current version until Johnson's work gained wide recognition.

---

[9] *John Baskerville, a Bibliography*, Cambridge, 1959, p. 71

HANMER 1771

This reprint of Hanmer on excellent paper, perhaps the best-produced Shakespeare edition of the 18th century, deserves more recognition than it has received. An advertisement at the start explained that the 1744 impression 'having been small, was suddenly bought up; and the original price advanced to a very exorbitant sum'.

> The great demand therefore of the publick for so elegant an edition induced the delegates of the university press to set about this republication: in which the inaccuracies of the first impression in punctuation and spelling are carefully adjusted; and, in order to obviate such other objections as have been made to it, at the end of each volume are annexed the various readings of the two most authentick publishers of our author's plays, Mr. *Theobald*, and Mr. *Capell*.

A fascinating move from Oxford – no thought there of Johnson; attention was restricted to the first literal critic, and the most recent. Warton and others contributed notes, sometimes at great length, to an extended Glossary at the end of volume six; the great respect felt by Johnson and Steevens for Warton caused a long Appendix to their edition of 1773. 'Had we foreseen the *Oxford* edition', Steevens wrote there, 'the assistance we expected from it might have persuaded us to pause; but our volumes were completely finished before its publication.'

It was not an easy system of reference; nobody could enjoy, as an alternative to footnotes, constant search down columns at the back to find what Theobald or Capell offered, or into volume six for Warton's latest contribution. The whole production showed Oxford at its laziest and finest; choosing the version everyone (Capell above all) condemned, adding scholarly equipment neatly but in such a way that it was the greatest nuisance to use; achieving artistically the most delightful edition of Shakespeare. Luckily Gravelot's plates had survived well through a quarter of a century:

> The editor has the further satisfaction to inform the reader, that the plates of the frontispieces to each play are in the very best preservation, the tail-pieces only being worn-out; which are reengraved by a very eminent artist.

BELL 1773–4

Jaggard described this more fully than any other 18th-century edition. Thirteen hundred were printed on 'ordinary' paper, and 134 people in the list of subscribers ordered large-paper sets. It 'scored a greater success than any previous issue, one week alone witnessing the sale of eight hundred sets'. The editor, an actor and hack playwright called Francis Gentleman, believed sadly that 'nothing but a pensioned defender of government, a sycophant to managers, or a slave to booksellers can do anything more than crawl'.

These nine duodecimo volumes form an attractive curiosity from that date, with engravings which caused the bibliographer to call it 'the first edition with artistic illustrations', and an engraved general title to each volume. The plays were printed 'as they are now performed at the Theatres Royal in London; Regulated from the Prompt Books of each House by Permission; with Notes Critical and Illustrative . . .' – and this seems true, so that the 1773–4 edition of Bell (like Tonson's in 1734) offered what audiences heard at Drury Lane and Covent Garden. Drury Lane productions were 'Regulated from the Prompt-Book, with Permission of the Managers, by Mr. Hopkins, Prompter', Covent Garden similarly from their prompter Mr. Younger; this until half way through volume five, after which the direct theatre connection ceased. Paging was volume by volume or play by play, which suggests two issues; my set in contemporary bindings is a mix. The ninth volume, *Poems*, with a different engraved title, has a Life of Shakespeare and invented names for every sonnet (for example, 'A good Construction of his Love's Unkindness', 'Error in Opinion', 'Love's Powerful Subtlety'). The first volume includes an essay on Oratory. Lists of Bell's books come between some of the plays.

This edition is an early example of Bell's arrival as book publisher. He had not yet given up the old form of s.

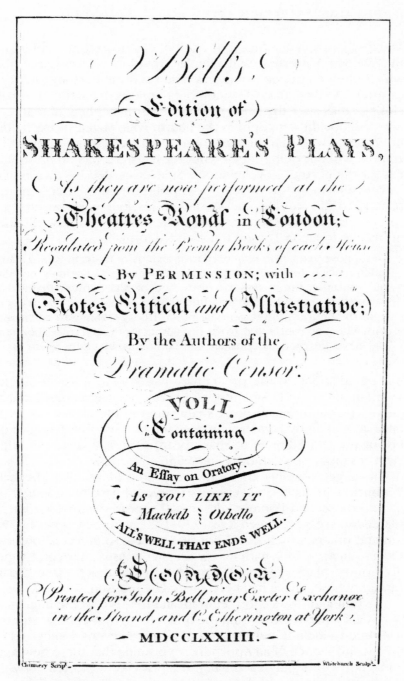

9 Engraved title page for the first Bell edition, 1774. [Actual height of *type* $5\frac{3}{4}$ inches]

JOHNSON AND STEEVENS 1773

The first Johnson and Steevens edition, extended to ten volumes as the 'Second Variorum' with ample provision of Steevens's notes which often contradict Johnson's. The variorum custom had begun to grow. No less than 33 publishers appeared on the title page, closing ranks after the death of Jacob Tonson, nephew of that Jacob who had bought copyright in the Fourth Folio Shakespeare; he died in 1767, and with him the firm. Johnson shared responsibility for this edition, without doing much work for it. There was no illustration, except the portrait in volume one. Steevens called his own preface 'Advertisement to the Reader' and printed two of them, the first relating to this edition, the second to his four volumes of Shakespeare quartos published six years earlier. In the new Advertisement his tribute to Jacob Tonson transcended formality:

> To suppose that a man employed in an extensive trade, lived in a state of indifference to loss and gain, would be to conceive a character incredible and romantic; but it may be justly said of Mr. Tonson, that he had enlarged his mind beyond solicitude about petty losses, and refined it from the desire of un-reasonable profit. He was willing to admit those with whom he contracted, to the just advantage of their own labours; and had never learned to consider the author as an under agent to the bookseller.

Among additions to the preliminary pages were a list of 'Ancient Translations from Classic Authors', because Steevens considered the old debate about Shakespeare's education in the classics as settled once and for all by Farmer who declared he used translation, and 'A List of the Old Editions of Shakespeare's Plays', a theme in which Steevens possessed authority and a fine collection.

The large assembly of footnotes produced by the Theobald–Warburton–Johnson–Steevens quartet would have been longer still if Oxford's second Hanmer edition had appeared a little earlier; the Clarendon Press produced it in 1770–1771, with new notes by Warton and others which could not be ignored; so Steevens observed them in an Appendix, with his own replies as usual. A second Appendix printed many comments provided by the much respected Dr. Farmer, whose advice had been invited by Johnson.

The timing of the Oxford edition, and this, is of some interest. As two years separated one from the other, it might seem that Steevens had time to include new notes and adapt. Steevens apologized 'for the inconvenience of an Appendix', explaining that these new notes 'were not within our reach when the plays were printed, to which they relate'. As none of the preliminary material in volume one was page-numbered, it looks again very much as if this impatient syndicate of publishers printed the long work as it came to them play by play, waiting until the last moment for their editor's complex array of Prefaces, Advertisements, Lists. The ten volumes which superseded all previous editions and became the standard for future editors and publishers'[10] must have been in the press for at least two years.

[10] Lowndes, quoted by Jaggard

JOHNSON AND STEEVENS 1778

Its title page called this 'the Second Edition, Revised and Augmented', assuming Johnson and Steevens 1773 to have been the first, though Johnson did not die until 1784 and might have reckoned his own edition of 1765 was the first. Printed labels on the spines over marbled paper boards in the bookshops read 'Shakspeare by Johnson and Stevens [sic] Second Edition', adding helpful lists of the plays in each volume. The production was similar to 1773, the publishing syndicate not quite the same but almost as numerous; preliminary essays, lists and soforth had grown substantially, to 346 pages; an 'Extract of Entries on the Books of the Stationers' Company' was followed by Malone's long 'Attempt to Ascertain the Order in which the Plays attributed to Shakespeare were Written'. Though Jaggard calls this the first edition edited by Isaac Reed, there is no evidence for that; Steevens consulted him constantly, as Theobald had consulted Warburton.

Malone's presence made the great difference, not Reed's. In 1780 the two volumes of 'Supplement to the edition of Shakspeare's Plays ... containing Additional Observations by several of The Former Commentators: to which are subjoined The Genuine Poems of the same author, and Seven Plays that have been ascribed to him; with Notes by the Editor and Others' appeared. Produced as additional volumes to the 1778 set, these marked Malone's major entry to the cast of 18th-century editors. 'This two-volume supplement contributed more to the understanding of Shakespeare than the ten volumes of the Johnson–Steevens edition,' writes Gary Taylor in his essay before the Oxford 'Textual Companion'.

Though this was not an illustrated edition, two portraits of Shakespeare and a facsimile of his handwriting appeared among the Prolegomena, and an engraving by Sherwin of Morris Dancers in volume five.

10   Original printed label for the spine of Johnson & Steevens, 1778. [Actual height of *label* 2½ inches]

STOCKDALE 1784

The first one-volume octavo Shakespeare, more than a thousand pages in double-column, decently spaced and clearly readable, was an interesting venture aimed at those who could not afford expensive sets – and at the servants of those who could. 'Many of the middling and lower ranks of the inhabitants of this country are either not acquainted with him at all, excepting by name, or have only seen a few of his plays, which have accidentally fallen in their way. It is to supply the wants of these persons that the present edition is principally undertaken ...'; But another social possibility was also imagined:

> It will be found serviceable even to those whose situation in life hath enabled them to pursue all the expensive editions of our great dramatist. The book now offered to the public may commodiously be taken into a coach or a post-chaise, for amusement in a journey. Or if a company of gentlemen should happen, in conversation, to mention Shakspeare, or to dispute concerning any particular passage, a volume containing the whole of his plays may, with great convenience, be fetched by a servant out of a library or a closet.

John Stockdale, born about 1749, blacksmith in Cumberland, valet in Cheshire, porter to a London publisher before starting on his own, was a remarkable example of social mobility in the 18th-century literary world.

P R E F A C E.

Nor is the utility of the present publication confined to persons of the rank already described. It will be found serviceable even to those whose situation in life hath enabled them to purchase all the expensive editions of our great dramatist. The book now offered to the public may commodiously be taken into a coach or a post-chaise, for amusement in a journey. Or if a company of gentlemen should happen, in conversation, to mention Shakspeare, or to dispute concerning any particular passage, a volume containing the whole of his plays may, with great convenience, be fetched by a servant out of a library or a closet. In short, any particular passage may at all times and with ease be recurred to. It is a compendium, not an abridgement, of the noblest of our poets, and a library in a single volume.

The editor hath endeavoured to give all the perfection to this work which the nature of it can admit. The account of his life, which is taken from Rowe, and his last will, in reality comprehend almost every thing that is known with regard to the personal history of Shakspeare. The anxious researches of his admirers have scarcely been able to collect any farther information concerning him.

11 Stockdale's one-volume 8vo, 1784: useful in giving orders to illiterate servants. [Actual *type height* $3\frac{3}{4}$ inches, *width* $4\frac{1}{2}$ inches]

ISAAC REED 1785

Continuing from the last, Isaac Reed's title page called this the Third Edition – the third Johnson and Steevens, 'revised and augmented by the editor of Dodsley's Collection of Old Plays'. Steevens had for this brief period announced his retirement from the Shakespeare scene, and Isaac Reed's retiring temperament kept his name from the general title. His own notes occur, discourse grew; Steevens was not allowed to hold the ground unchallenged by Reed, or more especially by Malone. The preliminary pages, substantially the same as in 1778, were increased by his own short but trenchant Advertisement and brief additions such as the names of the original actors in Shakespeare's plays. Though Reed's edition in the strangest way gave offence his reticence leaves an efficient impression, and volume ten closed at the end of *Othello*, without afterthoughts, Appendixes or, as in 1778, 'Accidental Omissions'. The 1778 version *with* Malone's supplements formed a more interesting assembly than this, but Malone was about to provide his own complete edition. Thirty-one publishers combined to form the syndicate for 1785.

THE PLAYS

OF

WILLIAM SHAKSPEARE.

IN TEN VOLUMES.

WITH THE

CORRECTIONS AND ILLUSTRATIONS

OF

VARIOUS COMMENTATORS;

TO WHICH ARE ADDED

NOTES by SAMUEL JOHNSON

AND

GEORGE STEEVENS.

THE THIRD EDITION,

REVISED AND AUGMENTED BY THE EDITOR OF

DODSLEY's COLLECTION OF OLD PLAYS.

ΤΗΣ ΦΥΣΕΩΣ ΓΡΑΜΜΑΤΕΥΣ ΗΝ, ΤΟΝ ΚΑΛΑΜΟΝ ΑΠΟΒΡΕΧΩΝ ΕΙΣ ΝΟΥΝ.
Vet. Auct. apud Suidam.

MULTA DIES, VARIUSQUE LABOR MUTABILIS ÆVI
RETULIT IN MELIUS, MULTOS ALTERNA REVISANS
LUSIT, ET IN SOLIDO RURSUS FORTUNA LOCAVIT.
Virgil.

LONDON,

Printed for C. BATHURST, J. RIVINGTON and SONS,
T. PAYNE and SON, L. DAVIS, W. OWEN, B. WHITE and
SON, T. LONGMAN, B. LAW, T. BOWLES, J. JOHNSON,
C. DILLY, J. ROBSON, G. G. J. and J. ROBINSON,
T. CADELL, H. L. GARDNER, J. NICHOLS, J. BEW,
W. STUART, R. BALDWIN, J. MURRAY, A. STRAHAN,
T. VERNOR, J. BARKER, W. LOWNDES, S. HAYES,
G. and T. WILKIE, SCATCHERD and WHITAKER,
T. and J. EGERTON, W. FOX, and E. NEWBERY.
MDCCLXXXV.

12 Isaac Reed's modest title page, 1785. [Actual height of *type* $7\frac{3}{16}$ inches]

BELL'S EDITION 1786–8

These 20 volumes made a more remarkable departure than is suggested in the bibliographies. John Bell, as publisher, responsible for his own books rather than working in committee, planned a different editorial arrangement which set a style for the long variorum editions of 1803, 1813 and 1821. He used the term Prolegomena, giving that title to his first two volumes, and the whole work extended to 20 volumes. Published in duodecimo format, clear type and good spacing make this the pleasantest of small editions to read. As the spread of notes up most small pages would have looked absurd, they were placed together at the end of every play like subsidiary volumes with their own title pages; indeed these are separately paged, and were no doubt completed at different times, for their title pages have different dates from the plays they note, sometimes a year later but more often the year before. *Hamlet*, for instance, has a 1788 title page, but the 'Annotations by Sam. Johnson & Geo. Steevens, and the Various Commentators, upon Hamlet, written by Will. Shakspere' is dated 1787; the notes filled 200 pages. There was no compromise or abbreviation; the general title to the plays (volume three) announced them 'With the Notes of all the various Commentators; printed complete from the best editions of Sam. Johnson and Geo. Steevens'. Copyright seems not to have obstructed the project.

As notes came after, 'Observations on the Fable and Composition' preceded; 'fable' applied alike to tragedy, comedy and history. Johnson's reflections after each play were thus brought forward, including his long summary of earlier *Merchant of Venice* stories. The Advertisement in volume one mentions that the notes were 'not only retrenched, where futile or needless, but interspersed with a variety of new illustrations.'

An a was removed from Shakespeare, robbed already of the first e, by making him Shakspere; the switch was made from old to new s throughout, for typographic reasons well explained:

> In the mode of printing too, he hath ventured to depart from the common mode, by rejecting the long ʃ in favour of the round one, as being less liable to error from the occasional imperfections of the letter ʃ, and the frequent substitution of it for the long ʃ; the regularity of the print is by that means very much promoted, the lines having the effect of being more open, without really being at any additional distance.

Engravings had distinguished Bell's less remarkable nine-volume edition of 1773–4; a different set is present here. 'In point of *exterior*, it is believed,' wrote the publisher, 'that it hath as yet no rival, either in ornaments, printing, or paper.' It was issued in 76 parts.

RANN 1786—91

Little is known about the history of this curious production, completed in six octavo volumes between 1786 and, according to the title pages, 1791; the last two volumes carry no date, but the Grolier Club exhibition catalogue of 1916 extends their date to 1794. Rann was vicar of St. Trinity, Coventry, and the usual sources have nothing to add. The first volume is dated 1786, the second 1787, the third 1789, the fourth 1791; as a note before volume one informed subscribers 'that the remaining five Volumes are completely ready for the Press; and will be printed with all convenient Despatch', it seems the Clarendon Press advanced with something short of enthusiasm. The imprint in volumes one to four of my set reads 'Oxford: at the Clarendon Press'; from five and six the Clarendon press dropped out, though Oxford remains, and the title page design changed a little.

What was Oxford's motive for printing the six stout octavo volumes? The Clarendon Press had a dubious record with Shakespeare editions, responsible only for Hanmer, the worst of them, in 1744 and Hanmer again in 1771, not a distinguished academic performance. Here at least was a decent text, including what Hanmer had relegated or deleted, but without other editorial merit: in an age of gathering finesse and hair-splitting Rann offered no preface or other Prolegomena, and, as the Grolier Club catalogue put it, 'little more than verbal suggestions in footnotes': no hint of collation or a new text, or new reflections in the notes, or of attribution when earlier editions were quoted. It may be agreeable now to handle Rann's edition, but one wonders whether a majority of delegates persuaded the Clarendon Press to cut its connection with a venture which had so little to contribute.

MALONE 1790

This first Malone edition is in ten volumes bound as 11; volume one was always split into two, with a second title page for the second part. The Prolegomena extend to about 825 pages, of which his 'Historical Account of the Rise and Progress of the English Stage' fills 284. Malone must have been a troublesome editor for Baldwin the printer, who had to cope with 45 pages of afterthought ('Emendations and Additions') when all this was set, and 150 pages of afterthought ('Appendix') when all the plays were set in type or printed. Malone also provided a glossary of 'all the Words and Phrases in [Shakespeare's] Plays and Poems, which have been explained or illustrated in the preceding Notes, and in the Appendix'. Volume ten included Shakespeare's poems, the first serious edition of the complete works to have them since Rowe's nine-volume duodecimos from 1714: his own supplements to the Johnson and Steevens 1778 set had stood to that as the additional volume of poems to Rowe 1709, or to Pope's 1723 quartos. Steevens showed his crotchety temperament again by rejecting the poems in 1793.

The small type of this edition with readable good paper almost prevented the common 18th-century defect of show-through. Notes, climbing ever higher up the pages, with adequate space between lines, remained legible. The plays were not illustrated, but several portraits including those of Southampton and of Lowin the comedian were added.

As Malone died before setting in order his chaotic notes for the 21-volume variorum, the task Boswell's son completed, this 1790 edition was the best memorial from his lifetime. He planned also a fine quarto edition, but that never appeared.

13   Original printed spine label for Malone, 1790. [Actual height of
label, $2\frac{9}{16}$ inches]

BELLAMY AND ROBARTS 1791

This delightful set in eight octavo volumes, first issued serially between 1787 and 1791, then identically as a set in 1791, had no note on the text and no notes but provided the most charming engravings among any of the 18th-century editions. After a biographical essay (mostly quoted from Theobald), an eccentric choice of poems, Shakespeare's Will and his Coat of Arms, the first volume (Comedies) opened with *As You Like It.* This remains a pleasant reading version.

BOYDELL 1791–1805

There can be no doubt that Boydell's Shakespeare, published by Alderman John Boydell and his nephew Josiah, was the most splendid of bibliophile editions undertaken in the 18th century or at any other time. *The Dramatic Works of Shakspeare Revised by George Steevens* with 100 engravings after paintings by Reynolds, Fuseli, Romney, Westall and other able artists of that moment, appeared in 18 parts between 1791 and 1802, printed by Bulmer 'from the Types of W. Martin'. Described as atlas folio, the nine bound volumes look modest beside a colossal binding of the *Collection of Prints, from Pictures Painted for the Purpose of Illustrating the Dramatic Works of Shakspeare, by the Artists of Great-Britain,* issued by the Boydells and printed by Bulmer, its two title pages dated 1803 and the Preface 1805. The publication price of a set of these prints was 60 guineas. Boydell's vision turned to commercial nightmare, but he could have said with Bottom 'The eye of man hath not heard, the ear of man hath not seen; man's hand is not able to taste, his tongue to conceive, nor his heart to report, what my dream was'.

The set of large prints was probably *not* 'intended to accompany', as bibliographies suggest, Boydell's edition of the plays, for many of them reproduced the same paintings on a different scale, but Josiah's 1805 Preface explained the genesis of this whole enterprise. They will be discussed later, though 'Man is but an ass, if he go about to expound this dream'. The typographic aspect of it is relevant here.

George Nicol, typefounder and King's Printer, had proposed the great scheme to Garrick many years before. Josiah Boydell quoted Nicol, whose account is more interesting than a précis of it, in the Preface:

> The conversation that led to the present undertaking was entirely accidental; it happened at the table of Mr. Josiah Boydell, at West End, Hampstead, in November, 1787: the company consisted of Mr. West, Mr. Romney, and Mr. P. Sandby; Mr. Hayley, Mr. Hoole, Mr. Braithwaite, Alderman Boydell, and our Host. In such a company it is needless to say, that every proposal to celebrate genius, or cultivate the fine Arts, would be favourably received.
>
> At the moment of the proposition, I had no idea of having any concern in the execution of the work, – and only offered to contribute my mite to so great and so expensive an undertaking. It was very soon however foreseen, that having involved my friends in so arduous a task, it was incumbent on me to lend every assistance in my power to the completion of it. The typographical part alone was the department wherein I could be of any use: of the mechanical part of printing indeed I knew but little; but from the general line of my profession, and my particular admiration of fine printing, I was acquainted with all the beauties, and all

the defects of the most eminent artists, from John Fust of Mentz, to John Baskerville of Birmingham.

Nicol interrupted this staggering claim with a footnote tribute to Bulmer who 'has so perfectly supplied this defect [Nicol's ignorance of mechanics], in the execution of the typographical part of the Shakspeare, that he has left nothing to desire: in so much, that it may be truly said, that no Printing Press, which has hitherto existed, ever produced a work *in nine large volumes in folio so uniformly beautiful*'. John Boydell in a prospectus dated 1789 left readers to guess the identity of Nicol's advisers 'who, were I at liberty to mention their names, would do him honour, and the undertaking credit'.

Robert Martin we have met before, printer of the Jubilee Shakespeare at Birmingham with Baskerville's types. William was his brother, employed by Nicol to cut types 'in imitation of the sharp and fine letter used by the French and Italian printers', as Timperley explained,[11] 'which Mr. Nicol, for a length of time caused to be carried on in his own house'.

Print seller and book publisher went into partnership. The 1791 title page reads: 'Printed by W. Bulmer and Co. \ Shakspeare Printing-Office \ for John and Josiah Boydell, and George Nicol \ from the Types of W. Martin'. 'This magnificent edition,' Dibdin wrote, 'which is worthy of the unrivalled compositions of our great dramatic bard, will remain as long as those compositions shall be admired, an honourable testimony of the taste and skill of the individuals who planned and conducted it to its completion.'

Nobody could complain about William Martin's work, or its use here. Bulmer called his place the Shakspeare Press, Boydell published from the Shakspeare Gallery; Martin's types, so successfully used elsewhere by Bulmer through the next decades, were designed for this edition.

---

[11] *A Dictionary of Printers and Printing,* 1839

JOHNSON AND STEEVENS 1793

The 15-volume variorum of 1793 marked Steevens's return as editor, stimulated by his quarrel with Malone. Except for four fold-out schemes of obscure plots of plays, this major work was minimally adorned.

> We boast therefore of no exterior ornaments [wrote Steevens in his new Advertisement] except those of better print and paper than have hitherto been allotted to any octavo edition of Shakspeare.

Jaggard quoted Lowndes as suggesting this was 'generally called *Steevens' own edition*', and 'is by many considered the most accurate and desirable of all'. It may still be among the most desirable, as many must have felt at the time, for it is not hard to find; as to accuracy, Malone's reputation now stands higher. This ministry of all the talents offered a final 18th-century summary, the last manageable edition before three variorum versions in 21 volumes; not yet too technical, unafraid of such general discourse as followed *Othello:*

> If by 'the most perfect' [Malone's phrase] is meant the *most regular* of the foregoing plays, I subscribe to Mr. Malone's opinion; but if his words were designed to convey a more exalted praise, without a moment's hesitation I should transfer it to *Macbeth.*

The first two volumes, filled with Prolegomena, extended Malone's assembly by adding Farmer's long 'Essay on the Learning of Shakspeare' and Colman's 'Remarks' on it. Print and paper, modest and sensible, justified Steevens's claim. A long Glossary was helpful – but the Rev. Samuel Ayscough had already produced nearly 700 pages of *Index to the Remarkable Passages and Words.* Johnson and Steevens 1793 approached the far borders of pleasant home reading.

HARDING 1798–1800

Harding's 12-volume duodecimo edition is in admirable taste, printed by Bensley; clear to read, with etched and stippled illustrations, Rowe's *Life*, Farmer's essay on Shakespeare's Learning, a Glossary, and before each play the 'Observations' as in Johnson and Steevens 1793. There were no footnotes. Each play was separately paged and issued; the whole assembly could be bought bound in 12 volumes, with or without illustrations. 'This Edition of Shakspeare's Plays is not only published in 38 Numbers, at 2s each, with elegant Engravings; but also in 12 Volumes, without the Plates; forming a complete and uniform Collection of the Dramatic Works of our immortal Poet'; publishers' blurbs descend unchanged through the centuries, from complete and uniform to not only but also. Bensley's title pages had a wood engraving of the swan. The plays were 'accurately printed from the text of Mr. Steevens's Last Edition'.

THE

PLAYS

OF

WILLIAM SHAKSPEARE.

VOLUME THE FIRST;

CONTAINING

LIFE...PREFACE...FARMER'S ESSAY...TEMPEST.
TWO GENTLEMEN OF VERONA.

LONDON:

Printed by T. BENSLEY, Bolt Court, Fleet Street,

FOR VERNOR AND HOOD, POULTRY; E. HARDING,
PALL-MALL; AND J. WRIGHT, PICCADILLY.

1800.

14   Title page for Harding, 1800. [Actual height of *type* 5¼ inches]

'FIRST VARIORUM' 1803

Johnson's was the first variorum, but this Johnson–Steevens–Reed edition in 21 volumes is often so called; it was the first of three 21-volume versions, comfortably winning the race against Malone's. Steevens had died in 1800. As to type and design the three were similar except in detail, not much to choose between them. J. Plymsell, Printer, Leather Lane, Holborn, London, printed his name at the back of the 1803 title pages and set the style; in small ways, as usual with imitation, first was best. As text Malone's made and keeps a higher reputation; 1803, a tremendous undertaking, fifth 'Johnson and Steevens' edition, so thoroughly worked over by Isaac Reed that he allowed his name on the title page, seems neglected. His short Advertisement opened volume one, four pages of Addenda before the Glossary were his. Forty publishers joined to produce it, the Prolegomena filled three volumes, including one substantial addition to Malone's history of the English Stage, *Further historical Account by Chalmers* (almost a hundred pages) and *Addenda by the same*.

From the start of the new century, editions of Shakespeare proliferated; editorial debate of the old sort gave way to selective comment, except in the unending 'New Variorum'. The three 21-volume editions completed a drama. Fifteen hundred copies were printed in 1803.

CHALMERS 1805

This admirable edition in nine volumes had a finer pedigree and more interesting place in the canon than has usually been acknowledged. 'No man ever edited so many works as Chalmers for the booksellers of London' says the *Dictionary of National Biography*, but his Shakespeare is remarkable in several ways. The 'Series of Engravings, from original designs of Henry Fuseli, Esq. R. A., Professor of Painting' has not passed unnoticed, but Chalmers was responsible for what he called 'the first attempt that has been made to concentrate the information given in the copious notes of the various commentators within a moderate space, and with an attention rather to their conclusions than to their premises'. It was the first modern edition, departing from the habit of variorum commentary. In this eclectic way Johnson's Preface and Pope's were printed, none of the others; the *Sketch of the Life of Shakspeare* was 'an attempt, and the first of the kind, to collect the *disjecta membra* of his biography scattered over the volumes of Johnson and Steevens', and there was a reduction of Malone's history of the Stage. Commissioned by the publishers of the 1803 variorum, it presumably satisfied in nine volumes those who felt daunted by so many footnotes in 21. Baldwin was the very able printer of both. The long *Glossarial Index,* nearly 40 pages, gave reference but no definition.

BENSLEY 1807

Lowndes called this Heath's Edition, because many of the plates were engraved by Heath after Stothard and others. Illustrations in this set varied, as will be mentioned later, but it holds a place among notable editions of the period because the six imperial quarto volumes were printed by Bensley in close imitation of the Boydell folios. The publisher was Stockdale, ever ready to copy another's success, conspicuous in business in spite of much eccentricity of conduct and great coarseness of manners' according to *The Gentleman's Magazine*. These from the two great printers of their day provide an interesting typographic comparison, Bensley replying to Bulmer, remarkably similar page for page but not the same. The Bensley type was heavier than Martin's which Bulmer used, a little less elegant with less white space. Bulmer's page possessed the classic excellence which Bodoni's folios achieved in Italy, Bensley missed it by the slight indefinables which elevate typography into art. He used Caslon, not having access to Martin's types. Comparing them with Bodoni, Laurence Siegfried wrote:[12] 'One would hardly say of the Bulmer that it "combines the best features of each", though in design it obviously lies between the two, but to this eye at least, there is a grace, a refinement, one could almost say an aristocratic quality about the Bulmer that is not evident in either of the others ... It is not a type to be used on any and every job, not a universal or all-purpose type, but rather an occasional, even a special-occasions face.'

Stockdale chose a smaller format than Boydell, but some sets were issued on large paper. Mine possesses a mixed batch of illustrations and sizes, a characteristic Stockdale product, bound at that time in six fat volumes. The subscriber must have changed his order from ordinary to large paper after a couple of volumes had appeared, keeping both uncut and getting the binder to open each book with two or three plays from the smaller format. In illustration there could be no comparison between Boydell's vision and Stockdale's theft, but that argument belongs to another chapter. Derivative and therefore uninspired, Bensley's 1807 Shakespeare remains among the finest ever printed.

---

[12] In his Introductory Note to *William Bulmer and the Shakspeare Press*, Syracuse University Press, 1957

FIRST FOLIO REPRINTED, 1807

The first attempt to reproduce the 1623 folio, same size and with original spelling. As all editions since 1709 had used modern spelling, this was a new and useful endeavour, though Upcott amused himself by finding 368 mistakes. E. and J. Wright of St. John's Square were the printers. They used a special making of Whatman paper with the watermark SHAKESPEARE, dated 1806 above Whatman's name. There was no attempt at type-facsimile, but design and foliation followed the original. The title page so faithfully imitated that of 1623 as to have been used by enterprising booksellers in completing an imperfect copy.

BOWDLER (1807), 1827

Thomas Bowdler, freely mocked from that day to this for preparing a *Family Shakspeare* purged of indecency, took a similar stance to that of Gerard Manley Hopkins and Robert Bridges. His edition, first appearing in 1807 with only 20 of the plays, was often reprinted – filled, in publishing phrase, a long-felt need. The fourth edition with a new Preface was issued in 1825, ten duodecimo volumes; this from 1827 (fifth edition), eight octavo volumes with the first and fourth edition prefaces, came from Longmans who had been responsible for all but the first. Bowdler dedicated his work to Elizabeth Montagu, Johnson's friend, first of blue-stockings, whose *Essay on the Writings and Genius of Shakespear* had appeared in 1769. Bowdler died in 1825. Well printed and with minimal notes, the provenance of this set was appropriate: W. H. H. Fairclough, The Vicarage, Barton-under-Needwood.

'SECOND VARIORUM' 1813

Steevens had died three years before his 21-volume edition appeared, Reed died in 1807. In other ways a reprint of the 1803 work, volume one opened with a tribute to Isaac Reed by the librarian of the Royal Institution, Harris, who had assisted in 1803; most of it quoted from Nichols's *Anecdotes*. Volumes one to ten were printed by Thomas Davison of Whitefriars, dependably good, the rest no less ably by a Weybridge printer called Hamilton, both of them similar in style to Bensley.

'THIRD VARIORUM' 1821

The three variorum editions together form a fine summary of 18th-century work on Shakespeare but this last, known as Boswell's Malone, has time and again been called the foundation of modern Shakespeare scholarship. James Boswell, younger son of Johnson's biographer, had a hard task in ordering Malone's papers – 'I may add,' he mentioned in the 50-page *Advertisement,* 'that it is not every one that could have deciphered his notes.' Boswell's biographical essay on Malone preceded the list of contents and customary run of prefaces, essays, lists, histories and comment. Alone among the three variorum editions this included a volume of the poems, with 'Memoirs of Lord Southampton'. Thirty-five publishers (counting Longman, Hurst, Rees, Orme and Brown as one) joined to produce it; Baldwin was the printer. At the founding of a bibliophile dining club 57 years later, the Sette of Odd Volumes, a curious rule limited membership to 21: 'The Sette of Odd Volumes to consist of twenty-one, this being the number of volumes of the Variorum Shakespeare of 1821: but Supplemental O.V.s to the number of Twenty-one to be elected, and to be incorporated in the Sette as vacancies arise'. It recalled the culmination of digestible completeness.

THE

PLAYS AND POEMS

OF

WILLIAM SHAKSPEARE,

WITH THE

CORRECTIONS AND ILLUSTRATIONS

OF

VARIOUS COMMENTATORS:

COMPREHENDING

𝔄 𝔏𝔦𝔣𝔢 𝔬𝔣 𝔱𝔥𝔢 𝔓𝔬𝔢𝔱,

AND

AN ENLARGED HISTORY OF THE STAGE,

BY

THE LATE EDMOND MALONE.

WITH A NEW GLOSSARIAL INDEX.

ΤΗΣ ΦΥΣΕΩΣ ΓΡΑΜΜΑΤΕΥΣ ΗΝ, ΤΟΝ ΚΑΛΑΜΟΝ
ΑΠΟΒΡΕΧΩΝ ΕΙΣ ΝΟΤΝ.　　*Vet. Auct apud. Suidam.*

VOL. I.

LONDON:

PRINTED FOR F. C. AND J. RIVINGTON; T. EGERTON; J. CUTHELL; SCATCHERD
AND LETTERMAN; LONGMAN, HURST, REES, ORME, AND BROWN; CADELL
AND DAVIES; LACKINGTON AND CO.; J. BOOKER; BLACK AND CO.; J. BOOTH;
J. RICHARDSON; J. M. RICHARDSON; J. MURRAY; J. HARDING; R. H. EVANS;
J. MAWMAN; R. SCHOLEY; T. EARLE; J. BOHN; C. BROWN; GRAY AND SON;
R. PHENEY; BALDWIN, CRADOCK, AND JOY; NEWMAN AND CO.; OGLES, DUN-
CAN, AND CO.; T. HAMILTON; W. WOOD; J. SHELDON; E. EDWARDS; WHIT-
MORE AND FENN; W. MASON; G. AND W. B. WHITTAKER; SIMPKIN AND
MARSHALL; R. SAUNDERS: J. DEIGHTON AND SONS, CAMBRIDGE: WILSON
AND SON, YORK: AND STIRLING AND SLADE, FAIRBAIRN AND ANDERSON,
AND D. BROWN, EDINBURGH.

1821.

15　Title page for the Boswell-Malone variorum, 1821. [Actual
height of *type* $6\frac{3}{4}$ inches]

3 The Editors and Their Prefaces

I BEFORE CONTENTION: ROWE AND POPE

'From Isaiah to Karl Marx,' Aldous Huxley wrote in one of his philosophical books, 'the prophets have spoken with one voice'. From
Rowe to Malone the editors worked with flawless intention, but
prophets and editors strayed in performance. Pope thought Rowe
the best of men, who 'would laugh all day long'. He could laugh
through eternity at the mixture of civility, passion and pedantry
which followed his own first innocent editing of Shakespeare's plays.

Benjamin Victor told Garrick that Rowe's 'attempts as an editor
were so trifling, as not to require the least notice'. In disagreeing
now, one recalls that Rowe attacked a new task which must then
have looked more delightful than formidable. Nobody had yet made
heavy weather of Shakespeare; from the last (Fourth Folio) edition
he was to prepare a manageable pleasant set and introduce it.

Rowe enjoyed a successful writing life, not too much troubled by
money. Educated for the law but choosing to write plays and poems,
he inherited £300 a year at his father's death in 1692 when he was 18
years old. As he wrote patriotic plays and verse it is not surprising
that under a Whig administration he succeeded Nahum Tate as Poet
Laureate in 1715. Rowe's verse translation of Lucan's *Pharsalia*
seemed so excellent that his widow received a pension of £40 a year.

Opinions about his plays varied, but his own remained constant.
Through the length of one of his comedies, a failure which received
no second performance, his loud laughter was heard. Johnson said of
another play that 'There is scarcely any work of any poet at once so
interesting by the fable and so delightful in the language', but
Addison referred to 'the amorous declamations of Rowe' and compared Shakespeare's touching economy of expression in *Lear* with

'the long and laboured speech, enumerating the causes of his anguish, that Rowe and other modern tragic writers would certainly have put into his mouth'.

As nobody else had edited Shakespeare, no rival existed; these innocent volumes are like children who have not yet experienced school. One or two matters of debate received attention, especially that difficult seed of doubt from Ben Jonson as to 'small Latin and less Greek', which grew to trouble the 18th century, and he put a point of view in *Some Account of the Life, &c. of Mr. William Shakespear* which preceded the plays. Rowe wrote no formal Preface, but expressed in a conventional Dedication his code of conduct as editor. He and Pope (before Theobald caused a disturbance) came to their tasks with calm of mind; from Pope to Johnson, who rose above smallness, the atmosphere for editors became turbulent and after Johnson's death editorial relations remained complicated.

Some account of Shakespeare's life struck Rowe in 1709 as more urgent than comment on his work. 'And tho' the Works of Mr. *Shakespear* may seem to many not to want a Comment, yet I fancy some little Account of the Man himself may not be thought improper to go along with them.' Rowe's *Life* in one form or another became part of every critical edition through the whole period. As the plays seemed not to want a comment he provided none; this alone among such editions has no footnote (Capell's *looks* as if it has none, but they followed in large volumes later). A state of mind has to be imagined, before 'Shakespeare scholarship' was born.

So Rowe's Dedication offers generalities as to method and purpose. Each Marx and every Isaiah writing on this theme would have said the same:

> I must not pretend to have restor'd this Work to the Exactness of the Author's Original Manuscripts: Those are lost, or, at least, are gone beyond any Inquiry I could make, so that there was nothing left, but to compare the several Editions, and give the true Reading as well as I could from thence. This I have endeavour'd to do pretty carefully, and render'd very many Places Intelligible, that were not so before.

And this statement was preceded by his true claim, 'I have taken some Care to redeem him from the Injuries of former Impressions'. His phrasing is vague about early copies he searched, collated, compared, for no such science in editing English authors existed yet. 'In some of the Editions, especially the last,' he says, 'there were many Lines, (and in *Hamlet* one whole Scene) left out together; these are now all supply'd.' He was not the first or last (I could be included) to write about a subject too large for him to compass. Rowe did no new work for the edition of 1714. He had no connection with the book next door, Gildon's edition of the poems, published to look like a seventh volume, in 1710 by Curll. Gildon advanced further into controversy upon both poems and plays, but Rowe made no reply.

Rowe was considered 'master of most parts of polite learning, especially the classic authors, both Greek and Latin; he understood the French and Italian languages'. From that position he viewed the problem of Shakespeare's 'learning'; and Mrs. Oldfield was quoted as saying that 'the best school she had ever known was hearing Rowe read aloud her parts in his tragedies'. Warburton, sour about most earlier Shakespeare editors, called him 'the ingenious Mr. Rowe'. As first editor of Shakespeare rather than Poet Laureate, it seems now he deserved his place in Poet's Corner above Pope's epitaph. A kindly temperament and critical discretion show through his essay on Shakespeare's life.

*   *   *

Pope, writing the first Preface to an edition of Shakespeare, mapping the contours of his huge task, concluded that one could view the plays as 'an ancient majestick piece of *Gothick* Architecture, compar'd with a neat Modern building: The latter is more elegant and glaring, but the former is more strong and more solemn. It must be allow'd, that in one of these there are materials enough to make many of the other'.

This brilliant essay has sometimes been under-estimated because Pope's edition is not in keeping with his list of promises. His temperate survey of the problems went further than Rowe in analysis, written before the period of contention but replying to points of controversy in Rowe's *Life*.

The 'Gothick' concept contained and forgave a notion of erratic taste in Shakespeare, and Pope invented that useful spectre 'the Players' who must have caused, he felt, most of the errors. Admiration and understanding stop against this great obstruction at last, the Players. Who were they? Heminge and Condell in 1623 must be held responsible for negligent blunders, lack of comprehension, the addition of vulgar passages, disarray in the order of scenes and lines, wrong distribution of speech among the characters, inability to know prose from verse. Pope was very snobbish in his style of criticism, when it came to the Players:

> Having been forced to say so much of the Players, I think I ought in justice to remark, that the Judgement, as well as Condition, of that class of people was then far inferior to what it is in our days. As then the best Playhouses were Inns and Taverns (The *Globe*, the *Hope*, the *Red Bull*, the *Fortune*, &c.) so the top of the profession were then meer Players, not Gentlemen of the stage: they were led into the Buttery by the

Steward, not plac'd at the Lord's table, or Lady's toilette: and conse-
quently were intirely depriv'd of those advantages they now enjoy, in the
familiar conversation of our Nobility, and an intimacy (not to say dear-
ness) with people of the first condition.

His language of Gentlemen and Players, with such coincidence as
Lord's and the Tavern, recalls a cricket fixture which suffered from
the same vice.

Pope's admiration took precedence over any problematic criticism of Shakespeare who 'is justly and universally elevated above all
other Dramatic Writers'; but the purpose of a Preface was not to
praise him, rather 'to give an account of the fate of his Works, and
the disadvantages under which they have been transmitted to us'. On
a tide of familiarity with Homer, for he had just finished translating
the *Iliad*, Pope in a splendid paragraph shared Rowe's view of Shakespeare's *originality*, as a writer who may never have possessed and
had not needed the conventional advantages of classical example:

> If ever any Author deserved the name of an *Original*, it was *Shakespear.*
> *Homer* himself drew not his art so immediately from the fountains of
> Nature, it proceeded thro' *Aegyptian* strainers and channels, and came to
> him not without some tincture of the learning, or some cast of the
> models, of those before him. The Poetry of *Shakespear* was Inspiration
> indeed: he is not so much an Imitator, as an Instrument, of Nature; and 'tis
> not so just to say that he speaks from her, as that she speaks thro' him.

Pope's terms of praise exceed formal appreciation:

> His *Characters* are so much Nature her self, that 'tis a sort of injury to call
> them by so distant a name as Copies of her ... To this life and variety of
> Character, we must add the wonderful Preservation of it; which is such
> throughout his plays, that had all the Speeches been printed without the
> very name of the Persons, I believe one might have apply'd them with
> certainty to every speaker.

Satirist and master of emotional distance, Pope experienced Shakespeare's '*Power* over our *Passions*':

> We are surpriz'd, the moment we weep; and yet upon reflection find the
> passion so just, that we shou'd be surpiz'd if we had not wept, and wept
> at that very moment.

Another major source of admiration was Shakespeare's intuitive perceptions or 'Sentiments':

> His *Sentiments* are not only in general the most pertinent and judicious
> upon every subject; but by a talent very peculiar, something between
> Penetration and Felicity, he hits upon that particular point on which the
> bent of each argument turns, or the force of each motive depends. This is
> perfectly amazing, from a man of no education or experience in those
> great and publick scenes of life which are usually the subject of his

thoughts: So that he seems to have known the world by Intuition, to have look'd through humane nature at one glance, and to be the only Author that gives ground for a very new opinion, That the Philosopher and even the Man of the world, may be *Born*, as well as the Poet.

Pope seems to have imagined him as a later generation regarded John Clare, described on the title page of his first book as 'the Northamptonshire peasant'; he knew of course that Shakespeare at the age of about 15 had left the grammar school at Stratford, and this is placed in perspective by Gary Taylor in the new Oxford edition:

> Its boy pupils, aged from about eight to fifteen, endured an arduous routine. Classes began early in the morning: at six, normally; hours were long, holidays infrequent. Education was centred on Latin; in the upper forms, the speaking of English was forbidden ... A boy educated at an Elizabethan grammar school would be more thoroughly trained in classical rhetoric and Roman (if not Greek) literature than most present-day holders of a university degree in classics.

Nothing in the history of Shakespeare criticism looks now so unnecessary as the debate about his learning, on which Pope took a commonsense position. Learning, he pointed out, was not the same as language. Some lingering taste of this meaning exists still, in a sense of inadequacy without Greek and Latin.

> There is certainly a vast difference between *Learning* and *Languages*. How far he was ignorant of the latter, I cannot determine; but 'tis plain he had much Reading at least, if they will not call it Learning. Nor is it any great matter, if a man has knowledge, whether he has it from one language or from another.

This liberal apologia from the translator of Homer, imitator of Horace, approached from a different angle the one discussion which had begun to generate some heat.

From that context one may travel back to Rowe, who wrote no Preface but put into the *Life* passages which belong to prefaces. The fuss appeared in Ben Jonson's affectionate poem in the First Folio, *To the memory of my beloved, The Author Mr. William Shakespeare: And what he hath left us*. After saying how far he outshone Lyly, Kyd, Marlowe, these lines follow:

> And though thou hadst small Latine, and Lesse Greeke,
>   From thence to honour thee, I would not seeke
> For names; but call forth thund'ring Aeschilus,
>   Euripides, and Sophocles to us ...

Jonson started (as Pope points out) a classical tradition of drama in England, envied Shakespeare's success, cherished his friendship and flourished his own trump card, classical scholarship. Rowe mentions

a Conversation between Sir *John Suckling*, Sir *William D'Avenant*,

Endymion Porter, Mr. *Hales* of *Eaton*, and *Ben Johnson;* Sir *John Suckling*, who was a profess'd Admirer of *Shakespear*, had undertaken his
Defence against *Ben Johnson* with some warmth; Mr. *Hales*, who had sat
still for some time, hearing *Ben* frequently reproaching him with the
want of Learning and Ignorance of the Antients, told him at last, *That if
Mr.* Shakespear *had not read the Antients, he had likewise not stollen
anything from 'em*; (a fault the other made no Conscience of) *and that
if he would produce any one Topick finely treated by any of them, he
would undertake to shew something upon the same Subject at least as
well written by* Shakespear.

Hales sounds an attractive spirit, classical scholar, at Eton with his
books, admired by Suckling for 'putting or clearing of a doubt'. He did
both on this occasion, and put down Jonson but not the controversy.
Rowe accepted beyond doubt that Shakespeare 'had no knowledge
of the Writings of the Ancient Poets', partly through leaving school
early but also because in his works 'we find no traces of anything that
looks like an Imitation of 'em', and Imitations were one staff of poetic
life in the first half of the 18th century. It is not an apt word, in
present usage; application or adaptation come closer. Horace or
Juvenal provided models, applied by Pope and Samuel Johnson to
current events. As Shakespeare was credited by Rowe only with such
school grammar memory as allowed one of his characters in *Titus
Andronicus* to recognize

Integer vitae scelerisque purus

as coming from Horace, he needed to name some other quality in
this poet they all loved, but who broke the rules, and originality
became the natural excellence. Hales took the notion of theft to
sting Jonson, who had regarded his power to steal as the height of
civility. Originality became a new virtue, as applied to Shakespeare;
in the late 20th century, with that older commodity, classical knowledge, depreciating faster than the currency, Shakespeare is reckoned to have possessed both abundantly.

Rowe, a good classicist, aware of any departure from Aristotelian
decorum, steered clear of fractious comment for 'finding fault is
certainly the easiest Task of Knowledge, and commonly those Men of
good Judgement, who are likewise of good and gentle Dispositions,
abandon this ungrateful Province to the Tyranny of pedants'. He
found it difficult to use three categories for Shakespeare's plays,
which 'are properly to be distinguish'd only into Comedies and
Tragedies. Those which are called Histories, and even some of his
Comedies, are really Tragedies . . .', but as the reverse was true too,
this argument led nowhere. Most people had come to prefer 'Trage-
Comedy', he believed, above pure tragedy; that vice of Shakespeare's

age, 'tho' the severer Critiques among us cannot bear it', is 'agreeable to the *English* Tast'.

Charles Gildon, editor of the spurious seventh volume of poems, felt Rowe's tolerance passed sensible limits in wondering whether Shakespeare's art actually gained strength through lack of education. This was the offending passage in Rowe:

> Whether his Ignorance of the Antients were a disadvantage to him or no, may admit of a Dispute: For tho' the Knowledge of 'em might have made him more Correct, yet it is not improbable but that the Regularity and Deference for them, which would have attended that Correctness, might have restrain'd some of that Fire, Impetuosity, and even beautiful Extravagance which we admire in *Shakespear:* And I believe we are better pleas'd with those Thoughts altogether New and Uncommon, which his own Imagination supply'd him so abundantly with, than if he had given us the most beautiful Passages out of the *Greek* and *Latin* Poets, and that in the most agreeable manner that it was possible for a Master of the *English* Language to deliver 'em.

In a period which rejected enthusiasm, 'beautiful Extravagance' was a bold phrase at which Gildon aimed his gun in *An Essay on the Art, Rise and Progress of the Stage in Greece, Rome and England.* Agreeing with Rowe that an earlier critic, Rymer, had been too severe upon Shakespeare's indifference to classical rules for drama, he wished to rescue their beloved author from 'the foolish Biggotry of his blind and partial Adorers'. Gildon's reply to Rowe, printed as a preface to the volume which acted as Rowe's seventh, began the long custom of editorial discussion within a single edition. Several opinions they held in common, but this notion of advantage from ignorance struck him as absurd.

> 'Tis my opinion, that if *Shakespear* had had those Advantages of Learning, which the perfect Knowledge of the Ancients wou'd have given him, so great a *Genius* as his, wou'd have made him a very dangerous Rival in Fame to the greatest Poets of Antiquity; so far am I from seeing, how this Knowledge cou'd either have curb'd, confin'd, or spoil'd the natural Excellence of his Writings.

Gildon's usage is sometimes unfamiliar now. He thought Shakespeare surpassed the ancients 'in the *Topics* or *Common Places*' of drama but fell short in the 'Beauties'. This theme of the Beauties of Shakespeare is worth following separately; though he relegated Shakespeare's to the second division, Gildon took a strange course in providing a list of them, with classical parallels to prove superior merit.

Dryden, accepting the sense of Rymer's criticism, had dismissed it with the splendid comment: 'Who minds the Critick, and who admires *Shakespear* less?' – and this too left Gildon sadly puzzled:

That was as much as to say: Mr. *Rymer* has indeed made good his Charge, and yet the Town admir'd his Errors still: which I take to be a greater Proof of the Folly and abandon'd Taste of the Town, than of any Imperfections in the *Critic.*

And that brought him to the problem which faced them all: despite his distressing ignorance they could not reject the truth that Shakespeare bowled them over and left them defenceless. Each in his turn confessed it. Here is Gildon:

> For, in spite of his known and visible Errors, when I read *Shakespear,* even in some of his most irregular Plays, I am surpriz'd into a Pleasure so great, that my Judgement is no longer free to see the faults, tho' they are never so Gross and Evident.

And Gildon was convinced he read Latin; that he chose not to write in imitation of Latin authors, Rowe's argument, proved nothing. Taste excused itself for yielding to the unorthodoxy of genius, by taking a new position on ground of Nature and Originality, romantic concepts with which critics felt more at ease a century later when beauty became truth, truth beauty. Gildon heard the new talk of Nature with grave suspicion, for 'what there is in any Poem, which is out of Nature, and contrary to *Verisimilitude* and *Probability,* can never be *Beautiful,* but *Abominable'.* About this he is amusingly satirical:

> *Nature,* Nature is the great Cry against the Rules. We must all be judg'd by *Nature,* say they, not at all, considering, that *Nature* is an equivocal Word, whose Sense is too various and Extensive ever to be able to appeal too, since it leaves it to the Fancy and Capacity of every one, to decide what is according to Nature, and what not. Besides there may be a great many things Natural, which Dramatick Poetry has nothing to do with. To do the Needs of Life, is as natural as any Action of it, but to bring such a thing into a Piece of History Painting, or Dramatic Poetry, wou'd be monstrous and absur'd, tho' natural; for there may be many things natural in their proper Places, which are not so in others.

And the rest of his long essay explained the meaning of dramatic rule in Aristotle.

* * *

As to Pope's originality in believing 'the Players' had caused so much damage to Shakespeare's text, they were the villains of his piece. 'They have ever had a Standard to themselves, upon other principles than those of *Aristotle* ... Players are just such judges of what is *right,* as Taylors are of what is *graceful.'* He pointed to such irritating ignorance in First Folio stage directions as *Actus tertia, Exit Omnes* and *Enter three Witches solus;* and with regard to that upsetting moment in *Troilus* when Hector is made to quote Aristotle, the Players must again be at fault.

Considering in Shakespeare the problem of 'trifling and bombast passages', of 'mean conceits and ribaldries', Pope found the Players guilty again; for in the quartos he had examined, 'the low scenes of Mob, Plebeians and Clowns, are vastly shorter than at present'. Equally, fine passages from the quartos were omitted in 1623.

> From liberties of this kind, many speeches also were put into the mouths of wrong persons, where the Author now seems chargeable with making them speak out of character: Or sometimes perhaps for no better reason, than that a governing Player, to have the mouthing of some favourite speech himself, would snatch it from the unworthy lips of an Underling.

Though the freshness of Pope's responses is not in question, Rowe and Gildon had praised the same qualities: originality (as alternative to imitation), truth to character, emotional power. Rowe dismissed Rymer's distaste for what looked like ignorance of Aristotle, Gildon felt less tolerant. Pope's first originality was to sweep every trouble into a pile at the door of the Players, his argument supported by Hamlet's wish that 'those who play the Clowns wou'd speak no more than is set down for them'.

His second was at least a *claim*, not accepted by later critics, to have collated and used the early quartos. Tonson, announcing the edition in the *Evening Post,* October 1721, appealed for news of the rare quartos: '. . . any person therefore who is possessed of any old Editions of single Plays of His, and will communicate the same to J. Tonson in the Strand, such Assistance will be received as a particular Obligation, or otherwise acknowledged in any manner they shall think proper.' Six months later Pope advertised for pre-1620 quartos of *The Tempest, Macbeth, Julius Caesar, Timon of Athens, King John* and *Henry VIII.* It was different from advertisements in 1709, preparing for Rowe's edition, asking in a general way that 'any gentlemen who may have any materials by them that may be serviceable to this design will be pleased to transmit them to Jacob Tonson at Gray's Inn Gate'. And a little detective work convinced Pope that quartos and folio were partly printed 'from no better copies than the *Prompter's Book,* or *Piece-meal Parts* written out for the use of the actors'.

This conclusion, first appearing in Pope's preface, opened two centuries of what Greg called 'pessimism' with regard to the First Folio text, until he and Pollard and MacKerrow used other techniques of detection. Pope's theory extended further than in applying his own taste to the text; for such passages as disappointed him he found a fine word, 'not properly Defects, but Superfoetations', defined in Johnson's Dictionary as 'One conception following another, so that both are in the womb together, but come not to the full time for delivery together'; bursting with ideas, was his diagnosis.

Pope rejected the spurious plays taken on board by the Fourth Folio publishers; he left out *Pericles* also, which stayed out for half a century until the Johnson–Steevens edition of 1778. *Titus Androni-cus* he suspected but included as they all did; in the same bracket he placed *Love's Labour's Lost* and *The Winter's Tale*. Though Johnson is credited with discovering a 'line of descent' – the uselessness of the Second, Third and Fourth Folios, which followed the First with more mistakes than authority – Pope seems to say the same thing. The latter part of his paragraph has attracted so much criticism that its opening is ignored but this is what he wrote:

> This is the state in which *Shakespear's* writings lye at present; for since the above-mentioned Folio Edition, all the rest have implicitly followed it, without having recourse to any of the former, or ever making the comparison between them.

His point is that all old blunders from 1623 were foolishly followed in later editions; Johnson said the same from a different point of view, by suggesting none but the First Folio carried authority.

There follows in Pope's preface a sentence he may have lived to regret:

> I have discharg'd the dull duty of an Editor, to my best judgement, with more labour than I expect thanks, with a religious abhorrence of all Innovation, and without any indulgence to my private sense or conjecture.

It was no doubt misunderstood; his becoming modesty had the face-value of flattery in a dedication, but that 'dull duty of an editor' caused trouble, awoke opposition. In context it seems to mean no more than that the humble job is done as well as possible: who would not breathe a sigh of relief at the end? Johnson, who heaved and rolled in anguish, and kept the publisher waiting, was not immune. Religious abhorrence of all Innovation was an amusing phrase, for Innovation had then a special frowning overtone in religious usage. The first example in Johnson's Dictionary, from Hooker, gives it: 'The love of things ancient doth argue stayedness; but levity and want of experience maketh apt unto *innovations*'.

Pope's innovations as explained in the Preface were impeccable:

> The various Readings are fairly put in the margin, so that every one may compare 'em; and those I have prefer'd into the Text are constantly *ex fide Codicum*, upon authority. The Alterations or Additions which *Shakespear* himself made, are taken notice of as they occur.

His stance was more free than Rowe's, because of those spectral 'Players'. If they had made such a hash of Shakespeare's text his duty as editor, poet, man of taste, was to correct and disinter. The period of greater emendation developed from this, from comparable openings created by successive editors. Pope cannot be blamed; it seems more proper to honour his perception which observed the need – and to quote again the new Oxford editor, 'since we do not *know* what Shakespeare wrote, someone has to *decide* what Shakespeare wrote, on the basis of the evidence available at a particular time. Editors are the people who decide.'

II   FROM THEOBALD TO WARBURTON

As Lewis Theobald brought life and controversy to Shakespeare editing, he is unlucky in reputation as the King of Dullness in Pope's *Dunciad*. Dullness changed its sense a little, in the course of that debate. Pope's apology for discharging the dull duty of an editor reads as the polite relief of one who completes his humble task, but 'dull' was so taken up and wrenched out that he cast it back with strength of meaning in the *Dunciad*, where it stands for long foot-notes on minimal matters. Johnson received the word thus, and it would be ridiculous to question his understanding:

> This was a work which *Pope* seems to have thought unworthy of his abilities, being not able to suppress his contempt of *the dull duty of an editor*. He understood but half his undertaking. The duty of a collator is indeed dull, yet, like other tedious tasks, is very necessary, but an emen-datory critick would ill discharge his duty, without qualities very differ-ent from dullness ... Let us now be told no more of the dull duty of an editor.

Johnson was perhaps less than just to Pope who had done his job 'with a religious Abhorrence of all Innovation, and without any Indul-gence to my private Sense or Conjecture'. It was relatively a 'dull' or humble task for a poet who suppressed temptation towards more imaginative treatment.

Theobald's complaint was against this restraint, not (as Johnson's) that Pope viewed his task as boring. The ambiguity suggests a pro-gression:

1. Pope apologizes conventionally for completing his humble labour inadequately.
2. Theobald attacks excessive restraint in the poet who might have provided imaginative restoration.
3. Pope satirizes Theobald as an unimaginative blockhead, King of boredom, a footnote maniac.
4. Johnson condemns Pope for reckoning editorial duties to be a bore.
5. *We* condemn Pope for daring to impose his own taste and changes upon the text.

And Theobald used a different word, *drudgery*, for Pope's 'dullness' of the *Dunciad* and Johnson's in the *Preface*. He experienced it in the chore of correcting punctuation.

> I am sorry that the Use and Intention of this Undertaking ties me down to the Necessity of one unpleasant Office, That of setting right the Faults in Pointing, and those meerly literal, committed by the Printer, and con-

tinued by too negligent a Revisal. This is the Drudgery of Correction, in which I could wish to have been spar'd, there being no Pleasure in the Execution of it, nor any Merit, but that of dull Diligence, when executed.

If Pope's dullness was mere restraint, it stung him to be attacked for seeming merit; he could satirize Theobald's definition of that quality, hence the *Dunciad.*

Theobald is so large a figure in 18th-century Shakespeare that it is easiest to approach him obliquely through Bentley, whose edition of *Paradise Lost* was published by Tonson and others in 1732. Similarities in approach seem to make Bentley the catalyst for Pope and Theobald. One year earlier than the 1733 Shakespeare,* his could be reckoned the first critical edition of an English author but the dates are confusing, because *Shakespeare Restored* (his attack against Pope's edition), 1726, and the related controversy, pre-dated it. Bentley's semi-scrupulous proposals may well show the influence of Theobald's book; his Milton came too late to have much effect upon the 1733 Shakespeare except for its Preface.

In large quarto format Bentley's *Paradise Lost* is among the most handsome of Tonson's books, like Pope's Shakespeare and quite unlike the very decent working efficiency of Theobald's. Pope, Bentley, Hanmer were aristocrats among men of letters. Vertue engraved two excellent portraits of Milton, aged 21 and 62. Though large-paper copies of the 1733 Shakespeare also exist, on good thick paper, they lack much sense of occasion.

Theobald became scrupulous, or tedious, in *Shakespeare Restored* by detailing every minimal change of punctuation; unlike Bentley, who declared in the second paragraph of his Preface that faults

> ... in Orthography, Distinction by Points, and Capital Letters, all which swarm in the prior Editions, are here very carefully, and it's hop'd, judiciously corrected: though no mention is made in the Notes of that little but useful Improvement.

Like Pope, Theobald and all the editors, Bentley promised no change had been made in the text itself, corrections and suggestions being confined to margins and notes. As margins of a good copy are wide enough, his strange proposals seem more distracting than unsightly. Where Pope invented the Players, Bentley imagined an appalling combination of amanuensis and printer as root of all the evils he detected:

> This Bookseller, and that Acquaintance who seems to have been the sole Corrector of the Press, brought forth their First Edition, polluted with such monstrous Faults, as are beyond Example in any other printed Book.

---

* Theobald's edition, dated 1733, was not on sale until 1734

THE

Examination *and* Correction

OF THE

TRAGEDY of *HAMLET*.

I. Act 1. Scene 1. Page 346.

.
HEN yon fame ftar, that's weftward from the pole,
Had made his courfe t'illume that part of heav'n
Where now it burns, - - - - -

Various
Reading.

SOME of the old Editions read, *t'illumine*; which feems to be the trueft deriv'd Word, (from *illumino* in the *Latin*,) and is the Word ufed by our Author in another Place.

TWO GENTLEMEN of *VERONA*, pag. 195.

> *If I be not by her fair Influence*
> *Fofter'd, illumin'd,*

C

In

16 Start of the offending passages in Theobald's *Shakespeare Restored*, 1726. [Actual height of *type area* 8¾ inches]

Thus providing ample ground, Bentley could exercise his speculative taste in such passages as this from Book Eight, where Milton wrote:

> Love refines
> The thoughts, and heart enlarges; hath his seat
> In Reason: and is judicious, is the scale
> By which to heav'nly Love thou may'st ascend,
> Not sunk in carnal pleasure . . .

and Bentley, convinced that 'and is judicious' sounded wrong, offered in the margin an amazing phrase, 'unlibidinous is'.

'Spurious verses' appear in the printed text, says Bentley, 'which the Poet, had he known of them, *vel furca ejecisset*, would have thrown out with a Fork'. It echoes the puzzle of editors facing Shakespeare's unconventional use of words – creating language, as it now seems; displaying vulgar origins, as it struck them.

Bentley's Preface has one absorbingly facile sentence which deserves a close look:

> But though the Printer's Faults are corrigible by retrieving the Poet's own Words, not from a Manuscript, (for none exists) but by Sagacity, and happy Conjecture: and though the Editor's Interpolations are detected by their own Silliness and Unfitness; and easily cured by printing them in the *Italic* Letter, and inclosing them between two Hooks; yet *Milton's* own Slips and Inadvertencies cannot be redress'd without a Change both of the Words and Sense.

So Bentley distinguished three categories of error: the Printer's Faults, the Editor's Interpolations, Milton's own Slips. The first, a large grey area, may be discreetly adjusted by Sagacity, and happy Conjecture; for the second and third, italic and parenthesis and footnote will serve. Perhaps this helps to explain the apparent inconsistency between Pope's promise to leave the text of Shakespeare untouched, and his performance. It would be absurd to suggest that he or Bentley set out to deceive.

As to the suggested emendations, an innocent game of using a mechanism devised for the classics upon English poetry, Bentley enjoyed himself as Theobald did. 'I made the Notes *extempore*, and put them to the Press as soon as made; without any Apprehension of growing leaner by Censures, or plumper by Commendations.' In Notes an editor gains his freedom; readers can make him lean or plump.

*   *   *

Theobald, in the 1733 Preface, compared his edition with Bentley's, making a distinction which seems to claim more; for where Bentley's

Preface accepted the impossibility of discovering what Milton had dictated, Theobald held 'Hopes of restoring to the Publick their greatest Poet in his Original Purity: after having so long lain in a Condition that was a Disgrace to common Sense'. If their practice was more similar than their theory, Theobald felt he had achieved 'the first Assay of the kind on any modern Author whatsoever'. He needed some such claim after the years of pioneering preparation, correspondence and controversy. His interpretation of Bentley is phrased like one of Thomas Edwards's satirical *Canons of Criticism*: 'The chief Turn of his Criticism is plainly to show the World, that if *Milton* did not write as He would have him, he ought to have wrote so'.

'Literal Criticism', Theobald's phrase for the footnote paragraphs of explanation and comment in which he and Bentley both indulged, had brought wounding attention from Pope. 'Another Expedient, to make my work appear of a trifling Nature, has been an Attempt to depreciate *Literal Criticism.*' Anyone finds difficulty in defending the temptation to become a bore in his own subject. Theobald felt the injustice, when for years critics of Greek and Latin authors had used that method:

> I should account it a Peculiar Happiness, that, by the faint Assay I have made in this Work, a Path might be chalk'd out, for abler Hands, by which to derive the same Advantages to our own Tongue: a Tongue, which, tho' it wants none of the fundamental Qualities of an universal Language, yet as a *noble Writer* says, lisps and stammers in its Cradle; and has produced little more towards its polishing than Complaints of its Barbarity.

The Preface to *Shakespeare Restored* wanted no defence, as its author at the time of writing had not been attacked; he was the aggressor, in a notion familiar to players of Boggle and Scrabble. Corrupt texts of Shakespeare needed attention and correction, most critics have agreed from that day to this; Theobald swimming in those waters complains that Pope only felt the temperature with his toe. Where some passages in Shakespeare struck Theobald as so obscure as to look like 'flat Nonsense, and invincible Darkness' a marvellous possibility appeared to him: 'I can, by the Addition or Alteration of a single letter, or two, give him both Sense and Sentiment'. And he wondered, with confident optimism the centuries have not always supported,

> ... what true Lover of this Poet, who shall find him so easily cur'd, will not owe his Thanks for a Passage retriev'd from Obscurity, and no Meaning? and say, Shakespeare must certainly have wrote so?

Much bitterness followed the publication of this large quarto which

Curll produced wittily to look like a final corrective volume of Pope's Shakespeare; so it is worth recalling how Theobald's argument differed from later criticism of Pope, who has been dismissed as negligent in collation and casual in adjusting the text to his taste. Theobald's objection to the 'dull Duty of an Editor'[1] was that Pope should have been more assertive, less apprehensive.

> I cannot help thinking this Gentleman's *Modesty* in this Point too *nice* and *blameable;* and that what he is pleased to call a religious *Abhorrence* of *Innovation*, is downright *Superstition:* Neither can I be of Opinion, that the Writings of Shakespeare are so *venerable*, as that we should be excommunicated from good Sense, for daring to *innovate properly;* or that we ought to be as cautious of altering *their* text, as we would That of the *sacred Writings.*

This sort of coarseness stung, making Pope's polite phrase about religious abhorrence of innovation sound pretentious, and elaborated the metaphor to offensive meaning. Theobald rocked the boat. Launched into enthusiasm, finding his subject after years of undistinguished theatre work, he brought an end to critical decorum in this theme until Johnson restored it for a while. The greater discourtesies came from Pope, after 1726, not Theobald who illustrated their different approach by the pleasant story of an old priest who for years had made a mistake in his Breviary, reading *Mumpsimus* instead of *Sumpsimus*, 'and being told of his Blunder, and solicited to correct it, *The Alteration may be just*, said he; but, however, *I'll not change my old Mumpsimus for your new Sumpsimus*'. It is apt for Shakespeare, where a familiar phrase often sounds more comfortable than some well argued emendation.

For the 1733 Preface Theobald has been criticized because, as time approached for this responsible end to the long task, he wrote diffidently to Warburton confessing that on any other matter advice was possible but in the Preface an author stands alone. Theobald could not be supposed incapable of a Preface in which with perfect lucidity he expanded the 1726 Introduction, defended himself against years of attack, replied by argument and instance and principle.

He responded as others had to Shakespeare's qualities, opening with eloquent tribute to the whole spectrum, comparing one's experience of Shakespeare with 'going into a large, a spacious, and a splendid Dome thro' the Conveyance of a narrow and obscure Entry'. In terms similar to Pope's he admired the truth and separation of character; unlike him, high and low form part of this overall gothic

---

[1] I have taken this to mean humble duty

acceptance of whatever the eye observes beneath the splendid Dome – 'Clowns and Fops' especially, 'different in Features and Lineaments of Character, as we are from one another in Face, or Complexion'.

Rowe's *Life* in 1709 had taken the place of a Preface. Theobald gave a summary of Rowe and continued his own critical essay. Rowe's choice of favourite passages is of course ignored; Theobald prints one which struck him as having 'a Pomp and Terror in it, that perfectly astonishes', seven lines from *Julius Caesar:*

> Between the acting of a dreadful Thing,
> And the first Motion, all the *interim* is
> Like a Phantasma, or a hideous Dream:
> The Genius and the moral Instruments
> Are then in Council; and the State of Man,
> Like to a little Kingdom, suffers then
> The Nature of an Insurrection.

Other than this instance, Theobald chose to leave readers to find their own marvellous passages in the plays.

Again like Pope, he judged that Shakespeare used Greek and Latin authors in translation. This 18th-century problem began as one of adjustment: how could such excellent art rise from ignorance of the springs of art? It evaporated into guesses about Shakespeare's equipment. Theobald opened with caution:

> Tho' I should be very unwilling to allow *Shakespeare* so poor a Scholar, as many have labour'd to represent him, yet I shall be very cautious of declaring too positively on the other side of the Question: that is, with regard to my Opinion of his Knowledge in the dead Languages.

Himself a good classical scholar, he took a new view of the controversy 'as it related to the Knowledge of *History* and *Books*' – ground less sacred than Latin and Greek – concluding that the abundance of errors was an aspect of art, intentional. This liberal attitude seems far from Theobald's reputation as petty pedant:

> A Reader of Taste may easily observe, that tho' *Shakespeare*, almost in every Scene of his historical Plays, commits the grossest Offences against Chronology, History, and Antient Politicks; yet This was not thro' Ignorance, as is generally supposed, but thro' the too powerful Blaze of his Imagination; which, when once raised, made all acquired Knowledge vanish and disappear before it. For Instance, in his *Timon*, he turns *Athens*, which was a perfect Democracy, into an Aristocracy; while he ridiculously gives a Senator the Power of banishing *Alcibiades*.

Such absurdities were not offered in ignorance, Theobald says, and Shakespeare observed accurate historical detail when the drama needed it.

The comparable worry about Anachronisms is faced later in the Preface with equal spirit. There had been that distressing moment in Act II Scene 4 of *Troilus* in Pope's edition, when in a speech by Hector 'graver sages think' was substituted for 'Aristotle thought' – not quite silently, for Pope gave the folio reading in a footnote, an instance of Pope's manners and his method. In *Shakespeare Restored*[2] and again in the Preface Theobald attacked, accepting the anachronism as art, poetic licence, and counter-attacked with examples from Pope's translation of Homer.

Each 18th-century editor gave poor report of his predecessor. Theobald declared Rowe had 'neither corrected his Text, nor collated the old Copies'; was capable of doing well, 'had but his Industry been equal to his Talents'. Upon Pope he was more severe, having suffered from the *Dunciad:* '. . . pretended to have collated the old Copies, and yet seldom has corrected the Text but to its Injury . . . I have made it evident throughout my Remarks, that he has frequently inflicted a Wound where he intended a Cure'. The wounds inflicted by Pope were not forgiven; Theobald's condensed phrasing almost conceals the power of his reply:

> Were it every where the true Text, which That Editor in his late pompous Edition gave us, the Poet deserv'd not the large Encomiums bestow'd by him.

Pope's complaisance struck him as more damaging than Rymer's criticism, because 'The Censure of so divine an Author sets us upon his Defence; and this produces an exact Scrutiny and Examination, which ends in finding out and discriminating the true from the spurious'. Pope confused him, Rymer stimulated. In a more private way he cannot forgive, for

> there are Provocations, which a man can never quite forget. His Libels have been thrown out with so much Inveteracy, that, not to dispute whether they *should* come from a *Christian*, they leave it a Question whether they *could* come from a *Man*.

It remains unpleasant to read satirical comment upon Pope's Catholicism and his deformity.

Theobald gave a closer analysis of the quartos than Pope, who had paid more attention than Rowe but largely dismissed them as 'the *Prompter's Book*, or *Piece-meal Parts* written out for the use of the actors', adding therefore to corruptions which confused his demon 'Players' in 1623. Theobald better understood their history as piracies, attributing errors to three causes: inaccurate short-hand

---

[2] Appendix, p.134

transcription, false recollection, theft of individual actors' parts from the theatres.

Emendation, explanation, and 'Inquiry into the Beauties and Defects of Composition' formed for Theobald the three duties of an editor; of these he attended especially to the first two, as the third 'lies open for every willing Undertaker'. No pointer to beauties of Shakespeare, no starred passages in Theobald; he was the first to avoid it, and Johnson the second. As to emendation, his originality lay in attempting to justify by science not taste; that anyway was the theory, not always evident in his long correspondence with Warburton. But the language of his resolve gave scope for escape. 'His genuine Text is religiously adher'd to, and the Numerous Faults and Blemishes, purely his own, are left as they were found'. Apart from the repeated use of 'religiously' which he had noted in Pope it remains subjective, he judging both the genuineness of text and which among the faults and blemishes were Shakespearean. The next sentence set him free to wander:

> Nothing is alter'd, but what by the clearest Reasoning can be proved a Corruption of the true Text; and the Alteration, a real Restoration of the genuine Reading.

They all began with similar promises, but what clear reasoning could prove corruption? It was the editorial problem, from that day to this, and no doubt computers get it wrong too. Pope's 'religious abhorrence of all Innovation, and without any indulgence to my private sense or conjecture' is by now familiar. Rowe, it will be recalled, set out 'to compare the several Editions, and give the true Reading as well as I could from thence'.

Rowe, Pope and Theobald must have reckoned that if they erred it was from excess of scruple. This 'Addition or Alteration of a Letter or two', a 1726 phrase repeated in the Preface, seemed to Theobald a minor matter – 'such Corrections, I am persuaded, will need no Indulgence'. Where he has taken 'a great Latitude and Liberty in amending', the change is supported by that method of 'parallel passages' which he had explored at length in *Shakespeare Restored*. In this he differed from Pope's faith in a private sense of fitness. Where the text was clear, 'tho', perchance, low and trivial', Theobald left it.

All this led to something like academic method, which Pope considered a boring travesty. Modern Shakespeare editing must stand beyond imaginable range of any explosive *Dunciad*. Though he and Rowe claimed to have collated against the quartos, Theobald was first to collect, examine and compare with any thoroughness; beyond doubt he stood first in the line of professional amateurs, followed by Capell and Steevens, Reed and Malone: scholars with their private libraries, widely read in the literature of 16th and 17th-century theatre, delighting in parallel passages. 'I have thought it my Duty, in the first place', wrote Theobald, 'by diligent and laborious Collation to take in the Assistances of all the older Copies.' The second and third places he mentioned towards the end of this long essay:

> Besides a faithful Collation of all the printed Copies . . . let it suffice to say, that, to clear up several Errors in the Historical Plays, I purposely read over *Hall* and *Hollingshead's* Chronicles in the Reigns concern'd; all the Novels in *Italian*, from which our Author had borrow'd any of his Plots; such parts of *Plutarch* from which he had deriv'd any Parts of his *Greek* or *Roman* story; *Chaucer* and *Spenser's* Works; all the Plays of B. *Jonson, Beaumont* and *Fletcher*, and above 800 old *English* Plays, to ascertain the obsolete and uncommon Phrases in him.

All this he did, enjoying the colossal task except for 'some Labour and Pains unpleasantly spent in the dry Task of consulting Etymological *Glossaries*'. Dry task among glossaries, drudgery of punctuation; Pope's term 'dull' meant something different.

All this reading, such total immersion in the period, made it poss-ible to distinguish three types of obscurity which justify the many long notes which characterize his edition. Those obscurities 'common to him with all Poets of the same Species' sprang from an English habit of humour and satire, which needed familiarity with Shakespeare's people and period, for

> These owing their immediate Birth to the peculiar Genius of each Age, an infinite Number of Things alluded to, glanced at, and expos'd, must needs become obscure, as the *Characters* themselves are antiquated, and dis-used.

Then there was the explosion of new thought, speculation, science which so fascinated writers who wandered among them that they 'declined vulgar Images, such as are immediately fetch'd from Nature, and rang'd thro' the Circle of the Sciences to fetch their Ideas from thence'. Shakespeare fell into this 'vicious Manner', needing the help of footnotes more than a century later:

> The ostentatious Affectation of abstruse Learning, peculiar to that Time, the Love that Men naturally have to every Thing that looks like Mystery, fixed them down to this Habit of Obscurity. Thus became the Poetry of Donne (tho' the wittiest man of that Age,) nothing but a continued Heap of Riddles.

And that second type of obscurity remains a puzzle for us in imagin-ing those mythical nut-cracking groundlings who could no more make head or tale of it then than a Stratford or Barbican audience can now, to the chronic embarrassment of producers who think of every

distracting device to override public boredom and win the applause
which never disappoints.

> The third Species of *Obscurities*, which deform our Author, as the Effects
> of his own Genius and Character, are Those that proceed from his
> peculiar Manner of *Thinking*, and as peculiar a Manner of *cloathing*
> those *Thoughts*.

These are really third and fourth types of obscurity tied together: a
tendency to range wide among new sciences (different from his
second obscurity, of employing scientific imagery), and to use difficult or unfamiliar diction. 'He therefore frequently uses old Words,
to give his Diction an Air of Solemnity; as he coins others, to express
the Novelty and Variety of his Ideas.' All offered scope for the footnote paragraphs which Theobald thoroughly enjoyed providing.

Appreciation rather than fault-finding appeared to him the duty of
a critic; Rymer and Gildon he bracketed as displaying 'the hypercriti-
cal Part of the Science of Criticism', Rymer's excesses 'have taught
me to distinguish between the *Railer* and the *Critick*... Extravagant
Abuse throws off the Edge of the intended Disparagement, and turns
the Madman's Weapon into his own Bosom'.

Theobald, more abused than abusing, expected a hostile reception
for his work, but 'Fact, I hope, will be able to stand its Ground against
Banter and Gaiety'. Its completion represented an alteration of
course since his 1728 *Proposals*, which had announced only an
extension of the kind of comment and instance which filled *Shakespeare Restored*, for 'some *noble* Persons then, whom I have no
privilege to name, were pleased to interest themselves so far in the
Affair, as to propose to Mr. *Tonson* his undertaking an Impression of
Shakespeare with my Corrections'.

Warburton's help is so amply acknowledged that nobody could
have imagined a cause for such rebuke as came in reply. He was not
then Bishop of Gloucester but a speculative theologian in his early
30s, 'the Reverend Mr. *William Warburton* of *Newark* upon *Trent*.'

> This Gentleman, from the Motives of his frank and communicative Dispo-
> sition, took a considerable Part of my Trouble off my Hands; not only read
> over the whole Author for me, with the exactest Care; but enter'd into a
> long and laborious Epistolary Correspondence; to which I owe no small
> Part of my best Criticisms upon my Author.

Courtesy in scholarship and fascination with detail which made
possible the achievement of this pioneer work may be imagined
from the few lines of thanks to his friend Hawley Bishop, mentioned
in a letter to Warburton[3] as 'another kind labourer in the vineyard'.

---

[3] Nov. 15, 1729

With Bishop he went through all Shakespeare. 'We join'd Business and Entertainment together; and at every of our Meetings, which were constantly once a Week, we read over a *Play*, and came mutually prepar'd to communicate our Conjectures upon it to each other.'

Johnson never showed himself more prejudiced by a man's position than when asked to compare Warburton as critic with Theobald: 'O, Sir, he'd make two-and-fifty Theobalds, cut into slices!' The reputation for dullness attached to Theobald by Pope, as a by-product of his own apologia for the dull duty of an editor, suggests little more than an 18th-century habit of using some word or phrase satirically, which in its place looked harmless. In 1728 a play called *Double Falshood* appeared, adapted by Theobald from manuscript which he claimed to have been Shakespeare's. Every sort of trouble could and did come from this; Theobald's judgement as a Shakespeare critic looked ridiculous, his motives were suspect and the title seemed to describe his claim; but Pope took from it one line, 'None but himself can be his parallel', as expressing the absurdity of Theobald. A correspondent in the *Gentleman's Magazine*[4] wrote pointing out learnedly that it was a translation from Seneca, and so not deserving Pope's malice:

> Theobald, the professed Rival of Pope in the Editorship of Shakespeare, and, probably, for *this* reason the *original* Hero of *The Dunciad*, by the escape of one unlucky line,
>
>> 'None but himself can be his parallel',
>
> gave that wicked Wit a real advantage over him, and justly exposed himself to the Keenest severity of his satire.

Of course, Pope would have fastened on some other phrase if that line had not come as a natural gift. Theobald is perversely reckoned the dull editor, because Pope threw that term back to him in the *Dunciad;* his irritation in the literal understanding of conventional diffidence made him do so. Johnson's eighth definition of the word, in his Dictionary, is 'Not exhilarating; not delightful; as *to make dictionaries* is dull *work'*. I doubt whether any of the three of them found editing Shakespeare dull in quite that sense; Theobald was exhilarated by most aspects, and delighted.

The recollection became bitter for Pope, through Theobald's sustained attack in *Shakespeare Restored;* upon it, wrote Johnson in his Life of Pope, 'he never seems to have reflected afterwards without vexation'. In the same essay Johnson called Theobald 'a man of heavy diligence, with very slender powers'. Pope's wit in the *Dunciad* had

---

[4] Rev. E. Kynaston, Vol I, p.507, quoted by Nichols

1   *The Tempest*, Rowe, 1709. [Actual height of *image* $6\frac{5}{8}$ inches]

Lud. Du Guernier inv.

v.1.p.1.

2 *The Tempest,* Rowe, 1714. [Actual height of *image* 5½ inches]

H. *Gravelot in & del.* G. *Vander Gucht scul.*

Vol.1 P.1.

3 *The Tempest,* Theobald, 1740. [Actual height of *image* 5$\frac{3}{16}$ inches]

F. Hayman inv.　　　　　　　　　　　　H. Gravelot Sculp.

The taming of the SHREW. Act. 4. Sc. 2.

4　*The Taming of the Shrew,* Hanmer, 1744. [Actual height of *image* $8\frac{1}{8}$ inches]

TITUS ANDRONICUS. Act. 4. Sc. 3.

F. Hayman inv.   H. Gravelot sculp.

5 *Titus Andronicus*, Hanmer, 1744. [Actual height of *image* 8$\frac{5}{16}$ inches]

6   *The Tempest,* Bell, 1773. [Actual height of *image* $5\frac{3}{16}$ inches]

Act 1. TEMPEST. *Scene 1.*

Ramberg Sherwin & Grignion fec.

MISS PHILLIPS in MIRANDA.

.... O! the cry did knock
against my very heart. Poor souls! they perish'd.

Printed for John Bell British Library Strand Janʳ nᵈ 1785.

7   *The Tempest,* from Bell's 20 volume edition, 1785. [Actual height of
image 3¾ inches]

Ramberg del.ᵗ   Hall sculp.ᵗ

Mᵣˢ SIDDONS in ISABELLA.

Justice, O royal Duke! vail your regard
Upon a wrong'd, I would fain have said, a Maid!

London Printed for John Bell British Library Strand, March 10ᵗʰ 1785.

8 *Measure for Measure,* from Bell's 20 volume edition, 1785. [Actual height of *image* 3½ inches]

Double Falshood;

OR,

The DISTREST LOVERS.

A

PLAY,

As it is Acted at the

THEATRE-ROYAL

IN

DRURY-LANE.

Written Originally by *W. SHAKESPEARE*;
And now Revised and Adapted to the Stage
By Mr. THEOBALD, the Author of *Shakespeare Restor'd.*

———— Quod optanti Divûm promittere nemo
Auderet, volvenda Dies, en! attulit ultrò.   Virg.

LONDON:

Printed by J. WATTS, at the Printing-Office in
Wild-Court near *Lincolns-Inn Fields.*

M DCC XXVIII.

---

17   Title page of the play for which Theobald made large claims,
1728. [Actual height of *type* 6½ inches]

done its job, its venom partly understandable from the novelty of Theobald's exercise: by what right did this hack-writer for the theatre put down Pope's Shakespeare? That form of literary criticism was nobody's province, certainly not his. A stanza among Notes to the *Dunciad* expresses it:

> 'Tis generous, *Tibbald!* in thee and thy brothers,
> To help us thus to read the works of others:
> Never for this can just returns be shown;
> For who will help us e'er to read thy own?

That form of abuse would not have been used upon the main highways of *classical* criticism, where he was very competent, but Theobald had an old connection with Nathaniel Mist, described by Nichols as 'Printer of a scandalous Weekly Journal bearing his own name'. In Mist's Journal he became The Censor, writing thrice-weekly essays, until that became itself an independent journal for a life of 96 issues. Those were peccadillos of Theobald's youth, but after *Shakespeare Restored* he resumed the habit of letters to Mist's Journal on the theme of Pope's Shakespeare, which inspired four famous and deadly lines in the *Dunciad:*

> Here studious I unlucky moderns save,
> Nor sleeps one error in its father's grave,
> Old puns restore, lost blunders nicely seek,
> And crucify poor Shakespear once a week.

Two and a half centuries later it reads painlessly. 'He seeks for one who hath been concerned in the Journals, written bad Plays or Poems, and published low Criticisms: He finds his name to be *Tibbald*, and he becomes of course the hero of the poem.' And the poem was addressed to

> Dulness! whose good old cause I yet defend,
> With whom my Muse began, with whom shall end!

Here are the six lethal lines aimed straight at Theobald, still addressing Dulness:

> For thee I dim these eyes, and stuff this head,
> With all such reading as was never read;
> For thee supplying, in the worst of days,
> Notes to dull books, and prologues to dull plays;
> For thee explain a thing till all men doubt it,
> And write about it, Goddess, and about it . . .

Thus was Theobald's formidable background in Elizabethan literature scorned, along with the tedium of his footnotes – as they struck Pope, who did not live to experience Warburton's! Such passages in the *Dunciad* display a Mumpsimus rather than a Sumpsimus attitude to English literature.

A brilliant note which opens 'Remarks on Book the Second' of the *Dunciad* may have inspired the comparable group called *Canons of Criticism* which Thomas Edwards devised to taunt Warburton twenty years later. It reads:

> Two things there are, upon the supposition of which the very basis of all Verbal criticism is founded and supported: The first, that an Author could never fail to use the best word, on every occasion: The second, that a Critic cannot chuse but know, which that is? This being granted, when-ever any word doth not fully content us, we take upon us to conclude, first that the author would never have us'd it, and secondly, that he must have used that very one which we conjecture in its stead.

It has become conventional to spell Shakespeare thus, as in the Folios, but Rowe deleted the final e and Pope followed his example; Hanmer and Warburton observed Pope's spelling of the name, in using his text. Theobald restored Shakespeare; the title of his book seems to carry that second sense, exciting Pope's sensitivity from the start, as is clear from his first Remark on the opening page of Book the First:

> The *Dunciad, Sic* M.S. It may be well disputed whether this be a right Reading? Ought it not rather to be spelled *Dunceiad*, as the Etymology evidently demands? *Dunce* with an *e.* therefore *Dunceiad* with an *e.* That accurate and punctual Man of Letters, the Restorer of *Shakespeare*, constantly observes the preservation of this very letter *e*, in spelling the Name of his beloved Author, and not like his common careless Editors, with the omission of one, nay sometimes of two *ee*'s [as *Shak'spear*] which is utterly unpardonable.

And that whole note is signed 'Theobald'.

From that time to this Theobald's reputation as critic has been as changeable as the weather. Nichol Smith was dismissive, modern editors naturally admire his pioneer work towards a computer Shakespeare.[5] Here is Gary Taylor[6] comparing him with Pope:

> Theobald was the better scholar, and indeed remains one of the finest editors of the last three centuries. His collection of early quartos was larger than Pope's his knowledge of Shakespeare's period wider, his enthusiasm for the task greater, his aesthetic preconceptions less obviously anachronistic.

Churton Collins in his *Dictionary of National Biography* entry believed it 'would not be too much to say that the text of Shakes-peare owes more to Theobald than to any other editor'.

---

[5] In 1990 an excellent book by Peter Seary was published (*Lewis Theobald and the Editing of Shakespeare*, Clarendon Press) providing a just assessment
[6] Introduction to the Oxford *Textual Companion*, p.54

While he lived it was reprinted in smaller format (1740, eight volumes) with reduced notes and shorter Preface; and there were later reprints, though his edition yielded to Johnson's after a while. In all, according to Nichols, 12,860 sets were sold. Theobald made money from his Shakespeare, but never enough; the large fee of six hundred and fifty-two pounds ten shillings he received from Tonson for the first edition was just ten shillings short of three times the fee Tonson paid Pope for his quarto edition, and a little less than twice Johnson's.

He was a man of formidable learning. Nichols judged that 'in an intimate acquaintance with the Greek and Roman Classicks, he was at least on an equality with Mr. Pope – perhaps even his superior; and in old English Literature, though sarcastically styled "such reading as was never read", he was scarcely excelled even by his very learned Friend Mr. Warburton'. The Shakespeare editions are his monument, though he had gone some way towards editing Beaumont and Fletcher before he died in 1744. His high expectations of election as Poet Laureate in 1730 were disappointed when Cibber got the job instead; poets laureate remained at a low ebb, for few would now trouble to read Eusden whose death caused the vacancy, or Cibber, or the poems of Theobald which Churton Collins called 'perfectly worthless'. He lived on as theatre hack, and the manner of his death was touchingly reported by a Covent Garden friend who lived nearby:

> He had laboured under a jaundice for some months, which, after several changes of amendment and relapses, terminated in a dropsy; which, about two days after his being tapped, carried him off. His death was very remarkable, not only in that he went off quietly without agonies, but also that he was so composed as not to alter the disposition of his body, being in an easy indolent posture, one foot out of bed, and his head gently supported by one hand. He was a man well versed in the learned languages, and tolerably well acquainted with the modern.

Buried in his books might have been more appropriate: Theobald in an easy indolent posture, one foot out of bed, and his head gently supported by one hand, seems less characteristic.

* * *

After Pope's quarrel with Theobald came Hanmer's with Warburton. The indignation of both becomes humanly understandable in long letters from each, illustrating attitudes to English literary criticism which had not yet sorted themselves out. Warburton, rising but not risen in the church, author of a most peculiar theory opposing the dogma of immortality because Jews seemed to manage adequately without it, was not a professional critic – none existed –

but Hanmer stood out as an amateur, a gentleman to Warburton's player, as Warburton had behaved towards Theobald. English class distinctions, absurd now because the gentleman is an extinct species, became recognizable and explicit in the 18th century, trivialities about which these two editors showed themselves hypersensitive.

After Theobald's edition was published, Warburton, who enjoyed Shakespearean discourse on small textual points, commenced a friendship with Hanmer, retired politician, Whig, for a brief while Speaker of the House of Commons; a different relationship from the earlier one with Theobald, professional writer in the theatre. Visiting Sir Thomas Hanmer at Mildenhall, his seat in Suffolk, was quite another story.

Both versions of the quarrel, one written almost 20 years after the other, provide human details which cannot have been invented – as in Warburton's recollection of asking for the return of his own letters, when Hanmer fussed about right of ownership as he had paid postage.

Hanmer was not last of the outsiders, but most prominent in what he produced and the way it was done. Two years before publication he wrote more in sorrow than anger (Warburton's later letter was the reverse) to Dr. Smith at All Souls, politely asking that the project be shelved along with his Shakespeares 'if you are not fully satisfied that some advantage may arise from it to the University'; with seeming indifference to Tonson's claims upon copyright, he had offered it to Oxford. Then, the most surprising sentence: 'I am satisfied there is no edition coming, or likely to come, from Warburton; but it is a report raised to serve some little purpose or other, of which I see there are many on foot'. Old Hanmer had dismissed from his mind the notion of a clergyman's scheme to pirate his notes.

To clarify that history for Smith he recalled the exchange of letters begun by Warburton who had asked the Bishop of Salisbury's introduction 'for this purpose only, as was then declared, that as he had many observations upon Shakespear then lying by him, over and above those printed in Theobald's book, he much desired to communicate them to me, that I might judge whether any of them were worthy to be added to those emendations which he understood I had long been making upon that author'.

A pleasant old notion of intellectual communion. Perhaps both met in that frame of mind, storing an unspoken possibility each was too reticent to mention. It did not long survive the Mildenhall visit, which lasted a week 'while I had no suspicion of any other design, in all the pains he took, but to perfect a correct text in Shakespear, of which he seemed very fond'.

This visit took place in May 1737; in October Warburton was writing to Thomas Birch in terms which suggest he had extracted from Hanmer such excellent notions as would make his own edition something of a scoop:

> You are pleased to enquire about my Shakespear. I believe (to tell it as a secret) I shall, after I have got the whole of this Work out of my hands which I am now engaged in, *give an Edition of it to the World.* Sir Thomas Hanmer has a true critical genius, and has done great things in this Author; so you may expect to see a very extraordinary edition of its Kind.

Hanmer in retirement from distinguished public life had the opposite approach to that of Warburton who appears in this passage as secretive, scheming. It is also possible that in Hanmer's house where hospitality and generosity prevailed, or soon after leaving it, his guest dreamed the desire to edit an edition and naively declared it, for 'not long after', Hanmer continued to Smith,

> the views of interest began to show themselves, several hints were dropt of the advantage he might receive from publishing the work thus corrected; but, as I had no thoughts at all of making it public, so I was more averse to yield to it in such a manner as was likely to produce a paltry edition, by making it the means only of making a greater sum of money by it.

In that intriguing sentence came the first mention of a matter prominent in Hanmer's mind, payment: amateur and professional. And if one accepts that he had at first no thought of making it public, the whole elaborate scheme for his Oxford edition was devised to oppose Warburton's. The code of a baronet led to unexpected motives. Hanmer assumed, rightly in the event, that the theft must 'produce a paltry edition'; visually Warburton's in 1747 deserved no better phrase; and it is implied that his own, though making no money, should be a fine affair.

'Upon this he flew into a great rage,' he told Smith, 'and there is an end of the story.' It is not the end of the letter, for Hanmer went on to emphasize his own absence of 'interest', in a way which later irritated those who could not afford the same patronage:

> As to my own particular, I have no aim to pursue in this affair: I propose neither honour, reward, or thanks, and should be very well pleased to have the books continue upon their shelf, in my own private closet. If it is thought they may be of use or pleasure to the publick, I am willing to part with them out of my hands, and to add, for the honour of Shakespear, some decorations and embellishments at my own expence. It will be an unexpected pleasure to me, if they can be made in any degree profitable to the University, to which I shall always retain a gratitude, a regard, and a reverence ...

Zachary Grey, vicar of St. Giles and St. Peter's, Cambridge, rector of Houghton Conquest in Bedfordshire, had the amateur scribbling rural life which a 20th-century reader envies. He passed his winters at Cambridge and lived during the rest of the year at Ampthill, the nearest market town to Houghton Conquest. Nothing could so stimulate as controversy to help forget the damp cold of a Cambridge winter; apart from theological books he edited *Hudibras* and in the process began a chronic quarrel with Warburton which perhaps influenced his view of his Shakespeare, and made him see Hanmer's in a friendlier light than most people. Grey wrote a pamphlet with the explicit title, *Remarks upon a late edition of Shakespeare, with a long string of emendations borrowed by the celebrated author from the Oxford edition without acknowledgement. To which is prefixed a defence of the late Sir Thomas Hanmer, bart, addressed to the Rev. Mr. Warburton.* With Hanmer he had a friendship of some standing; Nichols printed a letter addressed to Grey in 1742, in which the Oxford editor mentioned a problem in *Lear* and gave news of his edition:

> I must now acquaint you that the books are gone out of my hands, and lodged with the University of Oxford, which hath been willing to accept of them as a present from me. They intend to print them forthwith, in a fair impression adorned with sculptures; but it will be so ordered that it will be the cheapest book that ever was exposed to sale ... if you have any friends or neighbours who are desirous to secure a copy to themselves, perhaps it would not be amiss you should let me know who they are; for none are to go into the hands of booksellers, and I believe it is not intended to print a great many of them.

This was roughly what happened, though there is no evidence that Hanmer's Shakespeare could only be bought by subscription. With excellent engravings these six quarto volumes were sold for three guineas; Pope's had cost twice as much, and the price of Hanmer's rose to ten guineas before it was reprinted. Hanmer was the only editor who refused payment; Warburton came second in the league table provided by Benjamin Victor in 1771, with £500.

Long after this, when he was Bishop of Gloucester and it seemed that Hanmer's 1742 letter to Smith of All Souls, with its story of their dispute, might be published in the *Biographia Britannica*, Warburton provided his own very different version for the editors. Hanmer had died in 1746, after witnessing Tonson's compliment in pirating his text but a year before Warburton's edition appeared. He called the letter to Dr. Smith 'one continued falsehood from beginning to end'. A magistrate might find difficulty in judging between the two stories, as both have the ring of well-remembered indignation. The introduction was not of his own seeking, says Warburton, scenting the suggestion of a social climb; not through the Bishop of Salisbury but – maintaining the level of preferment – 'on an application of the present Bishop of London to me, in behalf of Sir T. Hanmer; and, as I understood, at Sir T. Hanmer's desire'. He was not unwanted or uninvited at Mildenhall but went 'at his earnest and repeated request', and it was 'false that the views of interest began to show themselves in me to this *disinterested gentleman'*.

Nothing neither way, so far. Nobody can know who introduced them; Sir T. Hanmer annoyed everyone by his excessive denial of 'interest' and fees; wealth, not a major matter in editorial equipment, was poorly used to create distance between friends. There followed specific detail, which was probably not invented: Hanmer had approached 'a bookseller [i.e., publisher] in London, of the best reputation' with his Shakespeare scheme

> on the following conditions; of its being pompously printed with cuts (as it afterwards was at Oxford) at the expence of the said bookseller; who, besides, should pay one hundred guineas, or some such sum, to a friend of his (Sir T. Hanmer's), who had transcribed the *glossary* for him.

Now that shows Sir T. Hanmer in a different light, professional as the rest of them but able to afford to go it alone; not the first or last to lick his wounds after rejection from a publisher, emerging later in different format. And Warburton's scornful phrase as to 'its being pompously printed with cuts' recalls Pope's dismissive lines in the *Dunciad* about illustrated books, where

> by sculpture made for ever known,
> The page admires new beauties, not its own.

The bookseller (Tonson probably, an obvious choice, Warburton's publisher and friend) spilled the beans by reporting this visit to Warburton, 'understanding that he made use of many of my notes, and that I knew nothing of the project'. At that point the request went out for letters to be returned, followed by Hanmer's reply about cost of postage in receiving them, and his right to property.

There seems no reason to doubt Warburton's circumstantial letter, well remembered long after the event. The episode showed two sides of a slightly sad human story, transmitting overtones recognizable to this day. Hanmer, with the detachment of independence, had put out of mind the recollection of that wretched visit to a bookseller in London, of the best reputation.

Hanmer's easygoing preface spread his air of patronage. What are we about to receive? Nothing less than 'a true and correct Edition of *Shakespear's* works cleared from the corruptions with which they have hitherto abounded'. How can this miracle take place? 'One of the great Admirers of this incomparable Author hath made it the amusement of his leisure hours' to go over the text and put it right; and this he managed by

> making his own copy as perfect as he could: but as the emendations multiplied upon his hands, other Gentlemen equally fond of the Author desired to see them, and some were so kind as to give their assistance by communicating their observations and conjectures upon difficult passages which had occurred to them.

Such courtesies existed of course, as for instance from the Reverend Mr. Smith of Harkston in Norfolk, not to be confused with Dr. Smith of All Souls, who 'was greatly assistant to Sir Thomas Hanmer in his edition of Shakespear'; but among these kindly assisting friends was Warburton. They urged him to publish this edition which had accumulated after all the careful reading, and 'he, who hath with difficulty yielded to their perswasions' offered it – to the bookseller in London who rejected it, according to Warburton.

Accepting Pope's history of the corrupt text as it came down to him, Hanmer defined the remarkably free frontiers of his own discipline in amending. If Theobald made the alteration of a letter or two achieve amazing results, by Hanmer's rules of restraint almost anything went: he promised

> that no alterations have been made but what the sense necessarily required, what the measure of the verse often helped to point out, and what the similitude of words in the false reading and in the true, generally speaking, appeared very well to justify.

As to Pope's habit of relegating to footnote italic such passages as he found too coarse to be truly Shakespearean, Hanmer followed that example 'and it were to be wished that more had then undergone the same sentence'. His one substantial addition to these condemned extracts was the whole charming scene in French in *Henry the Fifth*, 'that wretched piece of ribaldry in King Henry V. put into the mouths of the *French* Princess and an old Gentlewoman, improper enough as it is all in *French* and not intelligible to an *English* audience, and yet that perhaps is the best thing that can be said of it'. He also took on board Pope's fantasy of the unscrupulous Players who added and subtracted, shifted and transposed for their vain popular purposes, raising theory to assurance:

> There can be no doubt but a great deal more of that low stuff which disgraces the works of this great Author, was foisted in by the Players after his death, to please the vulgar audiences by which they subsisted.

The very genuine prose of Hanmer's Preface projects across 250 years a tone of voice, style of life, the Suffolk landowner genial but autocratic in his library. Perhaps that episode with the London publisher made him resolve to make this the most splendid edition of them all. After the newly erected statue of Shakespeare in Westminster Abbey ('at publick expence') he wished that his private financing of these volumes 'which hath cost some attention and care, may be looked upon as another small monument designed and dedicated to his honour'.

Though all this was lightweight compared with Theobald before, and seems vapid in relation to plodding Warburton, Hanmer's edition, visually excellent, was never negligible. It represents the last major edition of Shakespeare from a dilettante equipped with taste and flair.

*   *   *

Nichols called Warburton 'so colossal a Scholar', 'this colossal Writer'; his schoolmaster remembered him as 'the dullest of all dull scholars'. The status of Warburton remains mysterious – he loved mystery – his ascent to the See of Gloucester no easy ride. After caustic comment on Pope in a letter posthumously and rather maliciously printed by Malone, that had nothing to do with the Shakespeare volume in which it appeared, he became Pope's assiduous apologist, friend, executor, and, after a decision of the courts in 1759, sole owner of copyright in Pope's writing. His extraordinary major work, dedicated to the Jews, was called *The Divine Legation of Moses demonstrated on the principles of a Religious Deist, from the Omission of the Doctrine of a Future State of Rewards and Punishments in the Jewish Dispensation*. Reprinted often, never completed, the argument proposed that as Jews have no dogma about eternal rewards and punishments, and such dogma is necessary to good society, and yet as the Jewish religion survives, there must be something divine in the continued existence of Judaism. This convoluted system of thought, recalling Hume's satirical conclusions about Christianity, came of course from the heart as an apologia for inadequacies in that large part of the Bible which Christians were yet expected to accept, and was typical of 'this colossal Writer'. The list of his publications is colossal as varied and tactless. Pope died in 1744, a year before the Jacobite expedition. Had he lived to learn about Warburton's sermon in October 1745, *A faithful Portrait of Popery, by which it is seen to be the Reverse of Christianity, as it is the Destruction of Morality, Piety and Civil Liberty*, he might have chosen a different literary executor.

But this was the time for his climb. Pope had introduced Warburton to his friend Ralph Allen who owned an estate near Bath; in 1745, at the age of 47 he married Allen's favourite niece. A year later came his first preferment, as Preacher to the Society of Lincoln's Inn. As his literary and theological thrust advanced together, he succeeded in 1759 to Pope's copyright and the See of Gloucester.

With both Pope and Johnson his friendships were uneven. He had perceived the excellence of Johnson's first announcement of a Shakespeare edition (a rare charitable note in the Preface to his own edition), for which Johnson was ever grateful ('He praised me at a time when praise was of value to me'); but as many or most of Johnson's Shakespeare notes, when that edition came, demolished Warburton's, it is not surprising to find swingeing comments in his letter to a friend:

> The remarks he makes in every page on my Commentaries are full of insolence and malignant reflections, which, had they not in them as much folly as malignity, I should have reason to be offended with ... to discover the corruption in an author's text, and by a happy sagacity to restore it to sense, is no easy task; but when the discovery is made, then to cavil at the conjecture, to propose an equivalent, and defend non-sense, by producing out of the thick darkness it occasions, a weak and faint glimmering of sense (which has been the business of the Editor [i.e., Johnson] throughout) is the easiest, as well as dullest of all literary efforts.

Warburton in the same passage referred to 'that trifling part of the publick, which pretends to judge of this part of Literature, in which boys and girls decide'. His elaborate and thumping paragraphs of footnote carried the machinery to crush perception.

With Pope he began and ended on a discordant note, if the anti-Catholic sermon soon after Pope's death (unconnected with it) is recalled. It was less than charitable of Malone to print in the first volume of his *Supplemental Observations*,[7] 1780, the whole of that letter from Warburton to Concanen on the theme of plagiarism, including the comment: 'Dryden I observe borrows for want of leisure, and Pope for want of genius'. He had been writing there about Addison, not Shakespeare; a mellow sentence introduced the comment on Dryden and Pope:

> I used to make it one good part of my amusement in reading the English poets, those of them I mean whose vein flows regularly and constantly, as well as clearly, to trace them to their sources; and observe what oar [sic], as well as what slime and gravel they brought down with them.

Johnson was quoted in Boswell with occasional respect towards Warburton who had become a bishop six years before the appearance of his own Shakespeare, though conversational awe of a senior

---

[7] p.223

churchman could not banish literary integrity, calling him 'perhaps the last man who has written with a mind full of reading and reflection'. Some form of amnesia must have overcome him towards the close of his life (1784) in telling Dr. Adams in Oxford that 'I treated him with great respect both in my Preface and in my Notes'. If Johnson's notes had shown great respect for Warburton, his edition of Shakespeare would lack much of its fun. Boswell thought Warburton 'must be allowed to have shown uncommon ingenuity, in giving to any author's text whatever meaning he chose it should carry'.

He earned a reputation for eccentricity, breezing out from church services before receiving Communion. Nichols, quoting from the manuscript of one Rev. John Jones, thought it 'proper to disclaim the most distant idea of detracting from the transcendant merits of Bp. Warburton. It is merely given as an instance, among many others that might be produced, of his *singularity'*. Jones provided several instances:

> A gentleman of eminence in the Church assured me, that a daughter of his, being in the same pew with Warburton, then a Bishop, in a certain great church in London, both on a Good Friday and on the Easter-day next following, on both which days the Holy Communion was there administered, observed with concern the Prelate's leaving the church, both times, when that solemn act of worship was coming on, and not joining in it. This was his then parish-church. A worthy Dignitary of the Church observed, with equal concern, the *same* omission, or neglect, in the Abbey Church at Bath. The Right Reverend went out, to the surprize of the congregation, when the act of administering the Communion came on.

At this distance scruple rather than negligence seems a possible explanation for conduct which looked singularly casual in London and Bath. Jones was not prepared to excuse him so lightly, adding:

> This great Author upon the Sacrament, when he himself administers it, is said to be very precise and particular, drawing on a clean pair of white kid-skin gloves &c. I almost wonder why his Reverend Lordship should not rather have his gloves for this office made of lawn.

Johnson defined lawn as 'Fine linen, remarkable for being used in the sleeves of bishops', and quoted a passage from Pope with the line

> A saint in crape is twice a saint in *lawn.*

His singularity was familiar in the literary world too. Thomas Davies wrote to Grainger in May 1769 upon publication of a book which was to have wide circulation in the next half century:

> This day the Biographical History of England is published! – The Bishop

of Gloucester has bought the book, which he calls *an odd one*. This is praise from him; for, if he had not an intention to peruse it, he would have called it a *sad* book. I was honoured with a visit from him this day.

Warburton, a great figure in the foreground of the landscape, receives wretched appreciation now for his work on Shakespeare, his own *odd* essay much neglected. 'William Warburton's eight-volume edition of 1747 is now remembered if at all,' wrote Daiches, 'for the lively abuse of Theobald and Hanmer to be found in its Preface.' Arthur Sherbo[8] believes 'Warburton's is surely one of the worst editions of Shakespeare ever published, and contemporary critics were ready to apprise him of that fact.' They provide that service for writers in any period.

He came to the task after longer apprenticeship than previous editors. Rowe and Pope accepted commissions from Tonson, Theobald rushed into print upon the stimulus of Pope's blunders, Hanmer's leisured posture was far from attentive to detail. Warburton had corresponded at immense length with Theobald, shared his reflections with Hanmer, taken from both. Two decades passed, between the adventure of 'literal criticism' with Theobald and the appearance of his own edition. He had some right to reckon himself the greatest expert: 'The Genuine Text ... is here settled: Being restored from the *Blunders* of the first Editors, and the *Interpolations* of the two last'. His aggressive title page expressed a proper mood of that moment.

Hanmer's strange belief, when his own version was ready for printing in Oxford, that Warburton had no intention of editing Shakespeare ('I am satisfied there is no edition coming, or likely to come from Warburton'), makes one suppose he was carefully deceived; it had been publicly announced, so Warburton was then denying or playing it down. Hanmer may not have come upon the relevant *Works of the Learned*, but whichever bishop introduced the two of them must have mentioned the notion; yet at some boundary between rivalry and delight both forgot they competed in the same race. While they met, Warburton had only his living at what Nichols called 'the valuable rectory of Burnt (otherwise Brand) Broughton' in Lincolnshire, a powerful list of publications, and literary friendship. His altered prospects in the early 1740s, while Hanmer's Shakespeare was printed, may also have changed a distant resolve into rapid action. Prosperous marriage, promotion, Pope's will, these cleared the air and he taxied for take-off. Some such

---

[8] *The Birth of Shakespeare Studies*, p.12

explanation accounts for the noisy thrust of engines in Warburton's Preface.

He took a more extreme view than Pope of the textual history, 'left to the Care of Door-keepers and Prompters'. Door-keepers had not entered the problem before; one wonders about their function, or existence, or why he blamed them. As to its corrupt state, Theobald's pleasant story of *Mumpsimus* and *Sumpsimus* became a belief that textual errors first caused neglect, and were later regarded though meaningless with stupid affection:

> The stubborn Nonsense, with which he was incrusted, occasioned his lying long neglected amongst the common Lumber of the Stage. And when that resistless Splendor, which now shoots all around him, had, by degrees, broke thro' the Shell of those Impurities, his dazzled Admirers became as suddenly insensible to the extraneous Scurf that still stuck upon him, as they had been before to the native Beauties that lay under it. So that, as then, he was thought not to deserve a Cure, he was now supposed not to need any.

Then he arrived among those four who had attempted the task of editing already, wasting no time upon civilities before dismissing each in turn. In this matter of scaling off extraneous scurf Rowe scored no marks, and Pope few, though he 'without any particular Study or Profession of this Art, discharged the great Parts of it so well as to make his Edition the best Foundation for all further Improvements'. As to explanation and emendation, that was left 'to the Critic by Profession' – to Warburton, it is understood, though the phrase more truly described Theobald.

His release of resentment against Theobald and Hanmer provides now the most entertaining paragraphs in Warburton's Preface. Together the two of them 'left their Author in ten times a worse Condition than they found him'. His stance was insufferable as Malvolio's towards Sir Toby: 'to each of them at different times, I communicated a great number of Observations, which they managed, as they saw fit, to the Relief of their several Distresses'.

Warburton on Theobald reflected the confusion of status. If fees distinguished them Hanmer was the only amateur: Warburton received £500 and Theobald more than £650, both handsome payments in their day. All previous editors being dead Warburton felt free to strike, and a Malvolian disdain reappeared in his interpretation of Hanmer:

> For, having a number of my Conjectures before him, he took as many of them as he saw fit, to work upon; and by changing them to something, he thought, synonimous or similar, he made them his own; and so became a Critic at a cheap Expence.

Where Sir Thomas used his own judgement instead of Warburton's 'his Conjectures are generally absurd and extravagant, and violating every Rule of Criticism'. And apart from blundering corrections Hanmer, to complete the measure of short lines, contributed 'a set of harmless unconcerning Expletives'.

Much of this reads foolishly in view of the communion those three had enjoyed before rivalry ended it. He concluded this destructive part of the essay on Theobald and Hanmer:

> They separately possessed those two Qualities which, more than any other, have contributed to bring the Art of Criticism into disrepute, *Dulness of Apprehension*, and *Extravagance of Conjecture.*

Warburton in his more constructive mood, if less entertaining, deserves attention. Each editor distinguished between rational amendment and flight of fancy, clear enough then but far from simple now. 'I have indulged nothing to Fancy or Imagination,' he wrote; yet he had tried to restore the text 'where it labours with inextricable Nonsense'. One man's nonsense was another's comprehension; a high proportion of Johnson's notes was given to contradicting Warburton's suggestions, on the ground that the early texts might be understood without change and had no need of them. Warburton 'once intended to have given the Reader a *body of Canons*, for literal Criticism, drawn out in form'; he lived to regret that intention when Thomas Edwards supplied the omission in devastating satire. The uncharity of this Preface invited response by dark references to 'some who would needs exercise' the Art of Criticism 'without either natural or acquired Talents; and by the ill Success of others, who seemed to have lost both, when they came to try them upon English Authors'. Hanmer and Bentley were the phantoms there; Warburton possessing natural or acquired talents, or both, he would have settled in repute for either.

He was at his best in apologia for Shakespeare's obscurities, which in this edition he intended to preserve and explain; if these thoughtful distinctions had extended to an understanding of earlier editors this would have been a first-rate essay. Aspects of Shakespeare's grammar, propriety, 'learning', disturbed many critics from Rymer and Ritson to Hopkins and Bridges. Warburton's phrase, 'a *licentious Use of Terms'*, referred to mixed parts of speech. Theobald and Hanmer had mistaken these for corrupt passages and altered them, he says, which 'hath put me to additional Trouble' – nothing terrible, one assumes, for the earlier editions were there to guide him – but he cherished a sympathetic perception that Shakespeare's

> superiority of Genius less needing the Intervention of Words in the Art of Thinking, when he came to draw out his Contemplations into Dis-

course, he took up (as he was hurried on by the Torrent of his Matter) with the first Words that lay in his Way; and if, amongst these, there were two *Mixed-modes* that had but a principal Idea in common, it was enough for him . . .

This curved away a little from Pope's approach to editing, and no scholar now would disagree, though his phrase 'the first Words that lay in his way' suggests careless speed, which was probably not what Warburton meant.

Where the sense was hard to unravel, one must blame the period when public taste 'delighted . . . in the high and turgid', when language was developing and a writer might 'disguise a vulgar expression with hard and forced construction, whereby the sentence frequently becomes cloudy and dark'. Such instances could only be left as they stood; '*Shakespear* was too clear in frame to be suspected of a want of Meaning; and too high in fashion for any one to own he needed a Critic to find it out'. As to 'his far-fetched and quaint Allusions, these are often a cover to common thoughts', their footnote interpretation formed part of his critical duty, with the occasional bonus that 'in clearing the Obscurity, you frequently discover some latent conceit not unworthy of his Genius'.

Warburton as philosopher, after shedding the paranoia, showed a mellow charm of mind – as Hanmer 'hath made it the amusement of his leisure hours' to brush up his Shakespeare, so he himself recalled the pleasures of reading the old poets and critics, 'my Younger amusements, when, many years ago, I used to turn over these sort of Writers to unbend myself from more serious applications'. As critics interpreted 'Beauties and Defects in an author he has been concerned with explanations of both' but chiefly of his Beauties, following Pope's use of inverted commas to direct readers to such passages. Warburton's prose assumed a charitable tone. 'An odd humour of finding fault hath long prevailed amongst the Critics; as if nothing were worth *remarking* that did not, at the same time, deserve to be reproved . . . Men being generally more ready at spying faults than in discovering Beauties.' Unreasonable it would be to imagine the principle extended from poets to editors, or that Warburton himself possessed an odd humour of finding fault.

He thanked 'dear Mr. Pope' who 'was desirous I should give a new Edition of this Poet, as he thought it might contribute to put a stop to a prevailing folly of altering the Text of celebrated Authors without Talents or Judgement'. It did not, in Warburton or his successors down the many decades. As to the Baedecker system of pointing out parts to admire, 'I have done the same by as many others as I thought most deserving of the Reader's attention, and I have marked them with *double* commas'.

After thanking the publishers, with diplomatic words of respect for the doubtful legality of 'that security for their Property, which they see, the rest of their Fellow-Citizens enjoy', he turned to a worried justification of his own time spent away from his proper calling, upon literary minutiae. Saint John Chrysostom who slept with Aristophanes under his pillow provided adequate precedent perhaps, but near home and truth was the example of Oxford University which 'thought good letters so much interested in correct Editions of the best *English* Writers'; and if their publications had proved inadequate, it was not Oxford's fault but (a sour note returning) 'his, who thrust himself into the employment'.

Warburton used curious turns of phrase in emphasizing importance of self-knowledge above other sciences, thinking of this as a physical science among other kinds of universal knowledge; and he drew a comparison with one's own language, another self-knowledge of greater importance than knowing foreign languages. As Warburton in a rare moment of conciseness should be cherished, his sentence is memorable; he wrote about 'the Knowledge of our Nature':

> As this Science (whatever profound Philosophers may think) is, to the rest, *in Things;* so, *in Words,* (whatever supercilious Pedants may talk) every one's mother tongue is to all other Languages.

Shakespeare of all poets brought us closest to self-knowledge, the argument ran; parallel with this, his language merited exact study. And this brought Warburton to his final serious argument, the need for precise understanding because English had no adequate Dictionary. Every learned foreigner studied English literature:

> This must needs make it deserving of a critical attention: And its being yet destitute of a Test or Standard to apply to, in cases of doubt or difficulty, shows how much it wants that attention. For we have neither GRAMMAR nor DICTIONARY, neither Chart or Compass, to guide us through this wide sea of Words. And indeed how should we? since both are to be composed and finished on the Authority of our best established Writers.

It defined the motive for Johnson, whose Dictionary was distinguished from earlier attempts by instances of usage, from 'our best established Writers' where that was possible. The prospectus for that work, dedicated to Lord Chesterfield, appeared in 1747, same year as Warburton's Shakespeare. If one influenced the other, a larger debt is due to Warburton than has been acknowledged.

III   JOHNSON

Johnson's troubles in completing his Shakespeare edition appear in an anecdote which John Nichols told Boswell:

> In the year 1763, a young bookseller, who was an apprentice to Mr. Whiston, waited on him with a subscription to his Shakespeare: and observing that the Dr. made no entry in any book of the subscriber's name, ventured diffidently to ask, whether he would please to have the gentleman's address, that it might be properly inserted in the printed list of subscribers. 'I shall print no list of subscribers', said Johnson with great abruptness: but almost immediately recollecting himself, added, very complacently, 'Sir, I have two very cogent reasons for not printing any list of subscribers; – one, that I have lost all the names, – the other, that I have spent all the money'.

His first Proposals for such a work, abortive through spurious objections from Tonson who claimed copyright, but noticed perceptively by Warburton, appeared in 1745. Eleven years later, eminent with the great Dictionary labour completed, backed by Tonson as head of a small syndicate, his *Proposals for Printing, by Subscription, the Dramatick Works of William Shakespeare* were optimistic in promising publication 'on or before *Christmas* 1757'. He had probably done no more serious work towards an edition in the Dictionary decade, after his notes on *Macbeth* which formed most of the 1745 Proposals. Those subscribers whose money had been spent received their books eight years late. 'That the Book shall be elegantly printed in Eight Volumes in Octavo' was more easily accomplished.

Johnson's 1756 essay is an interesting document, breathing a liberal spirit towards his predecessors but also damning them concisely before concluding. The generosity is seen in a resolve to make this, as it became, the first variorum edition: he would include previous comments, for readers to judge, rather than dismiss them. Though an irresistibly open temperament blew that intention to the four winds Johnson meant what he wrote, and seemed later unaware of the dismissive character of his own notes, especially in dealing with Warburton's. 'I treated him with great respect both in my Preface and in my Notes,' he told old Dr. Adams at Oxford in 1784.

As to the duties facing an editor, 'to correct what is corrupt, and to explain what is obscure', Shakespeare's text had been subject to unique corruption: 'multiplied by transcript after transcript, vitiated by the blunders of the penman, or changed by the affectation of the player ... they suffered another depravation from the ignorance and negligence of the printers, as every man who knows the state of the press in that age will readily conceive ... in no other age was the art of printing in such unskilful hands'.

He distinguished two sorts of obscurity: colloquial usage of one kind and another in a period of change 'when the meaning of our phrases was yet in fluctuation, when words were adopted at pleasure from the neighbouring languages, and while the Saxon was still visibly mingled in our diction'; and a rush of poetic expression which defied precise phrasing, 'that fulness of idea, which might sometimes load his words with more sentiment than they could conveniently convey, and that rapidity of imagination which might hurry him to a second thought before he had fully conveyed the first'.

Warburton had a similar passage in his Preface, both seeming to be adverse comment upon an excess of poetic excitement which caused confusing language, as with anyone who writes so fast that his script becomes illegible. Yet Johnson believed 'that very few of his lines were difficult to his audience, and that he used such expressions as were then common, though the paucity of contemporary writers makes them now seem peculiar'. That sentence combined his two sources of obscurity; if one accepts that Shakespeare used such expressions as were then common, it may be questioned whether for his audience or Johnson's or ours 'very few of his lines were difficult'. It could strike us now or any critic then that no audience at first hearing understood the rapid complexity of Shakespeare's thought and imagery. Perhaps a high proportion of Shakespeare's plays is incomprehensible from the stage, and always was; Johnson held that interpretation and restoration would bring back understanding. Every editor probably forgot the sweat of understanding what he proceeded to explain.

Johnson in his Proposals promised a work he did not achieve, the scope of which he could not then have imagined, in providing 'all the observable varieties of all the copies that can be found', complaining that earlier editors left no such help for him. As to correcting 'by a careful collation of the oldest copies', Theobald had known them better than Johnson who possessed no collection of his own and found some difficulty in gaining access to others. Later, in his 1765 Preface, Johnson reported with disappointment:

> I collated such copies as I could procure, and wished for more, but have not found the collectors of these rarities very communicative.

Garrick, owning a notable collection, took the sentence as a reference to himself and complained to Boswell, who has an amusing anecdote about this, for Garrick assured him

> that Johnson was made welcome to the full use of his collection, and that he left the key of it with a servant, with orders to have a fire and every convenience for him. I found Johnson's notion was, that Garrick wanted to be courted for them, and that, on the contrary, Garrick should have

courted him, and sent him the plays of his own accord. But, indeed, considering the slovenly and careless manner in which the books were treated by Johnson, it could not be expected that scarce and valuable editions should have been lent to him.

Most of the 'literal critics' of Shakespeare through the 18th century formed collections, from which they worked; no chance then to spend days in the Bodleian, the Folger, the British Library, looking everything up. Editors may do that now, partly because such places received 18th-century collections: Malone left his to the Bodleian, Capell to Trinity College, Cambridge. Johnson took a strange line in expecting that scarce and valuable editions should have been lent to him.

After customary promises that he will not make changes 'as in the Oxford edition, without notice of the alteration', and wise acknowledgement of 'danger lest peculiarities should be mistaken for corruptions, and passages rejected as unintelligible, which a narrow mind happens not to understand', he produced a splendid Johnsonian sentence with polite opening changing to the sharpest barb:

> If in this part of his design he hopes to attain any degree of superiority to his predecessors, it must be considered, that he has the advantage of their labours; that part of the work being already done, more care is naturally bestowed on the other part; and that, to declare the truth, Mr. Rowe and Mr. Pope were very ignorant of the ancient English literature; Dr. Warburton was detained by more important studies; and Mr. Theobald, if fame be just to his memory, considered learning only as an instrument of gain, and made no further enquiry after his authour's meaning, when once he had notes sufficient to embellish his page with the expected decorations.

Terribly unjust to Theobald, whose youthful letters to Warburton showed the excitement of discovery in a new subject, by fresh means, like a biologist solving secrets of life.

On words and meaning Johnson, after the Dictionary decade, claimed 'some degree of confidence, having had more motives to consider the whole extent of our language than any other man from its first formation'.

Then there was the intriguing matter of Shakespeare's 'beauties', dating from Rowe's duodecimo edition of 1714 where the eighth volume concluded with *An Index of the most Beautiful Thoughts, Descriptions, Speeches, &c. in Shakespear's Works*. Pope used inverted commas, Theobald ignored all this, Hanmer followed Pope, Warburton added double inverted commas for his own favourite passages. The theme had taken a new turn with young William Dodd's two volumes published in 1752, *The Beauties of Shakespear: Regularly selected from each Play. With a General Index. Digest-*

ing them under Proper Heads. Illustrated with Explanatory Notes,
and Similar Passages from Ancient and Modern Authors.

'For this part of his task, and for this only,' wrote Johnson rudely,
'was Mr. Pope eminently and indisputably qualified.' He dismissed
this habit of picking out jewels and gems, in a fine ironic sentence:

> But I have never observed that mankind was much improved by their
> asterisks, commas, or double commas; of which the only effect is, that
> they preclude the pleasure of judging for ourselves, teach the young and
> ignorant to decide without principles; defeat curiosity and discernment,
> by leaving them less to discover; and at last shew the opinion of the
> critick, without the reasons on which it was founded, and without
> affording any light by which it may be examined.

'The former editors have affected to slight their predecessors,' he
wrote, and the Prospectus was not wholly free of this tendency; but
it ended with the important resolve to make this a variorum edition,
and so it became, in which 'all that is valuable will be adopted from
every commentator, that posterity may consider it as including all
the rest, and exhibiting whatever is hitherto known of the great
father of the English drama'.

Johnson had written an essay in his Prospectus which for anyone
of narrower outlook might have served as Preface to the edition; but
when eight years later that approached publication his view had
changed, his vision broadened and the first high hopes of thorough-
ness become much reduced by experience. A surprising impression
from the long 1765 Preface is of humility, not prominent in Johnson's
reputation:

> I was forced to censure those whom I admired, and could not but reflect,
> while I was dispossessing their emendations, how soon the same fate
> might happen to my own, and how many of the readings which I have
> corrected may be by some other editor defended and established.

That charming expression would not have entered Warburton's
head, or Theobald's. Johnson, in conversation contentious, produced
as his Shakespeare Preface a profound and gentle composition; formidably satirical towards his predecessors when tempted to assess
them, provocative only by his well-considered viewpoint in facing
common criticism of Shakespeare for ignoring or defying the classical conventions, and eccentric as it now seems in a few comments
about the tragedies. In philosophical reflection and breadth of view,
to read Johnson's Preface after the others is like breathing country
air after a journey on the London underground.

Ample rambling ambling early paragraphs stressing the ease of
admiration for antiquity led towards emphasis upon 'just represen-
tations of general nature', one of Johnson's major critical points,

dismissed in the *Monthly Review*[9] as 'veneration for antiquity, and on the general talents of Shakespeare; delivered in that pompous style which is so peculiar to himself, and is so much admired by some kind of readers'.

He developed at several levels a simple reduction that 'Shakespeare is above all writers, at least above all modern writers, the poet of nature; the poet that holds up to his readers a faithful mirrour of manners and of life'. Johnson was the first editor to interpret that well-worn phrase thus, admiring Shakespeare as poet of common behaviour, the ordinary day, natural responses, developing apparent simplicity into an argument which extended beyond the range of previous prefaces; for he found classical permanence, lasting art, in the middle and normal and natural, not in highflown set pieces. Around this rock the frothy or polluted waters flowed. Such a thesis included his ultimate defence of tragi-comedy, the mixture of forms, as belonging to the truth of anyone's day and elevating it as a vital artistic innovation, somewhat shocked at last by his temerity (or originality) in doing so.

He identified two false or passing sorts of language, the vulgar and the affected, between which Shakespeare steered a natural course, dialogue in his plays resting therefore 'above grossness and below refinement'. In this middle way joining and changing moods and scenes, Johnson discovered a classicism which broke classic rule; for we witness 'Life in its native colours', Shakespeare 'shews plainly, that he has seen with his own eyes', he 'has no heroes', offers 'human sentiments in human language'. The strong terms of his editorial discovery bear no relation to later and romantic ideas of nature or what is natural:

> As his personages act upon principles arising from genuine passion, very little modified by particular forms, their pleasures and vexations are communicable to all times and to all places; they are natural, and therefore durable; the adventitious peculiarities of personal habits, are only superficial dies, bright and pleasing for a little while, yet soon fading to a dim tinct, without any remains of former lustre; but the discriminations of true passion are the colours of nature; they pervade the whole mass, and can only perish with the body that exhibits them. The accidental compositions of heterogeneous modes are dissolved by the chance which combined them; but the uniform simplicity of primitive qualities neither admits increase, nor suffers decay. The sand heaped by one flood is scattered by another, but the rock always continues in its place. The stream of time, which is continually washing the dissoluble fabricks of other poets, passes without injury by the adamant of *Shakespeare*.

---

[9] Vol. 33, 1765

Such thoughtful phrasing was not constructed to describe any commonplace conclusion, Shakespeare as 'poet of nature'; Johnson's heavy opening paragraphs about antiquity were his avenue to a major idea. It took him to awkward ground between two notions which might seem to be opposed, nature and 'instruction', for the balance of nature may not turn out to be morally instructive but 'it is always a writer's duty to make the world better, and justice is a virtue independent on time or place'.

His vigorous list of about a dozen faults which mar the plays, interrupting the larger apologia, was more idiosyncratic. Some of it finds easy acceptance now; from other parts modern taste has moved away. Few will quarrel with Johnson or others before him on the tedium of Shakespeare's puns. Somebody must sometime somewhere have written a defensive book on the excruciating theme. Johnson hammered argument into oblivion:

> A quibble is to Shakespeare, what luminous vapours are to the traveller; he follows it at all adventures, it is sure to lead him out of his way, and sure to engulf him in the mire. It has some malignant power over his mind, and its fascinations are irresistible. Whatever be the dignity or profundity of his disquisition, whether he be enlarging knowledge or exalting affection, whether he be amusing attention with incidents, or enchaining it in suspense, let but a quibble spring up before him, and he leaves his work unfinished. A quibble is the golden apple for which he will always turn aside from his career, or stoop from his elevation. A quibble poor and barren as it is, gave him such delight, that he was content to purchase it, by the sacrifice of reason, propriety and truth. A quibble was to him the fatal *Cleopatra* for which he lost the world, and was content to lose it.

Other critical points reflected Johnson's taste. So weak in his plots and endings, 'that a very slight consideration may improve them ... he seems not always fully to comprehend his own design'; 'had no regard to distinctions of time and place'; over-elaborate in narrative, 'he affects a disproportionate pomp of diction and a wearisome train of circumlocution, and tells the incident imperfectly in many words, which might have been more plainly delivered in few'; poor in 'set speeches' because they do not form part of natural conduct in which Shakespeare excelled; muddled in expressing complexity, 'entangled with an unwieldy sentiment, which he cannot well express, and will not reject'; and, conversely, inflating some simple thought with elaborate phrase: 'trivial sentiments and vulgar ideas disappoint the attention, to which they are recommended by sonorous epithets and swelling figures'.

As Johnson ended all his Shakespeare labours by writing the Preface, this flow of critical rhetoric reads like some parting sigh of relief after a long struggle. The first complaint, that Shakespeare 'seems to write without any moral purpose', accorded with his view of a poet of nature. One other point is out of tune with most responses now, in judging his art incapable of sustained sorrow or pathos. Those who admire him

> have never less reason to indulge their hopes of supreme excellence, than when he seems fully resolved to sink them in dejection, and mollify them with tender emotions by the fall of greatness, the danger of inno-cence, or the crosses of love.

He complained that such passages suffered interruption from 'some idle conceit, or contemptible equivocation', but that was not all. As critic or person Johnson responded more to Shakespeare in comedy than in tragedy, making astonishing general statements in this essay on that theme, while rejecting those absolute categories for the plays.[10] Nobody suspects Johnson was for a jig, or tale of bawdry, but this response after intimate acquaintance with all the plays shocks by obtuseness and his airy freedom in confessing it:

> In tragedy he often writes with great appearance of toil and study, what is written at last with little felicity; but in his comick scenes, he seems to produce without labour, what no labour can improve. In tragedy he is always struggling after some occasion to be comick, but in comedy he seems to repose, or to luxuriate, as in a mode of thinking congenial to his nature. In his tragick scenes there is always something wanting, but his comedy often surpasses expectation or desire. His comedy pleases by the thoughts and the language, and his tragedy for the greater part by incident and action. His tragedy seems to be skill, his comedy to be instinct.

And if this seems like an aberration Boswell's recollection confirmed it: 'Indeed Garrick has complained to me, that Johnson not only had not the faculty of producing the impressions of tragedy, but that he had not the sensibility to perceive them'.

Yet his sensibility, perceiving as unnatural those tragic passages which he admired in Addison's *Cato*, created such a defence for Shakespearean tragi-comedy as destroyed petty debate about 'the unities' in English drama. Parts of the Preface are crotchety and curious but these several pages on theatrical time and place contra-dicted Aristotle with such force that no critic in England could take up that theme again. The conclusion alarmed him: 'I am almost frightened at my own temerity'. As sustained ironic prose it recalls the best of reported conversation in Boswell. Johnson on the unities

---

[10] They remain astonishing, even after reading the most recent and careful work of exposition

of drama was as final in its day as Farmer on Shakespeare's learning. If anyone could imagine himself in some other place or century, while he sits watching a play

> There is no reason why a mind thus wandering in extasy should count the clock, or why an hour should not be a century in that calenture of the brains that can make the stage a field.

Fresh from the Dictionary he could choose the apt rare word, quoted there from De Quincey as 'A distemper peculiar to sailors, in hot climates; wherein they imagine the sea to be green fields, and will throw themselves into it, if not restrained'.

Johnson rose to brilliance in defining tragedy's effect upon an audience, observing that 'The delight of tragedy proceeds from our consciousness of fiction; if we thought murders and treasons real, they would please no more'. The whole passage strikes at complaisant modern viewing, at us who relax by screens for news of the day's distress, our sensitivity to Johnson's distinction between fiction and reality lost, *voyeurs* of execution and heartbreak. His defence of mixed time and place in a theatre was by extension from other arts, rather than part of his 'poet of nature' theme; no reason why drama should obey conventions more strict than existed for books or paintings. 'When the imagination is recreated by a painted landscape, the trees are not supposed capable to give us shade, or the fountains coolness; but we consider, how we should be pleased with such fountains playing beside us, and such woods waving over us.'

From these heights Johnson wandered down towards a survey of his predecessors. As Shakespeare's uneducated audiences could not be expected to follow dialogue which lacked incident and episode, he had chosen tales of action they already knew; such complex plots *must* have been familiar, for they could not otherwise have been understood. It is an unexpected argument. In the Prospectus nine years before, Johnson had been convinced a Shakespearean audience followed and understood what it watched and heard; after so long with the plays he judged them incomprehensible unless familiar; and later in the Preface he wrote that they 'were transcribed for the players by those who may be supposed to have seldom understood them'. It is strange to find him supposing audiences followed language and imagery which literate scribes 'seldom understood', and that people who took on board Shakespeare's complexity of thought could be defeated by the twists of an unfamiliar story. If this looked irresolute nobody should blame Johnson, for it remains a mystery, the large questions unanswered. Where the folios were incomprehensible, did those two actor-editors not understand what was printed? If we find scribes and compositors guilty of phrases of nonsense, who ever gathered or absorbed the sense? Actors at Stratford and the Barbican may seem to have little notion of what many of their lines mean; Johnson faced the difficulty of Shakespeare's meaning in his notes, without going so far as to accept that actors and audiences misunderstood what they spoke and heard. Shakespeare's plots are less formidable than his philosophy.

And his astonishing indifference to publication, remarked by Johnson and every other editor, could relate (a private view, valueless, not Johnson's) to this complexity, profundity, the knowledge that he was not understood, Landor's weariness of 'I strove with none for none was worth my strife'; so the printers, actors, editors ever since have striven.

Take his rough language with the smooth, said Johnson, 'Life in its native colours' from the poet who 'shews plainly, that he has seen with his own eyes'. Imperfections abound: Shakespeare wrote for his audiences, good box office, seldom troubling to perfect or publish. 'He has scenes of undoubted and perpetual excellence, but perhaps not one play, which, if it were now exhibited as the work of a contemporary writer, would be heard to the conclusion.' This passage of the Preface, still part of the poet-of-nature stream, wandered and divided before a rush of criticism as Johnson looked back to earlier editions. The general message could now recall Cowper's line, 'England with all thy faults I love thee still', breaking through the mist with such clarity as this sentence:

> *Shakespeare* opens a mine which contains gold and diamonds in unexhaustible plenty, though clouded by incrustations, debased by impurities, and mingled with a mass of meaner minerals.

Each of the earlier editors, even Theobald, had meant to change no more than was corrupt or incomprehensible, and each broke that resolve. In mid-century Johnson, looking back upon their work, judged they had gone too far in their emendations and enjoyed to excess the vanity of exposition. 'Those who saw that they must employ conjecture to a certain degree, were willing to indulge it a little further ... now we tear what we cannot loose, and eject what we happen not to understand.'

About the five who preceded him he was trenchant at greater length than in the Prospectus; only towards Rowe did he show more understanding than others who had dismissed him as critically valueless, seeing his task as that of playwright upon playwright, rather than poet upon poet; and Rowe's emendations, silently made, were often as silently adopted by others who, had they themselves produced them

would have filled pages and pages with censures of the stupidity by which the faults were committed, with displays of the absurdities which they involved, with ostentatious expositions of the new reading, and self congratulations on the happiness of discovering it.

Johnson largely dismissed Pope's edition, recognizing that in 'verbal criticism' too little work was done – aware perhaps that in this vast task his own achievement stopped short of promise. Except for the Preface he condemned Pope's performance: 'Confidence is the common consequence of success. They whose excellence of any kind has been loudly celebrated, are ready to conclude, that their powers are universal'. Pope's 'dull duty of an editor' was bitten and shaken to pieces, with a lament from the heart that 'Conjectural criticism demands more than humanity possesses'. In successive paragraphs Johnson made the distinction between conjectural and verbal criticism, which Theobald had called literal criticism.

His contemptuous summary of Theobald's work faded behind a paragraph of critical excellence in which Johnson defined a single line of descent from the First Folio to the Fourth:

> ... the truth is, that the first is equivalent to all others, and that the rest only deviate from it by the printer's negligence. Whoever has any of the folios has all ...

His recognition of a line of descent, different from classical criticism in which each surviving manuscript deserved separate attention, has been much admired. In detail a complete dismissal of the later Folios was not accepted by Steevens or Malone, but the perception was true and points even now to these 18th-century editions as the first advances since 1623.

Johnson's impatience with Theobald remains inexplicable except by prejudice of rank, calling this scholar-collector 'a man of narrow comprehension and small acquisitions'. Appreciation went no further than to acknowledge him 'zealous for minute accuracy, and not negligent in pursuing it' which could now seem high praise for the necessary qualities Rowe and Pope lacked. In suggesting that 'A man so anxiously scrupulous might have been expected to perform more', one wonders what Johnson had in mind. Theobald found punctuation a chore, but worked through that boring aspect of revision; Johnson's thanks could have been expressed more gracefully:

> I have sometimes adopted his restoration of a comma, without inserting the panegyrick in which he celebrated himself for his achievement.

Commas shifted, as they both knew, change the sense of sentences. Johnson respected Warburton and Hanmer above their deserts, Rowe as an artist from the past, and he honoured the wider genius of Pope, but Theobald's literal criticism obstructed the path and caused extra work, had been for the length of his task an inescapable nuisance. His impatient summary betrayed relief in saying what he had felt for years:

> *Theobald*, thus weak and ignorant, thus mean and faithless, thus petulant and ostentatious, by the good luck of having *Pope* for his enemy, has escaped, and escaped alone, with reputation, from this undertaking. So willingly does the world support those who solicite favour, against those who command reverence; and so easily is he praised, whom no man can envy.

Johnson's acceptance of Hanmer rose from his awe of a baronet, master of an estate; it was perverse to call him 'eminently qualified by nature for such studies'. After the experience of editing, Johnson felt admiration amounting to envy for the man who arrived by sense and flair without excessive detail, and distaste for Theobald's scholarship.

> He had, what is the first requisite to emendatory criticism, that intuition by which the poet's intention is immediately discovered, and that dexterity of intellect which despatches its work by the easiest means.

Hanmer's absence of footnote reference to his own or earlier emendations, Johnson admitted, 'made his own edition of little authority'. True to the concept of this as a variorum, 'I have received all his notes, and believe that every reader will wish for more'.

It embarrassed him to write about Warburton's edition, for the Bishop was very much alive and 'Respect is due to high place'; yet in the notes he had shown least respect to Warburton. A curious emphasis of phrasing in praise of Hanmer ('intuition by which the poet's intention is immediately discovered') preceded similar words in different sense used *against* Warburton ('precipitation which is produced by consciousness of quick discernment'). And Johnson questioned, less wittily than Quin,[11] the wisdom of so much time stolen from religion and given to 'notes, which he ought never to have considered as part of his serious employments'.

After these restless passages of criticism Johnson rose to a larger view which better suited his essay; in easier manner looking back to the serious, the satirical and the self-assured, to editors and the critics of critics, grateful to all who had preceded him, for 'not one has left *Shakespeare* without improvement, nor is there one to whom I have not been indebted for assistance and information'. Johnson's ability to view the whole footnote issue in perspective helped to make his the wisest essay of them all:

> It is not easy to discover from what cause the acrimony of a scholiast can

---

[11] Quin wished, on behalf of actors, that Warburton had kept to his own Bible and left theirs alone

naturally proceed. The subjects to be discussed by him are of very small importance; they involve neither property nor liberty; nor favour the interest of sect or party. The various readings of copies, and different interpretations of a passage, seem to be questions that might exercise the wit, without engaging the passions.

No need for a Dictionary troubled him through the years of his task, but some scepticism about the vanity of notes and value of editors distinguished him from others, gave endearing self-doubt to the closing pages of his essay. Notes may be necessary but they are necessary evils, he argued; anyone making first acquaintance with the plays should read straight through without distraction; and, after all, the world appreciated Shakespeare's genius before literal critics went to work upon it. Johnson was vulnerable because undeceived by all these years of textual labour, and human in sharing the passions which he found inexplicable. He proposed a paradoxical answer:

> Perhaps the lightness of the matter may conduce to the vehemence of the agency; when the truth to be investigated is so near to inexistence, as to escape attention, its bulk is to be enlarged by rage and exclamation.

In this heartfelt theme of his Preface Johnson's prose has such splendour that it is hard to resist quoting to excess:

> A commentator has indeed great temptations to supply by turbulence what he wants of dignity, to beat his little gold to a spacious surface, to work that to foam which no art or diligence can exalt to spirit.

No less important than his perception about lines of descent was Johnson's faith in discovering the sense of obscure passages in earliest editions rather than embrace the temptation to emend, concluding that 'the reading of the ancient books is probably true', resolving 'always to turn the old text on every side, and try if there be an interstice, through which the light can find its way'.

To later criticism that the edition fell so far short of promise the Preface offered a modest reply: 'I have indeed disappointed no opinion more than my own; yet I have endeavoured to perform my task with no slight solicitude'. Collation he found 'safe and easy' though he might have done more of that by journeying to Garrick's fireside than by waiting for books to be brought to his own messy room; conjecture seemed by comparison 'perilous and difficult'.

Johnson's disillusion, his sense of vanity and fallibility, were worlds away from Warburton's 'Genuine Text . . . here settled . . . restored from the *Blunders* of the first Editor, and the *Interpolations* of the two last'.

IV   FROM CAPELL TO MALONE

If Gerard Manley Hopkins had considered people among 'all things counter, original, spare, strange', he might have included Edward Capell, who called his little book of 'antient Poetry' *Prolusions*, defined by Johnson as entertainments or performance of diversion. The Cambridge University bibliophile society, named after him, has (at this moment of writing) ceased to exist. Edward Capell is remembered there because he left his fine Shakespeare collection to Trinity. He was of Catherine Hall, which seemed to him an undistinguished place, so the books went to Trinity because, according to Samuel Pegge the antiquary, 'nothing but his industry could exceed his vanity'.

His edition of Shakespeare appeared after two industrious decades, inspired by the shock of reading Hanmer's. No accurate text could be constructed, he felt, from the old foundations laid by Rowe which all who succeeded him had used:

> The editor now before you was appriz'd in time of this truth; saw the wretched condition his Author was reduc'd to by these late tamperings, and thought seriously of a cure for it, and that so long ago as the year 1745; for the attempt was first suggested by that gentleman's performance, which came out at *Oxford* the year before: Which when he had perus'd with no little astonishment, and consider'd the fatal consequences that must inevitably follow the imitation of so much licence, he resolv'd himself to be the champion; and to exert to the uttermost such abilities as he was master of, to save from further ruin an edifice of this dignity, which *England* must for ever glory in.

His exertions produced the first new reading, based upon early quartos where these could be found, on the first folio when they could not. His eccentricity appeared equally in the style of his edition and of his life. As a man of taste and means he chose to be interested in architecture, building his house at Hastings. 'As he must show a taste in something,' wrote Pegge in friendly perplexity, 'he chose Architecture, and built a house on the faith of his own skill in that Science, for which he paid exceedingly dear, to the great disappointment of those who succeeded to his fortune.' This charming place, as we should judge now, seemed most peculiar to a society accustomed to 'diversity of prospect, lawns, groves, rivulets, &c.; for it was close to the sea, at the dirty port of Hastings'.

Another aspect of independence showed itself in concern for what he called 'the beauty of the page', and that also brought Capell into trouble. The preface to *Prolusions* was dated 20 July 1759, eight years before the dedication to his Shakespeare edition. Dates are relevant to his history, for several unfortunate reasons. As Johnson's

Shakespeare had appeared just before his own, too late for comment or correction, he could only note that Johnson's text was based like all its predecessors on Rowe and Pope. Capell's text lacked notes, which for the beauty of the page he kept for separate publication in quarto later, promising them with minimal delay as they were 'in great forwardness'; but opposition and a dearth of subscribers altered the plan which only reached completion after his death. The interval of 6 and 15 years between his text and publication of the notes caused public neglect of both, driving into deeper withdrawal 'a disposition that was naturally upon the fret, and easily fermented'. The unfashionable Hastings house, which had cost almost £5000, was sold after his death for about £1300. In it nobody else was allowed to poke the fire. A Baronet friend was asked to leave his cane 'in the vestibule, lest he should either dirt the floors with it, or soil the carpet'. Obsessive house-fuss was less common then than now perhaps; 'to remove and misplace the most trifling thing in his room was a heinous offence'.

Pegge described him as solitary, single-minded upon his favourite Shakespeare subject. If a little praise came his way, as when Lord Dacre in a letter called him the *Restorer of Shakespeare*, he was moved to tears; 'he was known to have wept whenever he read the letter'. Habits of retirement during winters in Brick Court and summers at Hastings brought no sympathy from the clubbable literary world; the seeming secrecy of his Shakespeare notes caused Steevens to raid them; Johnson thought his style obscure as his habits, remarking to Boswell that 'If the man would have come to me, I would have endeavoured to endow his purposes with words; for, as it is, he doth gabble monstrously'. Pegge sensed a conspiracy of injustice among others in the subject: 'there was a determination among them not to suffer a Brother too near the Throne; and Mr. Capell had not fair play'. Walpole received a letter from his friend and neighbour George Hardinge, inviting his subscription towards the volumes of Notes: 'There is a knot of Booksellers formed against him, because he is (I will not say the best, but) the only Editor of Shakespeare'.

The only Editor made things difficult for himself and his readers. As he offered after 20 years little more than text and Preface, it was unreasonable to complain about lack of public recognition. The title page of *Prolusions* had included a startling claim: *'Edward the third, a Play, thought to be writ by SHAKESPEARE'*. Presumably Capell shared the thought. One could agree, reading it now, that it seems no worse than most of the *Henry the Sixth* cycle, and in his Shakespeare preface Capell argued at length for Shakespeare as author of all *Henry the Sixth*; but his apologia in *Prolusions* for that title phrase was thin: 'after all, it must be confess'd that it's being his work is conjecture only, and matter of opinion; and the reader must form one of his own, guided by what is now before him, and by what he shall meet with in perusal of the piece itself'.

Then there was the puzzling 'beauty of the page', and Dryden Leach the father of English fine printing; for his page cannot really be called beautiful, as pages go; it has larger margins than most, cleaner because this editor cleared them of footnotes. The type is too small, and the hyphened break of words quite senseless (at random I find u-niformly, gr-eater and e-ditor). The print shows through, and is not back-to-back recto and verso; these were indeed poorly printed books, with an assumption of fastidious taste. In both *Prolusions* and Shakespeare the editor devised a crotchety system of punctuation; to learn it could have deterred anyone from reading further. 'A third mark is, the cross: This, when it has one bar only, is significant of a thing shown or pointed to; when two, of a thing deliver'd: and they are severally plac'd exactly at the very word at which it is proper the pointing be made, or the delivery should take effect . . .'[12] Not riveting reading.

'A regard to the beauty of his page, and no other consideration,' Capell wrote, 'has induc'd the editor to suspend the operation of his plan in two of the poems . . .'[13] In the Shakespeare preface (p.23) he provided a note to explain why emendations, though 'the rejected reading is always put below', were not attributed to their authors. It was a curious omission, recalling Tonson's anonymous 1745 edition of Hanmer, where Warburton's statement in the Advertisement insisted on acknowledgement of his own emendations. Capell, after saying the attributions existed in his manuscript, mentioned in the note that

> they are suppress'd in the print for two reasons; First, their number, in some pages, makes them a little unsightly; and the editor professes himself weak enough to like a well-printed book . . .

So he accepted the burden of delay and derision, rather than produce such note-heavy volumes as became common later in the century, and were already familiar in a thousand editions of the classics. All the Shakespeare editors knew the vanity of placing their paragraphs on a page with his scenes; Edward Capell alone among the later 18th-century scholars refrained, realizing 'that he himself is the most injur'd by it; whose emendations are equal, at least in number, to all theirs if put together; to say nothing of his recover'd readings, which are more considerable still'.

---

[12] *Prolusions*, Preface, p.vi
[13] *Prolusions*, p.iii

Capell's temperamental privacy, poverty as a writer and thorough-ness in research made him the very opposite of Johnson, his imme-diate predecessor. The merit of Capell's edition is in eccentricity, the book's and his own; when the notes came Johnson complained his talents 'were just sufficient to select the black hairs from the white for the use of the periwig makers'. In the texts he printed, drawn direct from the quartos and First Folio, lay his originality as editor, the first fresh approach to Shakespeare since 1623.

Capell's Preface (he called it *Introduction*) was not among the best of its kind, written at an uneasy halfway stage of publication. The table of plays from the First Folio he printed uncritically, not ques-tioning *The Tempest* as coming first. The poor 'Players' were blamed, as usual, for defects and deception; where their version differed from early quartos Capell jumped to a remarkable guess:

> And who knows, if the difference that is between them, in some of the plays that are common to them both, has not been studiously heighten'd by the player editors, – who had the means in their power, being masters of all the alterations, – to give at once a greater currency to their own lame edition, and support the charge which they bring against the quarto's? this, at least, is a probable opinion, and no bad way of account-ing for those differences.

His guess seems now most unlikely. Capell after two decades of study dwelt among casual suppositions, in such matters as this and the author of *Edward the Third*.

He followed earlier editorial custom in lightly dismissing Rowe, Pope, Theobald, and in knocking Hanmer hard, as has been men-tioned. For Warburton he was content to leave comment where it rested in publications which had already attacked him,[14] adding only that 'the edition is not much benefited by fresh acquisitions from the old ones, which this gentleman seems to have neglected'. He meant of course his own sources, the quartos and First Folio, all other modern editions being derived via Rowe from the Fourth Folio – except Johnson's, which arrived too late to be considered, for John-son recognized the 1623 line of descent.

One of Capell's rare footnotes gave the printing history of his Shakespeare, as evidence that he had no chance to adapt to whatever Johnson wrote. Capell's title page has no date, but the work appeared in 1767. The first sheet, his note revealed, '(being the first of volume 2) went to the press in September 1760: and this volume was follow'd by volumes 8, 4, 9, 1, 6 and 7; the last of which was printed off in August 1765'. Volumes 3 and 5 and presumably the

---

[14] *The Canons of Criticism* and *Revisal of Shakespeare's Text*

Introduction occupied the final years. A publisher in those days found it necessary to pay his costs and store the sheets, rather than wait for a completed manuscript before starting to print.

On the chronic problem of emendation he was scrupulous, but difficult in his categories and sub-divisions: often, where modern editors seemed 'incompetent, or else absolutely deficient', his own 'using judgment and conjecture' replaced them, and such instances went into his text, leaving the rejected readings below; more specu- lative changes were held back for the promised volumes of notes; others again, among the confidently rejected readings, were *not* given below but reserved for the notes, because 'being of a compli- cated nature, the general method was there inconvenient'. It could apply to the man himself, of a complicated nature and his general method inconvenient.

Paragraphs on Shakespeare's sources, a foretaste of the subject for one promised volume called *The School of Shakespeare*, occupied the second half of Capell's introduction. He was not first in this field, preceded by the amazing Charlotte Lennox, but best read and most thorough.

Before leaving him an immense 'Note' should be mentioned, on the old problem of Shakespeare's learning. With the distaste he expressed for notes it offers one more eccentricity, stretching across nine pages and almost unreadably small. Capell had nothing very fresh to add, agreeing that Shakespeare learned enough school Latin to serve his use of it in the plays and observing that it was com- monest in his early plays; that he might well have acquired a little Italian and French; that imitations were absent because not needed, as was pleasantly phrased at the conclusion of this note: 'he had the stores in himself, and wanted not the assistance of a foreign hand to dress him up in things of their lending'. Most of this had been written before, by Rowe and Pope in their Prefaces; Capell showed no originality in observing Shakespeare's.

*   *   *

The rest of the period was dominated by Steevens and Malone, whose friendship became tainted by rivalry, and the sympathetic background scholarship of Isaac Reed. Between them these three were responsible for four new editions preceding the three long variorums which, living or posthumously, they created.

Johnson, most serious of moralists, had enjoyed the company of Steevens and proposed his election to The Club. When Boswell suggested the lies he told habitually might be taken as 'amusing fiction' the severe reply was 'Sir, the misfortune is, that you will

insensibly believe as much of it as you incline to believe'; but Steevens inherited Johnson's watch, with an engraved Greek inscription
from the New Testament, 'The night cometh, when no man can
work'.

For Steevens that night came in the first month of the new
century, after a prodigious amount of work on ever-larger Shakespeare editions. He was suspected of plagiarism in his use of Capell's
unpublished material and of introducing a few obscene footnotes as
the work of two clergymen he disliked.[15] Apart from such problems
of his own temperament he enjoyed a delightful bachelor life at his
house in Hampstead which had been an inn called the Upper Flask
(Flask Walk is still familiar), looked after by a distant cousin and her
daughters. From that height he observed London, walking there and
back most days in a routine described by Nichols in volume two of
the *Literary History:*

> He was an early riser; and, unless prevented by extraordinary bad
> weather, rarely failed walking to London and back again. His usual
> custom was to call on Isaac Reed in Staple-Inn at or before seven o'clock
> in the morning; and then, after a short conference with his intelligent
> Friend, he paraded to John Nichols, in Red Lion-passage; then hastened
> to the shop of Mudge and Dutton, the celebrated watch-makers, to
> regulate his watch; and to his steady and judicious friend Thomas Long-
> man, in search of new publications, and literary news. This was in general
> his ultima Thule.
>
> In returning, he constantly visited his much respected Friend Henry
> Baldwin; and then generally passed some time in converse with the
> Paragon of Literature, Dr. Samuel Johnson; rarely omitting to call at the
> well-stored shop of Ben White; the political storehouse of George
> Kearsley, or the literary conversational lounge at Archibald Hamilton's.
> Thence occasionally at one, two, or more of the following noted Biblio-
> poles: Cadell, Peter Elmsly, Tom Davies, Tom Payne, Debrett, or Stock-
> dale. Regularly finishing in Bond-Street either with Robson or Faulder, he
> hastened to an early dinner at his pleasant residence on Hampstead
> Heath.

From the tremendous collection he formed of old plays and fables,
inherited by his sister who must have been only too glad to get rid of
it in a sale five months after his death, he was able to comment on
many passages in Shakespeare with closer understanding than Johnson had possessed. His father became a director of the East India
Company; Steevens owned wealth enough to follow his tastes as
collector and connoisseur, gathering a complete assembly of

---

[15] For a full examination of this strange affair, and sifting of truth from fiction, see
Arthur Sherbo *The Birth of Shakespeare Studies*, 1956, pp.56–70

Hogarth's engravings in fine state, together with a parallel collection in poor later state to point the contrast. Born and buried in Poplar, he went to Eton and King's; it was agreed that with his taste for satire went many generous actions and a courteous manner. He was a skilled draughtsman. Few managed, as Isaac Reed did, to keep his friendship, and as Nichols put it 'he would sometimes break off his longest habits without ostensible reason'.

One elaborate witticism he aimed at Richard Gough, director of the Society of Antiquaries, whose attention was drawn to a shop in Southwark which exhibited a marble with Saxon letters recording the death of Hardiknute 'and describing the manner of his death, which was that of dropping suddenly dead, after drinking a gallon flaggon of wine at the marriage of a Danish Lord'. Steevens was of course responsible for the deception, and wrote his account of it for the *General Evening Post*, 25 October 1790:

> This stone was carried to a founder's in Southwark, who was in the secret, and a private buz whispered about, that such a curiosity was found. The antiquarians instantly surrounded the house, to purchase it at any price; no, the owner loved antiquity too well himself to part with it. They might take drawings of it with pleasure, but the piece was invaluable. This, however, was some comfort; to work they went, and a very accurate drawing was taken of it, and sent down to one of the greatest antiquarians in Derbyshire for his approbation; he returned for answer, 'That it was a great discovery, and perfectly answerable to the spelling and cut of the Saxon characters in the eleventh century.' The joke having thus travelled far enough, an ample discovery was made, which occasioned a good deal of innocent merriment on all sides; and the original marble was shewn on Saturday night last at Sir Joseph Banks's Converzatione, for the inspection of the curious.

As Shakespeare editor, especially for the edition of 1793 in 15 volumes, taking up the old task with undiminished energy, returning from retirement after crossing swords with Malone, Steevens established a remarkable routine according to Nichols who knew him well:

> It is to his own indefatigable industry, and the exertions of his printer, that we are indebted for the most perfect edition of our immortal Bard that ever came from the English press. In the preparation of it for the printer, he gave an instance of editorial activity and perseverance which is without example. To this work he devoted solely and exclusively of all other attentions a period of 18 months; and, during that time, he left his house every morning at one o'clock with the Hampstead patrole, and, proceeding without any consideration of the weather or the season, called up the compositor and woke all his devils:

'Him late from Hampstead journeying to his book

> Aurora oft for Cephalus mistook;
> What time he brush'd the dews with hasty pace,
> To meet the printer's dev'let face to face.'

At the chambers of Mr. Reed, where he was allowed to admit himself, with a sheet of the Shakespeare letter-press ready for correction, and found a room prepared to receive him: there was every book which he might wish to consult; and on Mr. Reed's pillow he could apply, on any doubt or sudden suggestion, to a knowledge of English literature perhaps equal to his own. The nocturnal toil greatly accelerated the printing of the work; as, while the printers slept, the editor was awake: and thus, in less than 20 months, he completed his last splendid edition of Shakespeare, in 15 large 8vo volumes; an almost incredible labour, which proved the astonishing energy and persevering powers of his mind.

Resignation was not among Steevens's virtues, and the prospect of death came as a fearful intrusion upon his habits as collector and editor; Rowlandson and Combe could have remembered him as the archetypal antiquary in their Dance of Death. Dibdin recorded the occasion:

> He grew not only irritable, but outrageous; and in full possession of his faculties, he raved in a manner which could have been expected only from a creature bred up without notions of morality or religion ... His language was, too frequently, the language of imprecation; and his wishes and apprehensions such, as no rational Christian can think upon without agony of heart.

It was said that after his death 'strange noises and deep groans were heard at midnight in his room'.

In more than 30 years of Shakespeare work Steevens wrote several 'Advertisements' or prefaces, changing his mind on a number of points as he progressed. A note he signed after the reprint of his first essay, in the posthumous 21-volume variorum of 1803, explained that these shifting opinions appeared in deference to a wish Johnson had expressed, 'that all the relative Prefaces should continue to attend his edition of our author's plays'. It is an interesting note, evidence that Johnson was deliberately the first variorum editor.

Steevens had produced in 1766, the year after Johnson's edition, 20 of the early Shakespeare quartos in four volumes, a landmark in 18th-century criticism as lending weight to texts of earliest authority. Capell in the same line of thought was at the same time printing his version from early quartos and the First Folio; it is not surprising that Steevens was accused of plagiarising in his own edition, as Capell allowed so much time to pass before publishing his notes. The 1766 volumes brought Johnson and Steevens into collaboration for future editions, though Johnson's part went no further than discussion, acceptance and occasional letters of introduction.

The 1766 essay is an attractive, uncharacteristically reticent piece of work. Steevens believed Shakespeare's obscurity rose from a colloquial style of his time. 'To make his meaning intelligible to his audience seems to have been his only care, and with the ease of conversation he has adopted its incorrectness.' All the more necessary therefore to soak oneself in popular literature of that period. Previous editors 'wanted industry; to cover which they published catalogues, transcribed at random, of a greater number of old copies than ever they can be supposed to have had in their possession'. Apart from that thrust it was a calm performance, suggesting the bibliophile and collector, thanking Garrick for urging the use of his own precious collection of quartos or 'pamphlets'; it seems Garrick, who had been very ready for Johnson to view his collection but not to borrow from it, showed even greater generosity to Steevens:

> Mr. Garrick's zeal would not permit him to withold anything that might ever so remotely tend to show the perfections of that author who could only have enabled him to display his own.

Steevens as collector had appeared in his decision sometimes to print several versions of the quartos, 'as there are many persons, who, not contented with the possession of a finished picture of some great master, are desirous to procure the first sketch that was made for it, that they may have the pleasure of tracing the progress of the artist from the first light colouring to the finishing stroke'.

From the flourishing trade of conjecture and emendation Steevens in this first essay remained detached; in an edition of Shakespeare's quartos, not of Shakespeare, he stood beyond controversy. As 'the language of conversations can only be expected to be preserved in works, which in their time assumed the merit of being pictures of men and manners', those became important sources and he had read them; and because every sort of errors plagued the text's descent, rather than add to them he presented the quartos as they had survived, 'the performances themselves make their appearance with every typographical error, such as they were before they fell into the hand of the player-editors'. It was a surprising resolve in the light of his later work; that Steevens was presenting evidence, not judging it, is suggested also by his inclusion of the 1609 *Sonnets*, with which he was quite out of sympathy. In printing the six rejected plays, he sat on the fence; perhaps Shakespeare wrote them, perhaps not, and perpetuating unworthy material did no good service to an author's memory:

> There is perhaps sufficient evidence, that most of the plays in question, unequal as they may be to the rest, were written by Shakespeare; but the reason generally given for publishing the less correct pieces of an author,

that it affords a more impartial view of a man's talents or way of thinking, than when we only see him in form, and prepared for our reception, is not enough to condemn an editor who thinks and practices otherwise.

The neat and quiet 'Advertisement' Steevens wrote for the 1773 edition, his first, was repeated in 1778 with the addition of a chapter from the *Guls Hornbook* by Dekker, from 1609, 'How a Gallant should behave himself in a Playhouse', which one may take as allegory for how a critic behaves himself in an edition. For his text Steevens trusted all earliest versions – it was the decade of earliest versions – finding that in later Folios 'the errors in every play, at least, were trebled'. Extra syllables added for completion of the metre were deleted, prose changed to poetry by earlier editors was returned to prose and vice versa. For the length and number of instances he apologized, but only by taking them from multiple sources could the interpretation be justified; in this he quoted Warton on Theobald, defending him against Pope – though he believed Theobald had access to about 100 old plays, not 800 as was claimed.

On the multiplication of instances Steevens quoted 'Falstaff's allusion to *stewed prunes*', an indecency which had defeated Johnson who could only meander around it:

> The propriety of these similes I am not sure that I fully understand. A *stewed prune* has the appearance of a prune, but has no taste . . . These are very slender disquisitions, but such is the task of a commentator.

The line occurs in *Henry IV Part I*, Act III, scene 3. Steevens, tasteless as the prune, had a field day with ten instances. Farmer capped them with another, better than any, commenting:

> Mr. Steevens has so fully discussed the subject of *stewed prunes*, that one can add nothing but the *price*. In a piece called Banks's Bay Horse in a Trance, 1595, we have 'a stock of wenches, set up with their *stewed prunes*, nine for a tester'.

Thus the editorial club enjoyed itself, leaving Johnson far behind.

Steevens, in the 1773 essay, explained his reasons for rejecting many suggestions which had arrived in the course of his task:

> The majority of these were founded on the supposition, that Shakespeare was originally an author correct in the utmost degree, but maimed and interpolated by the neglect or presumption of the players. In consequence of this belief, alterations have been proposed wherever a verse could be harmonized, an epithet exchanged for one more apposite, or a sentiment rendered less perplexed.

He made an interesting proposal in distinguishing between treatment proper to Shakespeare on the stage, and in a book:

Lately Published,

In Ten Volumes, large Octavo,

(Price Three Pounds and Ten Shillings, bound)

T H E

P L A Y S

O F

WILLIAM SHAKSPEARE,

With the CORRECTIONS and ILLUSTRATIONS of

ROWE,	FARMER,	TYRWHITT,
POPE,	PERCY,	MALONE,
THEOBALD,	TOLLET,	COLMAN,
HANMER,	HURD,	KENRICK,
WARBURTON,	HARDINGE,	REED,
UPTON,	HOLT,	FOLKES,
GREY,	GOLDSMITH,	LETHERLAND,
EDWARDS,	COLLINS,	BARRINGTON,
RODERICK,	BURROW,	JAMES,
THIRLBY,	SMITH,	RAWLINSON,
BISHOP,	CHAMIER,	BOWLE,
HEATH,	HAWKINS,	J. WARTON,
RIDLEY,	MUSGRAVE,	MURPHY,
SEYWARD,	LANGTON,	T. WARTON,
SYMPSON,	OLDYS,	WEST,
GRANGER,	GUTHRIE,	WARNER,
WALPOLE,	REYNOLDS,	MONTAGUE,
		&c. &c.

To which are added, NOTES by

SAMUEL JOHNSON and GEORGE STEEVENS;

Together with

THE PREFACES OF FORMER EDITORS:
TWO PORTRAITS OF THE AUTHOR;
A FAC-SIMILE OF HIS HAND-WRITING;

A Plate, representing the Figures of ancient Morris-Dancers,&c. &c.

The Second Edition, revised and augmented.

—Τῆ; φύσεως γραμμαλεὺς ἦν, τὸν κάλαμον ἀποδέχων εἰς νῦν.

Vet. Auct. apud Suidam.

Multa dies variusque labor mutabilis ævi
Retulit in melius, multos alterna revisens
Lusit, et in solido rursus fortuna locavit,   Virgil.

Printed for J. NICHOLS, T. EVANS, and the rest of the PROPRIETORS.

18   Publisher's advertisement opposite the title page of Steevens's edition of six source plays for Shakespeare, 1779. [Actual height of *type* $5\frac{9}{16}$ inches]

There are yet many passages unexplained and unintelligible, which may be reformed, at hazard of whatever licence, for exhibitions on the stage, in which the pleasure of the audience is chiefly to be considered; but must remain untouched by the critical editor, whose conjectures are limited by narrow bounds, and who gives only what he at least supposes his author to have written.

The approach he rejected had of course been Pope's and Hanmer's.

In 1773, nominally assisting Johnson who read and discussed it all, Steevens referred with restraint to other critics and his predecessors, except for the opening broadside against 'Mr. Rowe's inattention to one of the first duties of an editor' in using the Fourth and worst Folio. His denial of plagiarism from Capell is less than convincing. He closed with a handsome tribute to Jacob Tonson, last of the dynasty, great-nephew of Jacob the copyright-purchaser, who had died in 1767.

Steevens's third and longest essay, opening the 15-volume edition of 1793, marked a return to Shakespearean debate after his earlier decision to hand over responsibility to Isaac Reed, following the mild fracas with Malone which brought him back to 18 months of nocturnal work.

He had the good sense to change his mind on several aspects across the decades as confidence came and went. In 1766 he had written as an antiquary, preserving the faults, with greatest respect for whatever came earliest. A quarter of a century later he no longer resisted the editorial desire to produce a better version, and though proud of his acquaintance with first printed sources he was far from uncritical in using them, and disagreed with Malone who dismissed the Second Folio as worthless. The posthumous variorum of 1803 altered course on another matter also: the 1793 Advertisement opened with a long rejection of any claims to authenticity for Shakespeare's portraits. 'As he was careless of the future state of his works', he wrote in a sentence of classical balance, 'his solicitude might not have extended to the perpetuation of his looks.'

In this edition with fearless absurdity he refused to print the sonnets, adding pedantry to folly in a footnote reference to Thomas Watson's sonnets which he admired above Shakespeare's. At the low ebb of editorial comment he suggested Shakespeare borrowed from Watson in *Venus and Adonis*, where the line

> Leading him prisoner in a red-rose chain

is traced back to Watson's 83rd sonnet,

> The Muses not long since intrapping love
> In chains of roases . . .

Steevens, who could perform better than that, enjoyed the dull duty of an editor. Not all the minutiae of his notes and points were printed, he reassured readers, nor all mistakes of his predecessors ignored; but the pleasure of refuting them was sometimes too great to be sacrificed:

> A few, manifestly erroneous, are indeed retained, to show how much the tone of Shakespearean criticism is changed, or on account of the skill displayed in their confutation; for surely every editor in his turn is occasionally entitled to be seen, as he would have shown himself, with his vanquished adversary at his feet.

Dr. Farmer was the only man he would have trusted through a whole edition, and he had never the time.

The most striking change since 1766 was in his attitude towards the First Folio and its editors. As to those 16 plays which first appeared there, in a paranoid footnote Steevens suggested a reason: Heminge and Condell, that scheming couple, had suppressed them.

> ... may not our want of yet earlier and less corrupted editions of these very dramas be solely attributed to the monopolizing vigilance of its editors, Hemmings and Condell? Finding they had been deprived of some tragedies and comedies which, when opportunity offered, they designed to publish for their own emolument, they redoubled their solicitude to withold the rest, and were but too successful in their precaution.

He recalled the names of their fellow actors which 'cannot fail to enforce respect, viz. William Ostler, John Shanke, William Sly, and Thomas Poope'.

Steevens was more amusing in comment about the whole world of petty editing, literal criticism, which he of all people knew well, calling the passionate disagreements 'so many games of literary push-pin', and 'haberdasheries of criticism'; after all it mattered little, as 'a few chipped or disjointed stones will not impair the shape or endanger the stability of a pyramid'. In maturity he shared Johnson's view of notes as necessary evils, for Shakespeare was generally easy to follow and anyone could get the drift without instruction.

> It is unlucky for him, perhaps, that between the interest of his readers and his editors a material difference should subsist. The former wish to meet with as few difficulties as possible, while the latter are tempted to seek them out, because they afford opportunities for explanatory criticism.

His critical stance as anti-antiquary represented a complete U-turn since the reprint of 20 quartos, converted it seems by conversation with the respected Dr. Farmer:

> Having on this subject the support of Dr. Farmer's acknowledged judgement and experience, we shall not shrink from controversy with those

who maintain a different opinion, and refuse to acquiesce in modern suggestions if opposed to the authority of quartos and folios, consigned to us by a set of people who were wholly uninstructed in the common forms of style, orthography and punctuation. – We do not therefore hesitate to affirm, that a blind fidelity to the eldest printed copies, is on some occasions a confirmed treason against the sense, spirit, and versification of Shakespeare.

In late middle age he moved towards understanding, at least, the state of mind in which Pope and Hanmer prepared their editions, but making a familiar distinction: certain liberties acceptable for stage production would not be proper in a printed edition.

Editors had been too prolix; he foresaw the time when only a choice among so many long notes would be sensible.

We may subjoin (alluding to our own practice as well as that of others) that they whose remarks are longest, and who seek the most frequent opportunities of introducing their names at the bottom of our author's page, are not on that account, the most estimable cricks.

On the whole this essay is precious as showing that wit and irony which caused Johnson to welcome Steevens as a member of The Club, and a degree of detachment from the fray. The friendships with Farmer and Reed survived unimpaired. Walking down from Hampstead to work on the notes, get his watch adjusted and call at the bookshops he also thought kindly of Malone, in a back-handed compliment which may close this account:

His additions to an author's Life, his attempt to ascertain the Order in which his plays were written, together with his account of our ancient Stage, &c. are here re-published; and every reader will concur in wishing that a gentleman who has produced such intelligent combinations from very few materials, had fortunately been possessed of more.

*   *   *

It cannot be difficult for a man who hates publicity to preserve his friendships with those who seek it. Isaac Reed, indispensable background scholar to many literary endeavours of the late 18th century, was almost unique in remaining intimate with Steevens, most cantankerous among them all; 'for the last 30 years,' Nichols testified, 'there has scarcely appeared any literary work in this country, of the least consequence, that required minute and extensive research, which had not the advantage of his liberal assistance, as the grateful prefaces of a variety of writers have abundantly testified.' Boswell thought his 'extensive and accurate knowledge of English literary history . . . wonderful; indeed his labours have proved it to the world; and all who have the pleasure of his acquaintance can bear testimony to the frankness of his communications in private society'.

In all this he was like Dr. Farmer whose detachment in Cambridge kept him beyond the fray. Reed used to stay with him at Emanuel for a month in the autumn. 'If ever there was a mind devoid of guile,' wrote Nichols, 'it was Isaac Reed's.'

To have been woken most nights by the arrival of Steevens on a mission to plunder his knowledge for the next Shakespeare edition was remarkable enough; in that phase of life Reed had the rarest of literary phobias, a horror of seeing his name on a title page. In a letter (1778) he wrote:

> I declare I have such a horror of seeing my name as Author or Editor, that if I had the option of standing in the pillory, or of standing formally before the publick in either of those lights I should find it difficult to determine which to choose.

In the 1785 Shakespeare he avoided that embarrassment with the formula: 'Revised and augmented by the Editor of Dodsley's Collection of Old Plays', for which he had been responsible five years earlier. He overcame the scruple at last, for the 1803 title page (Steevens being dead) has 'Revised and augmented by Isaac Reed' and his name appears below the notes he wrote. When the vast library was sold after his death in 1807 the auctioneer's catalogue described him as 'Editor of the Last Edition of Shakspeare'.

So, unlike Malone and Capell, Reed's collection did not pass into the public institutions for any scholar of the future; in the terms of his will it was sold as Steevens's had been, an extraordinary event lasting 39 days. His books and those of Brand the antiquary were auctioned at about the same time. 'Isaac Reed's and Mr. Brand's books, &c. will both be very curious,' wrote Andrew Caldwell, a Dublin literary figure, to Bishop Percy, 'and the Catalogues are to be very carefully digested. Malone says he will be broke.' Reed had been chiefly at ease with his bibliophile friends, Malone among them.

It is an amazing catalogue. His First Folio was sold for £38, and in those days a large-paper set of the 1793 Johnson and Steevens edition seemed almost as desirable (£29). It would be pleasant to own lot 8536,

> Shakspeariana, a large assembly of Tracts, by various Authors, relative to Shakspeare, neatly bound in 9 vol. N.B. this Article must be a most Desirable acquisition to any Gentleman wishing to compleat his Collection.

It went for £23. Rowe's edition of 1709 cost only £1.2s, Johnson's from 1765 £4, Malone's (1790) £7. By similar proportion in today's uninteresting theme of prices, as a decent First Folio is worth above half a million pounds, Malone should cost more than ninety thousand but it does not. Boydell's nine folio volumes were sold for £19, his set

BIBLIOTHECA REEDIANA

A

CATALOGUE

OF THE

CURIOUS & EXTENSIVE

LIBRARY

OF THE LATE

ISAAC REED, ESQ.

OF STAPLE INN.

Deceafed.

Editor of the Laſt Edition of Shakſpeare.

Comprehending a moſt Extraordinary Collection of Books, in Engliſh Literature; particularly relating to the Engliſh Drama, and Poetry, many of them extremely Scarce, and enriched by his MS. Notes, and Obfervations. Together with his Manu-ſcripts, Prints, Books of Prints, Book Cafes, &c.

Which Will be Sold by Auction,

By Meſſrs. KING *and* LOCHEE,

AT THEIR GREAT ROOM,

No. 38,

KING-STREET, COVENT-GARDEN,

On MONDAY, NOV. 2, 1807,

AND 38 FOLLOWING DAYS, (SUNDAYS EXCEPTED.)

AT TWELVE O'CLOCK.

May be viewed on Monday, Oct. 26, and till the Time of Sale, and Catalogues had at the Room, illuſtra-ted with a Portrait of Mr. Reed, price 5s.

J. Barker, Printer, Great Ruſſel-Street, Covent-Garden.

19   Isaac Reed's collection sold by auction, 1807. [Actual height of *type* $5\frac{3}{4}$ inches]

of the immense *Shakspeare Gallery* plates for £21.10s, but they had been published for 60 guineas. His great bookcase, last lot of all, went to Lum for the large sum of £16. At random among other treasure one notes lot 8699, 'The original copy of part of Gray's Poems, in his own hand-writing', picked up by Bindley for a guinea; or Triphook's purchase for 9s (lot 8673) of an octavo volume owned once by Shenstone, with a note in Reed's hand, 'I purchased it of Tom Davies, who bought his Library. The first two Epistles are in Shenstone's own hand-writing'.[16]

Reed, son of a baker in London, earned his living as solicitor and conveyancer but loathed it: 'The practice of the Law was intolerable'. He seems to have been ready to enter the field as Shakespeare editor at Steevens's request, to withdraw for the same reason and again to return, inheriting from him 200 guineas and his corrected Shakespeare text, riding above the storms; 'for I heartily detest all the squabbles and paltry tricks which are used by authors against one another, and which no one who gives his name to the publick has a right to suppose himself insignificant enough to be exempt from. Writing is very painful to me, and I do not know that I am perfectly intelligible'.[17]

Reed's short essays to introduce his 1785 edition and the 1803 variorum travelled no further than expressions of diffidence, though for the later version especially his textual notes grew in length and confidence. The tone was clear in 1785: 'He has added but little to the bulk of the volumes from his own observations, having, upon every occasion, rather chosen to avoid a note, than to court the opportunity of inserting one'. It was curious in the future editor-overseer of 21 volumes to quote Prior's belief

> That when one's proofs are aptly chosen,
> Four are as valid as four dozen.

---

[16] It has been tempting to linger over Reed's books, as I have the catalogue (on large paper) ruled and marked by King the auctioneer for the bookseller George Nicol, with King's note to him:

'With this you will receive the catalogue of the late Mr. Reeds Books marked, not probably you will think in the neatest manner, but I believe correctly as it passed through no other hand but mine. I have affixed a few names to some particular Articles, and remain

Dr Sir

Yours truly

My respects to Mrs. Nicol   Thos King

[17] Letter to Nichols, quoted above

*   *   *

Theobald, Warburton and Steevens, each conscious of the temptations, could not suppress the egoism of editing; Reed and Malone
were more detached. Boswell referred to 'my steady friend Mr. Isaac
Reed, of Staple-Inn, whose extensive and accurate knowledge of
English literary history I do not express with exaggeration, when I
say it is wonderful'; Malone was his steadiest friend, listening as
Boswell read passages from the unfinished *Life of Johnson*, encour-
aging him through periods of depression. The *Journal of a Tour to
the Hebrides* was dedicated to him. Both Steevens and Malone died
with their maximal editions of Shakespeare unfinished; Reed saw
Steevens through the press, Boswell's son repaid his father's debt of
friendship by a greater labour in completing the work of Malone.

Some 18th-century editors became so closely identified with their
notes and convictions as to resent alternative solutions, like printers
who buried, drowned or melted the types they designed rather than
risk their use in some alien context. Debate was acceptable, but the
announcement of a new edition offered another form of threat. It
had happened between Theobald and Warburton, Warburton and
Hanmer; again 40 years on, with Steevens and Malone, who had
worked and published at ease together.

This was no terrible quarrel, but a break in friendship after 1783
when Nichols put a note in the *Gentleman's Magazine* to announce
Malone's Shakespeare edition 'with select notes from all the commentators'. Malone's two Supplementary Volumes to the 1778 'Johnson and Steevens' had appeared in 1780 with no trace of discord, his
own notes supplementing or opposing Steevens's views; for example, each wrote long and differing explanations as to Shakespeare's
share in *Pericles*. Malone produced a third volume of notes in 1783;
Reed's 'Johnson and Steevens' came two years later with those few
notes of dissent by Malone which caused Steevens to demand that
they be reprinted verbatim in the forthcoming Malone edition, giving
him the opportunity to reply; and when Malone claimed freedom
of choice in printing or excluding his earlier judgement war was
declared. In Boswell's[18] account of it:

> Mr. Steevens persisted in requiring that they should appear with all their
> imperfections on their head; and on this being refused, declared that all
> communication on the subject of Shakspeare was at an end between
> them.

His reaction can only be understood by recalling the grey cloud of

---

[18] References in the following paragraphs refer to the son of Johnson's biographer

Malone's future edition. Steevens had withdrawn, leaving the field to Reed. Malone's 'Advertisement' in the first 1780 volume included passages which could suddenly have seemed equivocal, contradictory.

> By a diligent collation of all the old copies [he would have read with satisfaction] and the judicious restoration of ancient readings, the text of this author seems now finally settled. The great abilities and unwearied researches of his last editor, it must likewise be acknowledged, have left little obscure or unexplained.

Golden words.

> But the field of illustration is so extensive [Malone continued] that some time may yet elapse before the dramas of Shakspeare shall yet appear in such a manner as to be incapable of improvement.

Steevens may have felt as Macbeth in learning that Fleance had escaped, 'Now comes my fit again'. It drove him towards the frenetic energy of his 15-volume edition; each competed for space and time, both surrendered to the dance of death.

After Malone's ten volumes had appeared in 1790, poorly printed and without payment, he announced a splendid version in 15 royal quarto volumes; it never came, but very likely this caused Steevens with sudden alarm to walk to Reed's chambers from Hampstead and work through each night to produce his own 15 volumes, racing him to it, completing the great task in 18 months. Without engravings, Steevens asserted his 1793 Shakespeare was better than any as to paper and printing. It reads like a direct answer to Malone whose announcement of a 'splendid edition' included the promise

> that the same gratuitous zeal which induced me to undertake the former edition, will accompany this revisal of it, and that no diligence or care of mine shall be wanting to render this new edition of my work, which is to be ornamented with engravings, and to be printed in fifteen volumes royal quarto, worthy of our greatest English poet. The first two volumes are intended to be published next year.

It was Boaden's belief that Malone 'had in the year 1790 done the greatest possible injury to his eyes by selecting types both for text and notes for his edition painful and distressing to the great majority of readers'. The great majority suffered, if anyone, rather than Malone who could hand responsibility to his excellent printer Baldwin; anyway, the type is no smaller than that chosen by Capell for the father of fine printing in England, Dryden Leach.

This competition between Steevens and Malone, extending an earlier tradition to the century's end, reached its limit in Boswell's essays for the variorum of 1821 where a heartfelt bias against the later Steevens (after his cooperation with Malone ended) is strongly expressed. At first all was harmonious: 'They both professed to follow the old copies with scrupulous fidelity, except where a clear necessity compelled them to depart from the readings which they supplied'; but whereas Malone continued along these lines, 'his rival critick has latterly adopted maxims directly contrary to the opinions which he formerly maintained'. It was Boswell's view that Steevens in conformity to 18th-century taste altered Shakespeare's intentional irregularities of metre, supporting such editorial decisions with the irony and ridicule which came easily to him. In reply to all this, Malone was preparing an Essay on the Phraseology and Metre of Shakespeare, leaving a draft which Boswell took pains to complete. As to the reprint of early quartos for which Steevens had been responsible in 1766, which brought about his partnership with Johnson, Boswell found it 'one of the most grossly incorrect performances that I have ever seen' and the 1773 edition of Shakespeare 'scarcely less objectionable'.

The status of the Second Folio was their next bone of contention, shaken into analysis by Boswell. Malone had devoted much of his 1790 Preface to dismissing the Second Folio as useless; Steevens got his printer to add up the number of readings from 1632 which Malone had accepted for his edition; Boswell demolished the statistic because most were mere corrections of typographic errors. Then there was the matter of the portrait, attacked as nonsense by Steevens in 1778 because nobody had good reason for declaring any image of Shakespeare to be a likeness; but after Malone's acceptance of the Chandos portrait Steevens took an opposite course, and decided that the much more recently discovered Felton portrait was true.

Steevens's perversity and academic wit had no appeal for Boswell in defending Malone when both were dead. Steevens mocked the Chandos painting by calling it 'the D'Avenantico–Bettertonian–Barryan–Keckian–Nicolsian–Chandosan canvas', which argued nothing, and Boswell believed his promotion of the later painting, with the printing of Richardson's Proposals for engraving it, might show 'that the fabricator of the Hardiknutian tablet had been trying his ingenuity upon a more important scale'.

Perhaps one can now accept that from Theobald to Malone the editors had assembled their examples and their parallels from 16th-century minor literature to demonstrate the sense of obscure phrases in Shakespeare, a learned form of burrowing in which Steevens travelled far, Reed further and Malone furthest. For entertainment in footnote discourse the Theobald–Warburton–Johnson phase was followed most ably by Steevens. Capell, Jennens, Farmer, Edwards attract still by some eccentricity, humanity or wit; Malone, most respected among them all now for his accuracy, was not an entertainer.

Nobody could imagine a friend of Johnson, Burke and Reynolds, sharing evenings with them, to have been dull company but Malone resisted the temptations of wit in his editing. Just after his death and while he himself was ill, Nichols wrote 'this is the peculiar fame of Edmund Malone, that he could subdue the temptations to display his *own* wisdom or wit, and consider only the temptations of his Author's text'. Steevens's pleasure in needling him a little is understandable, though it drove the 1803 edition into errors which Boswell's version corrected 18 years later, nine years after the death of Malone.

The major additions, as these later sets of the plays grew in number of volumes, were Malone's. Those early and mighty 19th-century editions seem roughly similar because they each include Malone's long 'Life of Shakespeare' and his *History of the English Stage*, so it would be false to suppose in all the debate that one protagonist could perform independently of another; both belonged, at times literally, to the same club. Steevens in early years had given to Malone his precious collection of old plays, they never ceased to communicate. When Malone published a book demolishing the Ireland forgeries in 1796, he sent a copy to Steevens who thanked him warmly.

Sidney Lee thought Malone's editing suggested an insensitive ear, and that he lacked the alertness of Steevens, but sensitive ears are out of fashion now. After reading Malone's *Life of Dryden*, Walpole's friend George Hardinge derided his exactness, what he called 'minute history', as Pope had satirized the literal criticism of Theobald, in a tract called *The Essence of Malone; or, the Beauties of that fascinating Writer, extracted from his immortal Work; in 539 pages and a quarter, just published; and with his accustomed felicity intituled, Some Account of the Life and Writings of John Dryden.* In 1801 appeared *Another Essence of Malone; or the Beauties of Shakespeare's Editor.* Steevens was not the only fountain which sprayed him.

Malone's achievements were formidable as author of three sustained essays in the late editions, and as the critic who demolished two conspicuous forgeries of his lifetime, Chatterton's and Ireland's. With him the Shakespeare game arrived at critical maturity, less admirable as a spectator sport than when Theobald and Pope were in the field; one misses Warburton's wounded ego, Johnson's devastating calm, Capell's eccentricity, Steevens's mischief. Literal criticism becomes the routine of thesis life. Malone was the first modern Shakespeare critic.

Johnson's explicit phrases about notes as necessary but necessary evils struck him as incomprehensible, needing interpretation. Johnson directed this advice to beginners, he declared; the multiplication of instances was meat and drink to him. Capell had given small help to the cause by making his own notes incomprehensible. The Malone manner is as oppressive as tropical sun exposing every angle:

> While our object is, to support and establish what the poet wrote, to illustrate his phraseology by comparing it with that of his contemporaries, and to explain his fugitive allusions to customs long since disused and forgotten, while this object is kept steadily in view, if even every line of his plays were accompanied with a comment, every intelligent reader would be indebted to the industry of him who produced it.

So every intelligent reader pays his debt, while looking back in sympathy to that parish priest who still preferred his *Mumpsimus* to *Sumpsimus*. Johnson faced his manly task, with 'Let us hear no more of the dull duty of a critic'; Malone's sentence has a different overtone: 'Let us then hear no more of his barbarous jargon concerning Shakspeare's having been *elucidated* into *obscurity*, and buried under the load of his commentators'. Yet the editors after 1821 – and before – performed a rescue operation.

It seems surprising that from this background Malone rejected Tyrwhitt's advocacy of original spelling; not one among all the 18th-century editors, looking back to early and earliest versions of the plays, printed the old spelling.[19] Tyrwhitt, one learns from Malone's Preface, 'was of opinion, that in printing these plays the original spelling should be adhered to, and that we never could be sure of a perfectly faithful edition, unless the first folio copy was made the standard, and actually sent to the press, with such corrections as the editor might think proper'. Malone found this 'liable to many objections', no doubt in part from the inadmissible use of 1623 as a starting point; and when the whole problem was comprehension with a view to restoration, outdated orthography looked irrelevant. Yet it is odd that a succession of editor-antiquaries detached themselves from original spelling; even if regret for its charm were dismissed as insufferable, Tyrwhitt must have regarded spelling as one form of clue in the hunt for restoration.

Malone's 1790 Preface proposed no new principle of editing, only an extension of old practice: back to the earliest quartos or, where none existed, to the 1623 Folio, and multiplication of instances to prove meaning. Theobald had been first to work along those lines but Malone decided against printing any Preface before Johnson's 'because they appear to me to throw no light on our author or his

---

[19] Steevens had of course used it in his 1766 reprint of the quartos

works'. As to Warburton, 'let none of his admirers ever dare to write his name with that of Shakspeare'.

As to the Second Folio, Steevens was able to reply with teasing and misleading statistics produced after daunting labour by his printer. In taking up that thread Malone mentioned 'the editor's profound ignorance of our poet's phraseology and metre', and it pleased Steevens to say the Second Folio had no editor. Malone was best when roused, as on Pope and that phantom editor:

> This person in fact, whoever he was, and Mr. Pope, were the two great corrupters of our poet's text; and I have no doubt that if the arbitrary alterations introduced by these two editors were numbered, in the plays of which no quarto copies are extant, they would greatly exceed all the corruptions and errours of the press in the original and only authentick copies of those plays.

Malone formed a great collection of 16th-century English writing, much of which came after his death to the Bodleian; during his life he shared it generously. The son of an Irish judge, Ireland remained his home though he had settled as a young man in London, bored by the law as Reed was too but able with independent means to abandon that life. Spending his money on books, sharing his equipment, helping the elder Boswell, enjoying the friendship of that circle, Malone and Reed remain as peaceful figures among the turbulent.

> I scarcely remember ever to have looked into a book of the age of Queen Elizabeth, in which I did not find somewhat that tended to throw a light on these plays.

V   OUTSIDERS

Charles Jennens, Handel's friend who prepared the libretti for several of his oratorios including *Messiah*, embarked upon a Shakespeare edition but died after completing work on five plays. Last of the rich amateurs, he is an interesting minor figure in Shakespeare history, if only as the cause of extreme irritation to Steevens who called him 'the only Editor to whom the scenes of Shakespeare had not even the most inconsiderable obligation'. The comment was perhaps inspired by a hostile pamphlet and Jennens's slight reference to Steevens below the list of Editions Collated in his printing of *Hamlet:* 'N.B. As *Steevens* publishes from the quartos, for brevity's sake, I take no notice of him but when he omits giving the various readings of those quarto editions he professes to collate ...' That was in 1773, when the first Johnson and Steevens edition had just appeared.

No doubt Jennens aroused envy by possession of ample means, an independent life with his books at Gopsal in Leicestershire and a town house; assuming authority beyond his range, a lesser Hanmer outside his time. A non-juror, charitable and religious, according to Steevens he behaved with such ostentation

> that if his transit were only from Great Ormond-Street, Bloomsbury, where he resided, to Mr. Bowyer's in Red Lion-passage, Fleet-street, he always travelled with four horses, and sometimes with as many servants behind his carriage. In his progress up the paved court, a footman usually preceded, to kick oyster-shells and other impediments out of his way.

Jennens in his brief progress kicked both publisher and printer, but he was not a negligible editor. *Lear* appeared in 1770, followed by *Hamlet, Othello* and *Macbeth* three years later; *Caesar* was published in 1774 after his death at the age of 73. He could not have expected in his eighth decade to complete such a task by the method he had chosen, of taking from all editions and listing every variant.

The idea was not absurd but helpful; his page, clearly printed with a minimum of comment except in rare moments of expansion or quotation, most footnotes limited to variant readings, looks more rational than most others before that date. Notes for *Hamlet* were in two columns; those for *Lear*, 'published as a specimen', were not. The complaint against Jennens was that after such close acquaintance with each possibility he would commonly make a *wrong* choice for his text, a criticism which has some force – as for instance when he destroyed one of the wonderful casual metaphors in *Hamlet* by printing

> A moth it is to trouble the mind's eye,

sending a reader to his footnote: 'The 3d.q, R and all after, *mote* for *moth*'.

He used a coy device in keeping his name from the title page, by dedicating the book to himself: 'Charles Jennens Esq . . . under whose patronage, by access to whose library, and from whose hints and remarks, the editor hath been able to attempt An Edition of Shakespeare, the same is inscribed, with the greatest respect and gratitude, by his most obliged, and obedient humble servant, The Editor'.

A considerable collector of Shakespeare but without claiming wide acquaintance in Elizabethan literature, the stimulus for Jennens seems to have been Capell's negligence – or rather, the space of years when Capell's text was out and about, but not his supplementary publication of the Notes which would eventually include 'a collected body of *Readings* that were to go with these plays'. Jennens was not indifferent to appearance but thought it an aspect of convenience; it is perhaps a minor point but worth observing, as he himself noted it, that no earlier edition included Act and Scene in the running headline of each page opening – nor later editions, until the 1821 variorum. As to Capell's high-fallutin about the excellence of a page without notes, Jennens replied from commonsense:

> But he was afraid his notes placed with the text should spoil the beauty of the book. If they are good ones they would not: for that man must be greatly mistaken in his ideas of beauty, who prefers the handsome appearance of a page in black and white, to the quick and easy information of his readers in matters necessary to be known for their becoming proper judges of the sense of the author, and the goodness of the edition.

If this was Jennens's single originality in the Preface to his specimen publication of *Lear*, it sprang from good critical response to the latest edition, Capell's, where a new text appeared without support from argument or evidence for choice. 'No editor that I know of has a right to impose upon every body his own favourite reading, or to give his own conjectural interpolation, without producing the readings of the several editions.'

It was a large gesture by Handel's elderly friend, alone in the library at Gopsal, to set about correcting this lax state of affairs. Arranging the quartos and folios down the length of his great table, keeping them open with bars of wood, he hobbled from one to the next seeking variant phrases and words, punctuation and syllables; noting them all, in solitude perceiving now and then, as it seemed, insight which merited a paragraph. Steevens reported this sensible method of collation as 'a pleasant [i.e. funny] circumstance'.

In such conditions the duty of an editor became dull, as he confessed. "Tis no doubt a slavish business to proceed through so many editions of so voluminous a writer, in the slow and exact manner this editor hath done in King *Lear*, and proposes to do in the rest of *Shakespeare's* plays.' Nobody thanked him but Jennens deserves to be better remembered. Boswell in 1821 referred to 'the total want of discrimination with which he collected the most obvious typographical errors from the most spurious copies'. In the constant question of emendation no scruple deterred him, guided by taste, from changing a phrase.

*   *   *

The first edition to appear from John Bell as publisher, called *Bell's Edition of Shakespeare's Plays*, had 'Notes Critical and Illustrative by the Authors of the Dramatic Censor'. This meant a poor author and actor on whom Garrick sometimes took pity, Francis Gentleman. He liked to be remembered for two volumes of criticism, called *The Dramatic Censor*.

The commercial success of this edition was startling; having nothing to do with Shakespeare scholarship Isaac Reed condemned it as the worst ever published. Jaggard's phrase, that this was 'the first edition with artistic illustrations', is nonsense, but 800 sets were sold in a single week.

The reason must be that three decades before Thomas Bowdler's 'Family Shakspeare' this was the first bowdlerized edition: it should be known as the first Gentleman's Shakespeare. All through the century coarse phrases and scenes had disturbed the editors who wanted to print what Shakespeare wrote; they explained, apologized, or relegated to footnote level and deleted. If the foundation of Bowdler is to be found in Pope and Hanmer, Bell's edition built further by printing the plays as performed at Covent Garden and Drury Lane where it seems the vulgarities were dropped, becoming conveniently 'a companion to the theatre'. The publisher achieved success through a U-turn from editorial accuracy, for 'it has been our peculiar endeavour to render what we call the essence of Shakespeare, more instructive and intelligible; especially to the ladies and to youth; glaring indecencies being removed, and intricate passages explained; and lastly, we have striven to supply plainer ideas of criticism, both in public and private, than we have hitherto met with'.

In this form an attractively illustrated set could circulate in families, rescuing Shakespeare from that commercial servility to Elizabethan audiences which was supposed to have corrupted his naturally noble style.

After this short declaration of intent, volume one looks respectable rather than responsible by including a long and irrelevant *Essay on Oratory*, scattering such names as Demosthenes, Isocrates, Cicero, Fenelon, Malbranche, and extending it with 'a pamphlet, written by Mr. GENTLEMAN, some few years since'.

The *Life of Shakespeare*, appearing as a preface to volume nine, the Poems, has farcical passages but one finds there a genuine distinction between adaptation and emendation. Though Gentleman thought Theobald 'the only ingenious liberal Critic . . . he often went conjecturally too far' – a different matter from changing the final scenes of *Lear*, as they were printed in this edition. As to Pope and Rowe, their observations 'are a disgrace to the great abilities of those able authors, and place them in the contemptible light of booksellers tools'.

This final volume, dated 1774, was the first to print the poems as part of a collected edition since Rowe's duodecimo in 1714.

* * *

Some mention has been made of Zachary Grey, Hanmer's apologist who 'passed his winter at Cambridge, and lived during the rest of the year at Ampthill'. Though he never attempted an edition of Shakespeare, Grey rests among the editors because of two volumes 'Published for the Author' in 1754, *Critical Historical and Explanatory Notes on Shakespeare with Emendations of the Text and Metre*. He found it agreeable to go through the plays, pausing whenever a phrase or event reminded him of some volume in his library, noting and copying without contention his contributions to parallel passages. Johnson assessed him with that hint of irony which looks like commendation:

> Grey's diligent perusal of the old English Writers has enabled him to make some useful observations. What he undertook, he has well enough performed; but, as he neither attempts judicial nor emendatory criticism, he employs rather his memory than his sagacity. It were to be wished that all would endeavour to imitate his modesty, who have not been able to surpass his knowledge.

After much religious pamphleteering, in 1744 Grey had produced an edition of Hudibras which landed him in trouble with Warburton through points which found their way into his notes. It was the familiar Warburton trouble – Theobald, Hanmer, then Grey. A mutual Cambridge friend had discussed the text with Warburton, and repeated the argument in conversation with Grey. Warburton took the first opportunity (his Shakespeare Preface) to question whether so 'execrable a heap of nonsense had ever appeared in any learned language as Grey's commentaries on Hudibras'. Grey replied by attacking Warburton's edition of Shakespeare, 'with a long string of emendations borrowed by the celebrated author from the Oxford edition without acknowledgement'.[20] 'A free and familiar letter to that great refiner of Pope and Shakespeare, the Rev. Mr. W. Warburton' followed in 1750 – so Grey possessed a sting and used it, but quiet life suited him better. The Preface to his 1754 work defended Hanmer's version as that of 'a good *Christian;* who has treated every editor with decency'. Warburton he avoided on this occasion, having exhausted that issue, only looking to the day when those two who criticized him most effectively, Edwards and Upton, produced their own editions.

It is of some interest to watch several constants in 18th-century Shakespeare criticism, among which Zachary Grey put obscenity in first place, then lack of education, and last 'the *jingles, puns* and *quibbles*'. Puns and quibbles he viewed as a habit of that day, giving examples from sermons by Lancelot Andrewes; they recall the language of Polonius, such as this for Easter:

> I have my *seasons,* one of which *seasons* is this, the *season* of his birth, by which all were recapitulate in *heaven* and *earth;* which is the *season* of the *text,* and so this a *text* of the *season.*

Francis Gentleman's preface to Bell's edition which omitted coarse passages from the plays came 20 years later, but Zachary Grey in Cambridge and Ampthill was troubled by the same problem. There had been no need for Warburton to apologize he felt, for spending time on Shakespeare; no discredit 'can arise even to a *clergyman,* for writing notes upon *Shakespeare . . .* provided he makes no comment upon the *obscene passages,* or explains innocent ones in an obscene manner'. Perhaps that final notion provided a thought for Steevens, who wrote just such explanations above the names, true or false, of two clergymen.

*   *   *

John Monck Mason was author of a Preface which later editors included, and of notes intended for a Shakespeare edition in which he was forestalled by the Johnson–Steevens publication of 1773. His *Comments on the Last Edition of Shakespeare's Plays,* issued in 1785, referred to those volumes, not (as was assumed) to Reed's edition of 1785.

Mason, who lived from 1726 to 1809, held public office in Ireland; his attractive book was published in Dublin. Steevens, though criti-

---

[20] But Hanmer's changes had been exposed in the anonymous edition of 1745

cized and opposed in the notes, had some respect for Mason. 'He is often ingenious and sometimes right,' he wrote to Bishop Percy; 'but occasionally outdoes even Dr. Warburton in absurdity of conjecture.' Steevens followed with an observation which came ill from him: 'There is also somewhat of ferocity in his manner which had better been avoided'.

Mason came to Shakespeare with a poor reputation as editor of Massinger, for which in this Preface he blamed the printer. Though he had not attempted the dull duty of an editor in collating quartos and folios, merely finding fault with the recent editions, it was frustrating to see his plans for publication 'anticipated, by the labours and eccentric reading of Steevens, the ingenious researches of Malone, and the sagacity of Tyrwhitt. – I will fairly confess that I was somewhat mortified at this discovery, which compelled me to relinquish a favourite pursuit, from whence I had vainly expected to derive some degree of credit in the literary world'.

He found fault with text rather than comment in the recent edition, but criticized both; it seemed to him that Steevens had shown false taste in choosing one reading when his notes showed the superiority of another – 'admitting alterations, in some passages, on very insufficient authority, indeed, whilst in others he has retained the antient readings, though evidently corrupt, in preference to amendments as evidently just'.

This was ground for the dilettante, then and since, endlessly absorbing for more years than man is given. Consider Lady Macbeth's lines at the end of Act One, Scene IV, which Mason quoted:[21]

> Come to my woman's breasts,
> And take my milk for gall, you murdering ministers.

Johnson understood this to mean 'take away my milk, and put gall into the place', and his note reappeared without comment all the way through to 1821. Mason, correctly as anyone would now agree but without regard in his own day, called this

> a poor explanation! That debases a very noble image: Her meaning is this, 'come to my breasts, you murdering ministers, and suck my milk,' which will have the effect of gall to stimulate, and fit for your bloody purposes.

What was Johnson imagining, one wonders now? Some sort of clinical pump to suck out her milk and then replace it?

In another part of the same play Mason printed the phrase 'But no more fights' (When Macbeth had had his fill of witches' forecast), and comments:

---

[21] p.141

I suppose this to be an error of the press, and that we ought to read, 'But no more *sights*', alluding to the sights exhibited by the Witches to Macbeth.

In fact it was an error of Mason, in misreading the old s as f, for nobody printed 'fights' in that edition or others. How wise of Bell to change the printing custom!

Mason's other claim, a curious one, was to have studied every line in Shakespeare whereas Steevens attended only to passages which had been debated by earlier editors. Quite untrue of course, of Steevens or the others. Theobald never let a phrase pass without question, as is clear in many obsessional letters to Warburton.

Apart from his Shakespeare notes Mason might be remembered from the Preface for a sentence about literary critics who demolished his edition of Massinger, 'these learned professors of the art of teaching grown gentlemen to think'.

*   *   *

Thomas Bowdler, remembered for providing the English language with a word which now seems less respectable than those many he deleted from Shakespeare, belonged to a cultivated Shropshire family from the neighbourhood of Hope Bowdler. Seven of them, brothers and uncles and aunts and sons, find their way as authors into the *Dictionary of National Biography.* After a medical training at St. Andrews and varied travel in Europe he became Fellow of the Royal Society, and a member of Elizabeth Montagu's talented circle in London. When Howard the social reformer died in 1790, Bowdler tried to continue his good work by visiting prisons. After the success of his *Family Shakspeare* he completed a comparable edition of Gibbon, published posthumously and greeted with less enthusiasm as family reading.

The notion may now seem foolish, but 18th-century parents and audiences did not find it so. Bowdler died 12 years before Victoria's reign began; the first specimens of his *Family Shakspeare* had appeared in 1807, it rose to high popularity in the Regency period.

Bad puns and witless obscenity in Shakespeare disturbed all the 18th-century editors, and though Stratford producers celebrate them now, rating modern audiences at the Elizabethan level, 18th-century theatres cut them out. This point was made several times by Bowdler and we know it from the first Bell edition, printed from playhouse texts and similarly explained by Bell's editor.

> Those persons whose acquaintance with Shakspeare depends on theatrical representations [Bowdler wrote in his preface to the first edition] in which great alterations are made in the plays, can have little idea of the

frequent recurrence in the original text, of expressions, which, however they might be tolerated in the sixteenth century, are by no means admissible in the nineteenth.

He was writing in 1807, not for Victorian owners of draped piano-legs. For the fourth edition he wrote it again, to those who objected against challenge to detail in their sacred text:

> They have not learned, or they have forgot, that except in one, or at most in two instances, the plays of our author are never presented to the public without being corrected, and more or less cleared of indecency; yet, *Macbeth* and *Othello, Lear, Hamlet,* and *As You Like It,* continued still to exhibit the superior genius of the first of dramatic poets.

Bowdler felt that those who objected to his tinkering could go back to the original; the man who changed a painter's work, he suggested, would be guilty, his own excisions caused no damage. Its origin went back a generation to his father's family readings in Shropshire.

> In the perfection of reading few men were equal to my father; and such was his good taste, his delicacy, and his prompt discretion, that his family listened with delight to Lear, Hamlet, and Othello, without knowing that those matchless tragedies contained words and expressions improper to be pronounced.

It is irrelevant to dismiss the endeavour by asking what a parson's family made of the Bible, because he was changing words and expressions, not events; so Hamlet's open talk of incest stayed, but not the rank sweat of an enseamed bed.

Without dictating to the world or asking that passages which embarrassed a family be deleted from ordinary editions, Bowdler struck a chord as the success of his work demonstrated. Blasphemy worried him, not only indecency, but he found the latter more common in Shakespeare. God as an expletive he changed to Heaven – but not in prayer, so we have

> O God! O God!
> How weary, stale, flat, and unprofitable
> Seem to me all the uses of this world!

The Steevens text was followed, he claimed to have made no change except where the deletion needed a substitution. Poor Doll Tear-sheet disappeared entirely from *Henry the Fourth*; Elizabeth Montagu had described all her scenes as indecent 'and therefore not only indefensible, but inexcusable': how then could Bowdler, dedicating his book to her, be expected to retain them? *Measure for Measure* presented a special problem, for in it 'the indecent expressions with which many of the Scenes abound are so interwoven with the story, that it is extremely difficult to separate the one from the other'.

Othello was disturbing too, its message moral but the manner questionable; if after all the omissions 'it shall still be thought that this inimitable tragedy is not sufficiently correct for family reading, I would advise the transferring of it from the parlour to the cabinet, where the perusal will not only delight the poetic taste, but convey useful and important instruction both to the heart and the understanding of the reader'.

Bowdler was editing for children, remembering his childhood, the plays were acceptable in his edition; general censorship was not his idea, for all might yet be enjoyed in the cabinet.

*   *   *

Thomas Edwards never planned an edition of Shakespeare, but wrote such entertaining prefaces and notes that he has a place here. His reputation rests upon a quarrel with Warburton, which began in the library of Ralph Allen's house near Bath. An account of that episode, inaccurate in other ways, has the circumstantial look of truth:

> Mr. Warburton generally took the opportunity of showing his superiority in Greek, not having the least idea that an officer in the army understood anything of that language, or that Mr. Edwards had been bred at Eton;[22] till one day, being accidentally in the library, Mr. Edwards took down a Greek author, and explained a passage in it in a manner that Mr. Warburton did not approve. This occasioned no small contest; and Mr. Edwards (who had now discovered to Mr. Warburton how he came by his knowledge) endeavoured to convince him that he did not understand the original language, but that his knowledge rose from French translations. Mr. Warburton was highly irritated . . .

Not surprising that he was, thus exposed in the family home of his young wife. Edwards annoyed him as Theobald had upset Pope; a less than brilliant note to that effect was added by Warburton to the *Dunciad.*

Edwards used wit, not literal criticism, to devastating effect. He viewed Warburton's 1747 edition as an imposture, and proved it to be so. Warton called the case he made 'unrefuted and unanswerable'. Edwards was in legal practice.

His attack opened in 1747, very soon after Warburton's Shakespeare appeared, and was issued a year later as *The Canons of Criticism*, an amusing title because Warburton in the Preface wrote that he 'once designed to have given the reader a body of Canons for Literal Criticism, drawn out in form: – but these uses may be well

---

[22] Edwards was at Eton, but never in the army

supplied by what is occasionally said upon the subject in the course of the following remarks'. Edwards called his book, which was got up to look like Warburton's, 'a Supplement to Mr. Warburton's Edition of Shakespear. Collected from the Notes in that celebrated Work, And proper to be bound up with it'. His satirical Canons – 25 of them – distilled from the Shakespeare notes, must have disturbed Warburton more than their dispute in the library at Prior Park about competence in Greek.

Each canon was followed by a destructive array of quotations in support; Canon II, 'He has a right to alter any passage, which he does not understand', stood upon 37 examples, among which the following from *Hamlet* can serve as illustration of the Edwards style and method:

> 'And flights of angels *sing* thee to thy rest.

> 'What language is this, of *flights singing?* We should certainly read,

> 'And flights of angels *wing* thee to *thy rest.* i.e. carry thee to heaven.'
> WARB

> *What language is this?* why English certainly, if he understood it. A *flight* is a flock, and is a very common expression; as a *flight* of woodcocks, &c. If it had not been beneath a *profess'd critic*, to consult a Dictionary; he might have found it rendered, *Grex avium*, in Littleton; *Une volée*, in Boyer; and why a *flight* of angels may not *sing*, as well as a *flight* of larks, rests upon Mr. Warburton to shew.

Johnson, who did not bother to comment on that particular folly, chose metaphor for his view of Edwards and Warburton: 'a fly may sting and tease a horse; but yet the horse is the nobler animal'. In his own edition he took some pleasure in teasing the noble animal.

The Canons offered a stunning indictment of emendation – the sixth for instance:

> As every Author is to be corrected into all possible perfection, and of that perfection the professed Critic is the sole judge; He may alter any word or phrase, which does not want amendment, or which *will do*; provided He can think of anything, which he imagines *will do better*.

Satire need not be consistent in aim, and Edwards was not, for he respected the work of Pope who did not in the first instance attempt, as Warburton (however wildly), to discover what Shakespeare wrote. Edwards managed thorough demolition, following the canons with a Glossary of absurd definitions culled from Warburton's notes. Luckily he had, as the publisher phrased it in his Advertisement (1758) 'a liberal Education, and an independent Fortune'. From that height he could afford to pour down the boiling oil of perfect Augustan prose, and here is the conclusion of his Sonnet, opposite the opening of the Canons:

Much hast thou written – more than will be read;
   Then cease from *Shakespear* thy unhallow'd rage;
Nor by a fond o'erweening pride mis-led,
Hope fame by injuring the sacred Dead:
   Know, who would comment well his godlike page,
Critic, must have a Heart as well as Head.

We can leave Edwards with an echoing phrase at the end of his comment, in the Introduction, on Warburton's proposal to read, instead of 'th'*ear-piercing* fife', 'th' fear-spersing fife' –

which is such a word, as no poet, nor indeed any man who had half an ear, would have thought of; for which he gives this reason, which none but a Professed Critic could have thought of; that piercing the ear is not *an effect on the hearers*.

4 Styles in Editing

Theobald on Shakespeare descends to us through his editions (1733 and 1740), and *Shakespeare Restored* (1726) and the very long series of letters to Warburton which fill most of the second volume of Nichols's *Illustrations of the Literary History of the Eighteenth Century* (1817). There were other letters, both private and public, but most of him survives in those three sources.

His prevailing mood, in contrast to Pope, was of delight in the subject he had discovered, 'the *first Essay* of *Literal Criticism* upon any Author in the Engligh Tongue', as he claimed in the final pages of *Shakespeare Restored*. Theobald loved the work, an example of pleasure in labour if ever there was, sharing his explorations with Warburton through the five years before and just after his edition appeared. Time and again a conflict between civilized sharing and the resolve to publish took Warburton by surprise, but nothing of that entered the correspondence with Theobald. Though with few exceptions only one half survives, ease and intimacy prevailed.

> I entirely come into your thoughts, that this epistolary intercourse should be kept up with all the negligence of conversation (Theobald to Warburton, 29 May 1729)
>
> You bring back to my mind the time of a love-correspondence; and the expectation of every fresh Letter from you is the joy of a mistress to me (Theobald to Warburton, 6 November 1729)
>
> I am drawing so near the end of my task, that, like a boy with a dear sweet morsel, I am afraid of eating it quite up; and am for extending my pleasure in spite of gluttony (Theobald to Warburton, 10 March 1729–30).

There was never any doubt that so much teasing of the text for sense and accuracy beat a path towards Theobald's edition, in which Warburton provided willing help; only later it struck him that too much

146

had been given away, that his own version after so many years of questing thought could replace it. Nichol Smith, with limited respect for Theobald, accepted that Warburton gave 'ungrudging assistance and was plainly interested in the success of the edition'.

Theobald was not his pupil, they wrote as equals; Warburton is told that a change he had suggested in *Antony and Cleopatra* 'is very fine: but, I much fear, it is bettering Shakespeare'.[1] In many points of detail they courteously differed, as in the first half of a long letter of 29 May 1729. In 1731 Theobald replies with patience to Warburton's contorted interpretation of a phrase in *Love's Labour's Lost*, and 'cannot think the lines are in any degree obscure'. It occurs in Biron's wonderful speech about the love learned from women's eyes, the long passage beginning

> Have at you then, affection's men at arms,

when all courtly academic vows of chastity with which the play opened are exploded sky-high. Pope had punctuated that opening line with a full stop after 'affections'. The lines which made Warburton pause appeared thus in the folio:

> For when would you (my Leege) or you, or you?
> in leaden contemplation have found out
> Such fiery Numbers as the prompting eyes,
> Of beauties tutors have inrich'd you with:

No crux for an editor there perhaps, punctuation a touch casual but Rowe set that right and Pope reduced the capitals to convention. Theobald saw no need for a note either, but this is what he wrote to Warburton in 1731:

> You call these obscure lines, and imagine they contain an allusion I cannot possibly discover in them. On the strength of this supposition, you have given me a very ingenious note; which I wish could properly find a place, for the reason on which you desire it. But, indeed, I cannot think the lines are in any degree obscure; and I can but wonder as yet how my dear friend is become so metaphysical to fancy *fiery numbers* have any relation to the *stars*. I am either more dull than usual; or I am persuaded, upon looking back to the passage, you will expound it thus with me . . .

And he proposed the straightforward paraphrase of a few lines, taking fiery numbers to be 'verses of fire and spirit'.

Warburton was not put down or his fire put out so easily; 16 years later his own edition has the note:

> Alluding to the discoveries in modern astronomy; at that time greatly

---

[1] Feb. 19, 1729–30

improving, in which the ladies eyes are compared, as usual to *stars*. He calls them *numbers*, alluding to the *Pythagorean* principles of astronomy, which were founded on the laws of harmony. The *Oxford editor*, who was at a loss for the conceit, changes *numbers* to *notions*, and so loses both the sense and the gallantry of the allusion. He has better luck in the following line, and has rightly changed *beauty's* to *beauteous*.

This richly absurd note, typical of Warburton's tendency to mislead where no ambiguity or obscurity existed, managed also to reject one unneeded emendation made by Hanmer and to accept another. No doubt the two of them had been through it all, at Mildenhall. Johnson set things in order again ('*Numbers* are in this passage nothing more than *poetical measures*'), adding a characteristic comment: 'The Astronomer, by looking too much aloft, falls into a ditch'. Malone restored Hanmer's wretched 'beauteous', preserved also by Chalmers and Singer, removed by Knight.

It is easy to wander along the byways of Warburton's eccentricity; one other instance appears properly here, as its source was in a letter to Theobald (14 October, 1734), quoting four unproblematic lines from *Midsummer Night's Dream:*

> The spring, the summer,
> The chiding autumn, angry winter, change
> Their wonted liveries; and th' amazed world,
> By their increase, now knows not which is which.

They worried Warburton. '*By their increase?*' he asks, 'whose increase! or what increase? there is nothing preceding to which *increase* can be referred so as to make sense.' So he proceeded, correcting and altering:

> We must read,
>   By their INCHASE, now knows not which is which.
> It comes from the French, *enchassure*, a term in use amongst the jewellers to signify the setting a stone in gold or silver; to this the word *inchase* metaphorically alludes . . . And the Poets in their *Prosopopoeiae* represent Spring as adorned with emeralds, the Summer with the pyropus, the Autumn with the topaz, and Winter with diamonds.

Theobald, in his next edition (1740), took no notice of this. One never knows what went on between Hanmer and Warburton, but Hanmer in 1744 changed 'increase' to 'inverse' without any explanation. The anonymous edition a year later, using Hanmer's text but making good that deficiency ('the Editor of that not having thought proper to point out the Alterations he has made from the former Copies') has 'inverse' but gives the original reading below. Warburton in 1747 stood by his 'inchase' for '*Enchassure*, a term in use amongst Goldsmiths for the setting a stone in Gold'. Johnson had the briefest of footnotes: '*By their increase*. That is, *By their produce*'.

Shakespeare often made his own words, but when Warburton rejects them his substitutions commonly look unapt and inept. Nobody else was troubled by that short passage. The two of them must have paused to discuss it, in polite disagreement, at Mildenhall.

Theobald is always a good starting place for viewing the editors, because he founded the industry. Working from Pope, who had corrupted the incorrect rather than studied for accuracy, the field was open for emendations speculative, conjectural, wrong or right, accepted and rejected. Warburton's position between Theobald and scholarship and the *Dunciad* became equivocal; there was no doubt where his future lay, yet the correspondence pleased them both. Nothing in Shakespeare, familiar or remote, as they went through it, was exempt from challenge.

The best-known emendation when Theobald's name crops up, 'a' babbled o' green fields' was not truly his own (Theobald substituted babbled for 'talked' at the suggestion of a friend), and seems less acceptable now than to sentimental taste a century ago. Falstaff babbling of green fields as he died might have suited a Victorian painter, without sounding apt or accurate. Changing a letter, supposing a mistake in transcription, could lead alike to nonsense, brilliance or the truth. It keeps its place.

More surprising, because so familiar, is a change in Macbeth's line

> But here, upon this bank and shoal of time.

Johnson's note tells all: 'This is Theobald's emendation, undoubtedly right. The old edition has *school*, and Dr. Warburton *shelve*'. Warburton's proposal was not absurd, could even have been right, but Theobald had supported his phrase with a parallel from *Henry the Eighth*,

> And sounded all the depths and shoals of honour.

in a letter to Warburton dated 23 December 1729, and expressed himself well:

> *Bank* and *school*! What a monstrous *couplement*, as Don Armado says, is here of heterogeneous ideas! I venture to read,
> — on this bank and SHOAL of time.
> i.e. this shallow, this narrow ford of human life, opposed to the great abyss of eternity.

This was an inspired guess, gaining general acceptance, with the mandate of one parallel use. Speculative ingenuity based on the habits of scribes could produce results far less convincing.

When Theobald found a manifest blunder in Pope's edition he swooped like a hawk – for instance, in a couple of lines from *Henry the Eighth* which he punctuates thus for emphasis –

> – I'le *startle* you
> Worse than the SCARING bell. –

and continues

> Now is it not wonderful that Mr. Pope (who is a Roman Catholic, if any thing, in Religion) should know so little of the SACRING bell, as to substitute this tautological silly epithet instead of it, in opposition to the best copies?

He himself could be at times unimaginative, literal-minded and unwise. When every phrase was subject to question, imagination quickly suffered both death and birth among editors. The meaning of Antony's response to Cleopatra's death is so powerfully abbreviated, expresses such sudden descent to despair, as almost to defy analysis:

> Now all labour
> Marrs what it does, yea, very force entangles
> It self with strength; seal then, and all is done.

Thus Theobald's text (1733). In his letter to Warburton, 21 February 1729–30, he had noted in exasperation '*Seal* what? I do not see that this allegory agrees at all with *marr, force, entangle, strength*'. None of the editors was troubled by the extreme concentration of 'very force entangles / It self with strength', a phrase of mood rather than meaning, but several offered their different understandings of seal or seel. That now seems to give no difficulty, just a comprehensive finality from the sense of seal: pack it in, close it; life and the document – or letter, or parcel – are done. The word looks sudden as Antony's despair, all passion spent, struggle ended. The sealing will be his own life's ending. Theobald arrived there, in his edition, by a roundabout route. His note reads:

> *Antony* had offended *Cleopatra* with his Suspicions; he is here about doing something to deserve her Pardon: and he thinks, stabbing himself will *seal* That Pardon.

Warburton's note seems to have got it right:

> Metaphor taken from civil contracts, where, when all is agreed on, the sealing compleats the contract; so he hath determined to die, and nothing remained but to give the stroke.

Johnson, always credited with massive common sense, felt moved by habit to oppose Warburton with a quite unnecessary suggestion which marrs what Shakespeare had done:

> I believe the reading is:
> –seel then, and all is done. –
> To seel *hawks*, is to close their eyes, The meaning will be:
> Close thine eyes *forever, and be quiet.*

Hanmer had changed seal to 'sleep'. In 1773 Steevens brought back seal; Malone, keeping the old reading, pointlessly produced an earlier example from this play in support of Johnson. A condensed, difficult passage flew past them all, for the minor conflict which needed no attention.

Literal-mindedness was an attribute of the editor, thinking aloud as he combed through – as for instance in Act V of *The Tempest:* 'The entrance of the Cell opens, and discovers Ferdinand and Miranda playing at chess'. Theobald had a passing thought:[2] 'May it not reasonably be asked, where they got their chess-board?' Steevens was the only other to pause there, with useless evidence of his wide reading: 'Shakespeare might not have ventured to engage his hero and heroine at this game, had he not found *Huon de Bordeaux* and his Princess employed in the same manner . . .'.

Such examples are not hard to find; the field is rich, choice alone difficult. On 27 May 1729, Theobald fastened upon a word in *Hamlet* which had not troubled him before; the Ghost reveals that he was murdered and Hamlet pleads:

> Haste me to know it; that I, with wings as swift
> As meditation, or the thoughts of Love,
> May sweep to my revenge.

As the start of the story it needs to be understood, though there seems no obscurity. Theobald discovered one:

> Here is either, I suspect, a most barbarous tautology, or a great mistake in terms. *Thought,* indeed, is swift; but *Meditation* is not so. That is, I take it, a deliberate action of the soul, by which we weigh and ponder our first simple ideas, and so form a judgement upon them. I imagine our Author wrote,
>   As *Mediation,* or the *Thoughts* of Love.
> So a tautology will be quite removed; and a beauty, in my poor opinion, added to the thought.

Though there is no such note or change in any edition, the letter perhaps caused Warburton to ponder the phrase and admire it, Johnson thought, to excess.

> This similitude is extremely beautiful [Warburton's note records]. The word *meditation* is consecrated, by the *mysticks,* to signify that stretch and flight of mind which aspires to the enjoyment of the supreme good. So that Hamlet, considering with what to compare the swiftness of his revenge, chooses two of the most rapid things in nature, the ardency of divine and human passion, in an *enthusiast* and a *lover.*

It was a ponderous note, stretching Hamlet's urgency ('Haste me to

---

[2] To Warburton, May 29, 1729

know it') into thoughtful considerations. Johnson, receptive to a religious reading, damped down the fire a little:

> The comment on the word *meditation* is so ingenious, that I hope it is just.

Theobald's emendations could be visual, oral, or inspired by a simple instinct towards improvement. Highly questionable proposals were sometimes introduced by such a phrase as 'I make no doubt . . .'. In *Troilus*, Act V Scene 4, Thersites rails against 'The policy of those crafty swearing rascals, – that stale old mouse-eaten dry cheese, Nestor; and that same dog-fox, Ulysses, –', and Theobald asked[3] 'why *swearing*? What did Nestor and Ulysses *swear*? I make no doubt it should be, SNEERING rascals . . .', – and Mason later agreed with the sense of that comment but Johnson threw out the emendation which appeared in Theobald's text and was accepted by Warburton.

An earlier conjecture similarly introduced has been generally received, though it still looks questionable. Concanen had paused over Prospero's lines to Ferdinand in *The Tempest*:

> If I have too austerely punish'd you,
> Your compensation makes amends; for I
> Have given here a Third of my own Life,
> Or that for which I live.

Why a *third*, they both wonder? Why not half, Miranda's mother being dead? It seems now a futile point, for Prospero could still think of his daughter as one third, and her mother a third whether quick or dead, but Theobald concluded 'he has given him, in his daughter, his very life and heart-strings . . . I have no doubt therefore but the Poet wrote,

> – for I
> Have giv'n you here a *Thread* of my own Life,
> Or that for which I live.'

And his thread was woven into the fabric, from 1733 to the new Oxford edition. That was not strictly a scribal or oral error, but one word which Theobald decided to change under the protection of a frail hypothesis:

> The change will be still more minute, if we allow for the old way of spelling this word *Thrid* from its Saxon derivation; and the error has arisen plainly from a bare transposition of the letters.

If at other times his speculation had stronger support from literary

---

[3] to Warburton, 6 March 1729–30

parallel or scribal theory, it is likely that instinct showed the way and structure confirmed it. He wrote to Warburton[4] about the end of Bottom's soliloquy after waking from his paradisal donkey dream, Act IV Scene 1,

> And I will sing it in the latter end of a play before the Duke: peradventure, to make it the more gracious, I shall sing it at her death.

– which the new Oxford editors accept, but Theobald rejected:

> At her death! – At whose? In all Bottom's speech there is not the least mention of any she-creature, to whom this relative can be coupled. I make not the least scruple but Bottom, for the sake of a jest, and to render his *voluntary*, as we may call it, the more gracious and extra-ordinary, said,
> – I shall sing it *after* death.
> He, you know, as Pyramus, is killed upon the scene; and so might promise to rise again at the conclusion of the interlude, and give the Duke his Dream by way of song. If this conjecture be right, the source of the corruption is very obvious. The *f* in *after* being sunk by the vulgar pronunciation, the copyist might write it from the sound – *a'ter;* which the wise Editors not understanding, concluded two words were falsely got together, so splitting them, and clapping in an *h* produced the present reading – *at her.*

With this form of scholarship, seductive then and later, old pronunciation and dim-witted editors and 'clapping in an *h*' all pulled in to shore up the delicate structure, Theobald was less at ease than when he questioned for better or worse a difficult meaning. This emendation – 'after death' for 'at her death' – appealed to several of the editors. Theobald of course included it, with a note copied almost verbatim from his letter quoted here. Warburton, Johnson and Capell all accepted it. In 1773 Steevens brought back the old reading with a note: 'He means *the death of Thisbe*, which is what his head is at present full of' – and that should have been that, but Theobald's guess lingered in the memory of Steevens who changed the phrasing of his note for the 1803 variorum:

> He may mean *the death of Thisbe*, which his head might be at present full of; and yet I cannot but prefer the happy conjecture of Mr. Theobald to my own attempt at explanation.

He searched for a tempting change if the sense seemed to need it.

> O Harry, thou hast robbed me of my youth

Hotspur says, dying after his fight with the Prince. Theobald could not think why Hotspur's brain turned to the loss of youth, rather than of title and fame. 'I have a strong suspicion that our Poet wrote:

---

[4] 27 May 1729

O Harry, thou has robbed me of my WORTH.

i.e. thou has cut off the fame of all my budding honours, by this conquest of thine'. This was in the easy exchange of letter-writing[5] and he let it pass without comment as editor; but Warburton remembered, and provided his different gloss in 1747: 'I fancy *Shakespear* wrote *growth*, i.e., honours in the bud'. Nobody accepted that, or troubled to refute him.

Though they all recognized that Shakespeare used words unconventionally, his habit troubled them. In the opening scene of *Richard the Second*, Mowbray challenges Bolingbroke and would meet him

> were I ty'd to run a-foot
> Even to the frozen ridges of the *Alps*,
> Or any other ground inhabitable.

As they faced each other that very moment there was no need for such a marathon, but the notion of frozen ridges as *inhabitable* worried Theobald. 'I doubt not but we should read UNHABITABLE. For *habitable*, you know, is an English word as well as *inhabitable*'[6] – and sure enough, below the text is one of his longish learned notes. This time Warburton paid no attention, and Johnson provided a definition: '*Inhabitable*. That is, *not habitable, uninhabitable.*'

The analysis of each expression inevitably produced a large number of wrong readings. It has become very improper to choose one reading rather than another on grounds of taste, as seeming more Shakespearean, but often the rational solution took force from the sound of a phrase. Falstaff asked the Prince not to let him and his friends be known as bad characters 'when thou art King', stuffing his speech with circumlocution: 'gentlemen of the shade' they were, 'minions of the moon: And let men say, we be men of good government; being governed as the sea is, by our noble and chaste mistress the moon, under whose countenance we – steal'. It is the introduction to Falstaff's character, and his style, and so of some importance that he be understood. 'Marry then,' he has said, 'sweet wag, when thou art King, let not us, that are squires of the night's body, be called thieves of the day's beauty.'

'I do not know how they can be said Thieves of the *Day's Beauty,*' wrote Theobald to Warburton.[7] 'Should it not rather be, BOOTY?' Into his edition it went, not a terrible blunder but simply wrong. The old phrase 'conveys no manner of Idea to me' his note says. 'They robb'd by Moon-shine; they could not steal the fair Day-light.' Be that

---

[5] to Warburton, 23 December 1729
[6] 10 January, 1729–30
[7] 13 January, 1729–30

as it might, Warburton stole 'booty' without a note of emendation or origin – it had also been taken by Hanmer, and only accredited in the anonymous edition of 1745. Johnson used booty, with Theobald's note on which he made no comment. Capell put beauty in its place again, and Steevens in 1773 added an excellent note which established it for ever, concluding: 'To take away the beauty of the day may probably mean to disgrace it'. Malone's final contribution was to suggest 'a pun on the word *beauty*, which in the western counties is pronounced nearly in the same manner as *booty*'.

Consistency may be the hobgoblin of little minds but one episode in Theobald's history injured his record as scrupulous editor of Shakespeare. In 1727 a play was acted at Drury Lane, and published a year later, called *Double Falshood; or, The Distrest Lovers*.[8] Its title page bore the legend 'Written Originally by W. Shakespeare; And now Revis'd and Adapted to the Stage by Mr. Theobald, the Author of *Shakespeare Restor'd*'. In 1727 it had been produced with some success, and there was a benefit performance (Pope refused to contribute) the year after publication. Theobald, at a time of critical intimacy with every phrase of the plays, claimed that this boring and lifeless piece was the work of Shakespeare's late maturity, writing to Dodington in the conventional style of a Dedication:

> I bear so dear an Affection to the Writings and Memory of SHAKE-SPEARE, that, as it is my good Fortune to retrieve this Remnant of his Pen from Obscurity, so it is my greatest Ambition that this Piece should be received into the Protection of such a Patron: And I hope, Future Times, when they mean to pay *Shakespeare* the best Compliment, will remember to say, Mr. DODINGTON was that Friend to his *Remains*, which his own SOUTHAMPTON was to his *living Merit*.

Future Times wondered how such a fastidious scholar as Theobald ever dared in his height of concentration pass off this semi-rubbish as Shakespeare's. Some saw a double pun in the title, the Preface may be read as a study in duplicity; and in the middle of such examination as was shown in *Shakespeare Restored*, how could Theobald ask the world to accept this text without a word of editorial discussion?

One would like to give him the benefit of several doubts, in which the first is nothing more extraordinary than a human bibliophile truth, that possession may breed enough enthusiasm to bend judgement. Theobald was an enthusiast and owned three manuscript copies of this feeble play. Here is the collector at work:[9]

There is a Tradition (which I have from the Noble Person, who supply'd

---

[8] See also p. 82 in Chapter 3
[9] These two passages are from the printed Preface, 1728

me with One of my Copies) that it was given by our Author, as a Present of Value, to a Natural Daughter of his, for whose Sake he wrote it, in the Time of his Retirement from the Stage. Two other Copies I have (one of which I was glad to purchase at a very good Rate,) which may not, perhaps, be quite so Old as the Former; but One of Them is much more perfect, and has fewer Flaws and Interruptions in the Sense.

He could also boast that delightful quality, provenance, for

one of the Manuscript Copies, which I have, is of above Sixty Years Standing, in the Handwriting of Mr. *Downes*, the famous Old Prompter; and, as I am credibly inform'd, was early in the Possession of the celebrated Mr. *Betterton*, and by Him design'd to have been usher'd into the World.

He was the perfect victim of credible information and of the Noble Person who provided a manuscript. As to the play, its revision and adaptation and absence of explanation, this was a text for theatre performance in which different standards prevailed. If Shakespeare at this period was commonly cut and changed for the stage, nothing eccentric marked the presentation of this. His editor, who had worked for the theatre before turning critic, was two people in one.

Theobald was the pioneer of detailed discourse over Shakespeare; an occasional winding journey from him through one small textual question gives the taste of different editorial styles. In his letter to Warburton of 27 November 1729, he questioned the correctness of an unimportant line in *Comedy of Errors*, towards the end of the Second Act,

We talk with goblins, owls, and elvish sprights.

'They might fancy they talked with goblins,' Theobald wrote, 'but why with *owls*, in the name of Nonsense? I make no doubt but we must read, with goblins, *ouphes*, and elvish sprights.' And he quoted two appearances of that word in *The Merry Wives*. It was odd to take exception to the owls, when that line had a more questionable history. There was no prior quarto for *Comedy of Errors*, which was first printed in 1623 where the line reads

We talke with Goblins, Owles and Sprights.

Rowe, probably taking from the Fourth Folio a reading which descended from the Second, printed

We talk with Goblins, Owles and Elves Sprights

– completing the line of course, and meaning, it would seem, the spirits or sprights of elves. But neither owls nor elves established themselves without a fight; nothing in the new game of Shakespeare criticism was simple.

Elves (to take the second problem first) were changed by Pope – who relegated that speech by Dromio of Syracuse to small print below the text, as un-Shakespearean – to elvish, making the sprights elvish rather than the elves sprightly. Steevens in 1778 mentioned that the 'epithet *elvish* is not in the *first* folio, but is found in the *second*'. This slight error he changed and corrected in 1793, his new note reading: 'The epithet *elvish* is not in the first folio, but the second has – *elves*, which certainly was meant for *elvish*'.

Any appeal to the Second Folio was a red rag to Malone who took the occasion to point out that 'All the emendations made in the second folio having been merely arbitrary, any other epithet of two syllables may have been the poet's word, Mr. Rowe first introduced – elv*ish*' [sic]. But he was wrong, for Rowe had introduced elves. The 1803 variorum brought a last plea from Steevens, quoting an *elvish* from *Richard the Third* and adding: 'Why should a book, which has often judiciously filled such vacuities, and rectified such errors, as disgrace the folio 1623, be so perpetually distrusted?'.

Meanwhile the owls were turned by Theobald into ouphes. Dromio had continued with two pleasant lines:

> If we obey them not, this will ensue,
> They'll suck our breath, and pinch us black and blue.

The note in 1733 repeated his question from four years earlier, adding: 'Or could *Owls* suck their Breath, and pinch them black and blue? I dare say, my Readers will acquiesce in the justness of my Emendation here'. They did not, only Capell choosing ouphes.

Warburton predictably wrote a long note, opening for once with a poisoned arrow:

> Here Mr. *Theobald* calls out *in the name of Nonsense*, the first time he had *formally* invoked her, to tell him how *Owls could suck their breath, and pinch them black and blue.*

and continuing in more characteristic style:

> He did not know it to be an old popular superstition, that the scretch-owl sucked out the breath and blood of infants in the cradle. On this account, the *Italians* called Witches, who were supposed to be in like manner mischevously bent against children, *Strega* from *Strix*, the *Scretch-owl.*

And he went on to quote nine lines from Ovid.

Johnson had nothing to add to the last statement. Warburton's paragraph appeared in all future variorum editions, but Tollet was quoted also as finding that *'Ghastly owls* accompany *elvish ghosts*, in Spenser's *Shepherd's Calendar for June'*. Steevens found another reference in *Cornucopiae or Pasquil's Night-cap, or Antidote for the Headach*, 1623. Malone achieved the commonsense last word:

How, it is objected, should Shakspeare know that *striges* or screech-owls were considered by the Romans as witches? The notes of Mr. Tollet and Mr. Steevens, as well as the following passage in *The London Prodigal,* a comedy, 1605, afford the best answer to this question: 'Soul, I think, I am sure cross'd or *witch'd* with an *owl'*.

Yet they were unjust to Warburton, who had found authority and validity to turn out the ouphe for the owl.

As the examination of minutiae pioneered by Theobald grew ever more neurotic, one other instance from a thousand may be followed without abuse of space. At the start of Act IV in *Julius Caesar,* Antony and Octavius have a brief exchange which threatens to become explosive; Antony, in fractious mood, describes his general Lepidus as a useless aesthete:

> A barren-spirited fellow; one that feeds
> On objects, arts, and imitations;
> Which, out of use, and stal'd by other men,
> Begin his fashion.

Bitter, concise, these lines are not now difficult to understand; modern manners and vocabulary have alike grown to meet them. In the neighbourhood of Bond Street just such people may be seen, any day of the year; they define the collector. Shakespeare despised affectation, and saw through fashion. In a soldier it would have seemed especially contemptible.

In this instance, 18th-century usage found obscurity where none now exists. Theobald to Warburton, 14 February 1729:

> I do not conceive why he should be called a narrow-spirited fellow, that can feed either on *objects* or *arts; i.e.* as I presume, form his ideas and judgements upon them: *stale* and *obsolete imitation,* indeed, reasonably fixes such a character. I have long suspected the text; and with great deference and diffidence, I will submit to you my emendation:
>
> On ABJECT ORTS, and imitations.
>
> *i.e.* on the scraps and fragments of things rejected and despised by others.

Thus it appeared in the 1733 edition. He was certainly changing meaning, for 'orts' is explained there as 'not so much antiquated, tho' corrupted in the Pronunciation, but that Children are warn'd to this Day of leaving *Orts* on their plate'. They sound disgusting, one would not now blame the children, but Theobald's word has been devoured by time.

Johnson left 'abject Orts' on the plate, printing Theobald's note without comment; Warburton kept them, merely noting the change as Theobald's, and Capell chose them, giving the old reading below. Steevens brought back objects and arts in 1773, and extended his note in the next edition, but the terms carried a different sense at that time, for he paraphrased objects as 'speculative knowledge', and arts as 'mechanick operations'. He wondered also whether it might have a meaning similar to the present-day noun *rejects*: '*Objects*, however, may mean things *objected* or thrown out to him'. Far from the collector in Bond Street, but at least Steevens was wise to throw out the orts. Malone brought the sensible conclusion: 'Objects means, in Shakspeare's language, whatever is presented to the eye'.

The impossibility of discovering absolute Shakespeare is accepted by modern editors; Theobald and the rest of them used their best endeavours, hitting, missing, struggling. A favourite line may still be dredged from quarto or folio, drowned to death by Theobald more than two and a half centuries ago. In *Antony and Cleopatra*, here is part of her epitaph for him:

> for his Bounty,
> There was no winter in't. An Antony it was,
> That grew the more by reaping.

It was the second time that Cleopatra used this form of speech, Antony as a concept beyond description turned into a descriptive noun; earlier she had complained:

> Oh, my oblivion is a very Antony,
> And I am all forgotten.

One passage balances the other. Theobald found no problem in the syntax but 'there is no consonance of ideas betwixt a Winter and an Antony; nor, I am afraid, any common sense in an Antony growing by reaping'.[10] So it disappeared from the edited texts, and remains absent. But Theobald searched too often for common sense in poetry; Cleopatra's phrase meant more than that Antony's bounty was, as might easily be said, inexhaustible; it grew the more by reaping. Usage stretches to meet imagination.

Theobald could not manage that. 'I shrewdly suspect, our Author wrote:

> – For his Bounty,
> There was no Winter in't. An *Autumne* 'twas,
> That grew, &c.

I appeal to you with some diffidence in it; though certainly this restores an uniformity of metaphor, and conveys some meaning in an Autumn still growing by reaping.'

In fact it conveys none, for neither autumns nor corn (which did Theobald have in mind?) grow by reaping. But science follows:

---

[10] to Warburton, 8 April 1729

nor is the variation from the traces of the letters very great, especially if we consider the old way of spelling the two words Antonie and Automne.

All the equipment is there, giving in scholarly style a highly question-able answer which has deleted the old form. None of them demurred, or had much to add.

Theobald was too original and delightful (because he took delight) to be dismissed on such a note, nor was he always buried in minutiae; he had favourites among the plays and made general judgements. *Titus Andronicus* most obviously he dismissed, 'something so bar-barous and unnatural in the fable, and so much trash in the diction';[11] he held a low opinion of *Richard the Third*, 'a Play, that, unless Shakespeare's, would be as execrable to me as the character of its Hero';[12] and he was not alone at that time in turning a blind eye to the merits of *Love's Labour's Lost*:[13]

> The next in order, I do not know whether we may not pronounce the very worse in the whole set. And it is no less corrupt throughout in the text, than it is vicious in the composition. But the badness of the coin shall not affright me from bringing it to the touchstone.

Theobald remains the most attractive of early editors, the first to write long notes of doubt, interpretation, speculation, emendation, for which his preliminary thought survives in *Shakespeare Restored* and the letters to Warburton. Neither Rowe nor Pope was a note-writer, Theobald began the habit; his criticism, often intemperate, is the guide to what Pope had done. It would be beyond the range of this book to attempt general criticism of such silent editors as Rowe or Pope, but Theobald left his own record of precious detail.

In *Shakespeare Restored* he made a splendid claim: 'The Cause of SHAKESPEARE is here engaged, and the Restitution of him con-cern'd'.[14] On four fronts he set out to engage Pope:

> The exceptionable Conjectures of the *Editor*, I think, may be ranged under these Heads; as, where he has *substituted a fresh Reading*, and there was no Occasion to depart from the Poet's Text; where he has *maim'd* the Author by an unadvis'd *Degradation*; where he has made a *bad* Choice in a *Various Reading*, and degraded the better Word; and where he, by *mistaking* the *Gloss* of any Word, has given a wrong Turn to the Poet's Sense and Meaning.

It was a poorly organized Appendix, written at heat from notes, 60

---

[11] To Warburton, 24 February 1729–30
[12] To Warburton, 29 January 1729–30
[13] 6 December 1729
[14] Appendix, p. 133

quarto pages of multiple instance and overkill; spreading steadily from criticism of Pope's emendations to supplying a largish crop of his own.

*   *   *

As Warburton's edition was published after 20 years of such textual examination, privately or with Theobald first and later with Hanmer, the phrasing of his title page expressed understandable impatience.[15] By 'first Editors' he meant Heminge and Condell; 'the two Last' were Theobald, and Hanmer whose changes were silent as Pope's. Warburton in his text no more respected Pope than had Theobald, but as literary executor he could not quite reject Pope who had died three years before. The edition 'By Mr. Pope and Mr. Warburton' needed Pope's Preface; after Warburton's paragraphs about Theobald and Hanmer in his own, he would scarcely have elected to print theirs.

In looking at footnote evidence for editing, the succession is from Theobald through Warburton to Johnson; Rowe, Pope and Hanmer in their quiet ways doctored the text, with minimal mention of problem or solution. Warburton waited 14 years after Theobald's edition before the publication of his own, which held the field for 18 until Johnson's appeared, though the others were reprinted several times and commonly available. After two decades of background work Warburton needed to display an advance, the final solutions, a weight and a width of scholarship. He did so in pedantic enormous notes, which Johnson often as not reprinted and with casual mastery knocked apart.

Johnson wrote a few sentences of general reflection after most of the plays, simple impressions he carried from long and exact attention to them. On the whole he was most at ease in comic scenes of the histories, and could not rise to great occasion in the more complex tragedies; the two parts of *Henry the Fourth* were probably his favourite plays. 'Perhaps no authour has ever in two plays afforded so much delight,' he reflected; and his long note at the end on Falstaff must have been written in release from tears of laughter:

> But Falstaff unimitated, unimatable Falstaff, how shall I describe thee? [There was really no need to describe him.] Thou compound of sense and vice; of sense which may be admired but not esteemed, of vice which may be despised, but hardly detested. Falstaff is a character loaded with faults, and with those faults which naturally produce contempt. He is a thief, and a glutton, a coward, and a boaster, always ready to cheat the

---

[15] 'The Genuine Text ... is here settled: Being restored from the *Blunders* of the first Editors, and the Interpolations of the two Last.'

weak, and prey upon the poor; to terrify the timorous and insult the defenceless. At once obsequious and malignant, he satirises in their absence those whom he lives by flattering. He is familiar with the prince only as an agent of vice, but of this familiarity he is so proud as not only to be supercilious and haughty with common men, but to think his interest of importance to the duke of Lancaster. Yet the man thus corrupt, thus despicable, makes himself necessary to the prince that despises him, by the most pleasing of all qualities, perpetual gaiety, by an unfailing power of exciting laughter, which is the more freely indulged, as his wit is not of the splendid or ambitious kind, but consists in easy escapes and sallies of levity, which make sport but raise no envy. It must be observed that he is stained with no enormous sanguinary crimes, so that his licentiousness is not so offensive but that it may be borne for his mirth.

No other character in Shakespeare received such attention from Johnson, it is an extraordinary note from the flood tide of enjoyment. Drink and obesity two centuries later have lost their power as props for wit, and we turn with more interest to the Porter in *Macbeth* whom Pope relegated, or the Clown in *All's Well that Ends Well*, pathos has gained upon heartiness; but Johnson wheezed and rollicked at Falstaff's 'perpetual gaiety', while to *As you Like It*, for example, he gave slender praise with a few condescending moral reflections. Falstaff also trailed a moral truth in Johnson's final paragraph which seems to arrive with a sober clearing of the throat:

> The moral to be drawn from this representation is, that no man is more dangerous than he that with a will to corrupt, hath the power to please; and that neither wit nor honesty ought to think themselves safe with such a companion when they see Henry seduced by Falstaff.

The Tempest, Midsummer Night's Dream, Merry Wives, Comedy of Errors, Much Ado received no general observations from him. *The Taming of the Shrew* he thoroughly enjoyed, reprinting a long plagiarism from that story which had amused him as appearing innocently and ignorantly in *The Tatler*. He could not accept Theobald's assumption that Shakespeare must have had a finger in the writing of *Titus Andronicus*, but a logically excellent note on the authorship of the *Henry the Sixth* plays defended Shakespeare's presence there: 'From mere inferiority nothing can be inferred; in the productions of wit there will be inequality'. From a long note, that is extracted as an instance of irreproachable logic which yet fails to complete or advance the argument.

Though it would be absurd to call anything Johnson wrote puerile, his summary of *Measure for Measure* was at best excessively simple: 'Of this play the light or comick part is very natural and pleasing, but the grave scenes, if a few passages be excepted, have more labour than elegance': no word of Claudio's predicament which so appealed to the Victorians, nor of Isabella's passion and persuasion. The problem of *The Winter's Tale*, that sudden birth of jealousy found also in *Cymbeline* and *Othello*, had no place in his afterthought: 'This play, as Dr. Warburton justly observes, is with all its absurdities, very entertaining. The character of Antolycus is very naturally conceived, and strongly represented'. No word for the enchanting pastoral of Perdita. Johnson failed to respond profoundly to the emotional passages in Shakespeare, and his comments were often vacuous. 'The comick part raises laughter,' he wrote after *The Merchant of Venice*, 'and the serious fixes expectation.' A very mild conclusion. *Antony and Cleopatra* meant little to him: 'the power of delighting is derived principally from the frequent changes of the scene; for, except the feminine arts, some of which are too low, which distinguish Cleopatra, no character is very strongly discriminated'. *Julius Caesar* gave him no great pleasure: 'I have never been strongly agitated in perusing it, and think it somewhat cold and unaffecting, compared with some other of Shakespeare's plays'. Two paragraphs on *Troilus and Cressida* are of the most chilly sort, beginning:

> This play is more correctly written than most of Shakespeare's compositions, but it is not one of those in which either the extent of his views or elevation of his fancy is fully displayed.

Johnson's generalities (the comic characters in Troilus 'are copiously filled and powerfully impressed') make empty reading now. Except in laughing enormously at Falstaff, his response to the finest scenes in Shakespeare (as most people would now view or read them) was shallow. Character mattered more to him than poetry. His fuller appreciation of *Othello* was based upon the just characterization in that play.

The excellent apologia in his Preface dealt with a variety of accumulated worries as to decorum in Shakespeare: obscenity, poor education, the consequent defiance of classical custom in constructing a play, attention to natural life rather than formal art. If Johnson's wider responses now look inadequate, his strength as editor of the plays was often in commonsense assessment of the passions and pedantry of his predecessors. Johnson in judgement upon Theobald, Pope, Hanmer and Warburton was at his best; summing up, delivering a verdict, dismissing the evidence, passing sentence. His originality lay in calm appraisal, his decisions upon tedious argument were often given with devastating brevity, and as in any court his own conclusion was not beyond the range of challenge.

Trivial moments may provide better examples than familiar passages, so here is a minor typical instance from the opening scene of *Cymbeline*. Leonatus Posthumus, future husband of Imogen, is praised highly by one Gentleman to another. The several lines were printed thus in 1623:

> 1 I do not thinke,
> So faire an Outward, and such stuffe Within
> Endowes a man, but hee.
> 2 You speak him farre.
> 1 I do extend him (Sir) within himselfe,
> Crush him together, rather than unfold
> His measure duly.

Requiescat in pace, one might feel; no problem or complexity there, but that was not the way it struck the editors. Rowe, blind to the phrases which followed, changed *far* to *fair* and Pope copied him. Theobald put a stop to that, in a note which caused further fuss:

> I don't know what Consonance our modern Editors could find betwixt *speaking fair* and *extending*. No more, I believe, than they have Authority for the Reading. I have restor'd with the old Books;
>   *You speak him* farr.
> i.e. You speak widely, with Latitude, in his Praises: and then the other answers with great Propriety; "Sir, as *widely* as I speak of him, I *extend* him within the Lists and Compass of his own Merit".

This would not do for Warburton, who quoted Theobald, then rambled on:

> To *extend* a thing *within* itself is the most insufferable nonsense: because the very etymology of the word shews, that it signifies the drawing out any thing BEYOND its *lists and compass*. Besides, a common attention was sufficient to perceive that Shakespear, in this sentence, used *extend and crush together*, as the direct opposites to one another; which, in this Editor's sense, they are not; but only different degrees of the same thing. We should read and point the passage thus,
>
>   I DON'T EXTEND him, Sir: within himself
>   Crush him together –
> i.e. I do not extend him; on the contrary I crush him together.

One is often grateful to Warburton for providing Johnson's cue. The pattern is familiar: reformation, counter-reformation, judgment of the magistrate. Johnson more often adjudicates than initiates. Here is his reply now:

> I am not able to perceive that the old reading is *insufferable*. I extend him within himself: My praise, however *extensive*, is *within* his merit. What is there in this which common language and common sense will not admit?

But nothing was beyond challenge, in that period when every phrase in Shakespeare lay open to question. One of the Blagden family, close to Johnson's circle of friends, who owned my set of this edition, added his notes and amendments in balanced sentences and a neat hand down the margins.

> To *extend*, in a *legal* Sense [he wrote] is to *Value* Lands, Goods, or Tenements. If the Reader carries this in his Eye, Shakespeare's Meaning, as it stands in the original, is as elegant & sensible, as Dr. Johnson's is forced & unnatural.

Malone and Steevens added more interpretation and parallel, though none was needed.

The character of Warburton's notes might have been very different if he had prepared his edition in about 1730, when Theobald was launching his own upon a full tide of discovery; generous in sharing the analysis of phrases and difficulties with Theobald through years of their long correspondence, when no competitive sense of recognition or acknowledgement intervened, with Hanmer it was different, a friendship cultivated on both sides with some quiet thought towards future use. After 20 years of such intercourse, giving his answers and offering suggestions, Warburton assumed a greater authority than any which had preceded him and a compulsion to write obscure notes or suggest unneeded variants. Without Theobald's equipment of parallel instances in Elizabethan literature, or any finer mandate than his own judgement for urging emendations, he proposed changes where it struck him the text might be improved, providing ample ammunition for Edwards's *Canons of Criticism.*

Examples of Warburton being witless and absurd are not hard to find, though tedious to read. Here is one, from Act IV Scene 2 of *All's Well That Ends Well.* Diana very properly refuses Betram's oaths of affection. 'How have I sworn!' he says; her answer has no obscurity, appearing thus in the Folio of 1623:

> Tis not the many oaths that makes the truth,
> But the plaine single vow, that is vow'd true:
> What is not holie, that we sweare not by,
> But take the high'st to witness . . .

We always swear by the highest name, she is saying, and even then the vow has to be true. We do not swear by that which is not holy. Warburton rambled and made an expedition, when there was no reason for venturing out at all, changing the line and its punctuation to

> What is not holy, that we swear, not 'bides, –

proposing a typically awkward improbability.

> Yes, nothing is more common than such kind of oaths [he wrote]. But Diana is not here accusing Bertram for swearing by a Being not holy, but

for swearing to an unholy purpose; as is evident from the preceeding lines,

> 'Tis not the many oaths, that make the Truth;
> But the plain simple vow, that is vow'd true.

The line in question, therefore, is evidently corrupt, and should be read thus,

> What is not holy, that we swear, not 'BIDES,

i.e. If we swear to an unholy purpose the oath abides not, but is dissolved in the making. This is an answer to the purpose. She subjoins the reason two or three lines after,

> *– this has no holding,*
> To swear by him, whom I protest to love,
> That I will work against him. –

i.e. That oath can never hold, whose subject is to offend and displease that being, whom, I profess, in the act of swearing by him, to love and reverence. – What may have misled the editors into the common reading was, perhaps, mistaking Bertram's words above,

> By love's own sweet constraint, –

to be an oath; whereas it only signifies, *being constrained by love.*

That is a minor example, from the dull end of a poorly constructed play, but Warburton sought occasions for change; so it is surprising to find Johnson welcoming his blunder warmly, as 'an acute and excellent conjecture, and I have done it the due honour of exalting it to the text', though he expressed misgiving. Steevens in 1773 kept it there, but changed his mind five years later on the authority of Benjamin Heath's *Revisal of Shakespeare's Text.* Capell had dismissed it already; Malone quoted the long paragraph from Heath. Thus was much made frequently of nothing.

Warburton's emendations were after the school of Pope, sprung from his own taste rather than literary parallel or scribal evidence – and that was not an impossible principle of criticism, except for his claim to have restored Shakespeare from the blunders of former editors; but his taste was less interesting than Pope's, his guesses often foolish, and his notes both spurious and enormous.

Sometimes one may still feel inclined to follow Warburton, when modern taste ignores him. 'I am now, Sir,' Parolles says sadly to the Clown,[16] 'muddied in fortune's mood, and smell somewhat strong of her strong displeasure.' Warburton thought this a misreading for fortune's *moat*, which was possible and (irrelevant point) perhaps an

---

[16] *All's Well,* Act V Scene 2

improvement. Johnson, Capell, Steevens accepted fortune's moat which survived until the 1803 variorum; Malone had thrown it out in 1790, and Boswell of course followed him in 1821. In an example which displayed such intelligent sense, it comes as no surprise to discover that the suggestion was first made by Theobald in 1733, his note paraphrased by Warburton without acknowledgement. It could be interesting to count how many of Warburton's *sensible* emendations were taken thus from Theobald. He was much disturbed when Hanmer failed to attribute his own suggestions, in the quarto Oxford edition.

Many of Johnson's notes expressed his preference for leaving an older reading, quarto or folio, to stand. Notes are necessary but they are necessary evils. After a long proposal by Warburton in *The Winter's Tale*[17] he wrote:

> This emendation is one of those of which many may be made; it is such as we may wish the authour had chosen, but which we cannot prove that he did chuse; the reasons for it are plausible, but not cogent.

Better to leave things as they were. In the opening scene of *Love's Labour's Lost*, Johnson replied simply to another lengthy Warburton emendation:

> That there are *two ways of setting* a passage *right* gives reason to suspect that there may be a third way better than either . . . I cannot see why the passage cannot stand without disturbance.

It was his common judgement. Warburton ended one particularly silly suggestion with a priggish verdict: 'The epithet is proper and the compound not inelegant'.[18] 'Much less elegant than the present reading,' Johnson wrote.

He was at his best in giving judgement calmly between the warring factions; his emendations were no wiser than theirs, carried no special authority, though his labours with the Dictionary enabled him sometimes to make corrections in verbal definition. A couple of lines from *Macbeth* moved most of the editors to interpret or emend, though there was no need for so much thought to be given. After Duncan's murder Macbeth had also killed the King's two servants and, framing them as murderers, dipped their daggers in blood; in the old spelling of the Folio,

> There the Murtherers,
> Steep'd in the Colours of their Trade; their Daggers
> Unmannerly breech'd with gore;

---

[17] Act V Scene 1
[18] *Love's Labour's Lost*, Act V Scene 10

and nobody found any problem there until Warburton started a hare, offering his rather repellant note:

> This nonsensical account of the state in which the daggers were found, must surely be read thus,
>
> UNMANLY REECH'D with gore:
>
> *Reech'd*, soiled with dark yellow, which is the colour of any reechy substance, and must be so of steel stain'd with blood. He used the word very often, as *reechy hangings, reechy neck*, &c. So that the sense is, that they were *unmanly* stain'd with blood, and that circumstance added, because often such stains are most honourable.

Warburton at his worst, one would say. Johnson thought otherwise, adding a note of approval: 'Dr. Warburton has perhaps rightly put *reech'd* for *breech'd*.' His own needless alternative was no more persuasive:

> An *unmannerly dagger*, and a *dagger breech'd*, or as in some editions *breach'd with gore*, are expressions not easily to be understood. There are undoubtedly two faults in this passage, which I have endeavoured to take away by reading,
>
> – *daggers*
> Unmanly drench'd *with gore;*
>
> *I saw* drench'd *with the King's blood the fatal daggers, not only instruments of murder but evidences of cowardice.*
> Each of these words might easily be confounded with that which I have substituted for it by a hand not exact, a casual blot, or a negligent inspection.

Worse than the wilder shores of Theobald. Over the next half century, explanations of this passage proliferated. 'Every one has tried his skill at it,' Farmer remarked as prelude to his own, 'and I may venture to say, no one has succeeded.' Was there ever any reason to think twice about those lines? Blagden wrote dismissively up the margin of his Johnson volume:

> To *breech* is to *clothe* or to *cover*, and *unmannerly* is neither more nor less than *unseemly* – The Reader has Shakespeare's Idea, if he can form the disagreeable one of a *Dagger covered with blood.* – Is not this one of the plainest Passages in Shakespeare?

Apparently not, for on they went, but rather to explain than alter. Capell kept the old reading; so did Steevens in 1773 who began his note irreproachably:

> I apprehend it to be the duty of an editor to represent his author such as he is, and explain the meaning of the words he finds to the best advantage, instead of attempting to make them better by any violent alteration.

He continued in a sense close to Blagden's but not the same (daggers 'covered with blood, quite to their *breeches,* i.e. their *hilts* or *handles*'), equating daggers with cannon where 'the lower end ... is called the *breech* of it', and quoted in distant support a passage from Beaumont and Fletcher.

This history is worth following only because each contributor was true to himself. Malone, unable to resist appearing on stage, produced a thought both flawless and useless:

> Though so much has been written on this passage, the commentators have forgotten to account for the attendants of Duncan being furnished with unmannerly daggers. The fact is, that in our author's time a dagger was a common weapon, and was usually carried by servants, suspended at their backs. So, in *Romeo and Juliet*: 'Then I will lay the *serving creature's dagger* on your pate'.

The fact was, that as servants commonly carried daggers, the commentators found nothing worth mention. Warton, Heath and at last the great Farmer added their voices. Farmer, too tedious to quote at length, found a bilingual French book from 1605 and concluded that Shakespeare 'even as a *learner*' misunderstood the translations of *haut-de-chausses* and *bas-de-chausses*, breeches and stockings; deceived by the punctuation, 'evidently supposes *breaches* to be a new and affected term for *scabbards*'. Even if Shakespeare had seen the book, the misunderstanding remains misunderstood. Farmer, so highly respected by them all, must have been a genial old bore.

It would be false to suggest that after Johnson any kind of editorial decline began, but a certain style of debate gave way to the accumulation of literary parallel. Theobald's sense of discovery, Warburton's more distant excursions, Johnson's higher judgement upon 'the learned Commentator' (Warburton) and 'the Oxford Editor' (Hanmer) perhaps concluded the early editing of Shakespeare. Nichol Smith wrote that 'with the advance of detailed scholarship the Prefaces deteriorate in literary merit'; whether or not one agrees about the Prefaces it would be true of the notes. The most prominent among later editors, Steevens and Malone, providing a mass of literary parallel to support interpretations, also contributed their running dispute on such general issues as emendation and the use or worthlessness of later Folios. Steevens in his *List of the Old Editions of Shakespeare's Plays* (1766) had given his view that 'the only authentick edition is the folio of 1623, from which the subsequent folios never vary but by accident or negligence' but he changed his mind. In a note near the beginning of Act V in *Measure for Measure* for instance he regrets that 'the value of the second folio, it seems, must on all occasions be disputed'. In a note to *Othello* (Act I scene 3) he mentions with stronger emphasis that 'my sentiments concerning the merits of the second folio are diametrically opposite to Mr. Malone's opinion of it'.

They did not cease from mental strife, nor did their swords sleep in their hands. The debate continued, and is not finished. Through most of five pages in the 1821 variorum long editorial notes argued the authenticity of one word from Iago's lines

> O, beware, my lord, of jealousy;
> It is the green-ey'd monster, which doth make
> The meat it feeds on.

So Malone, following Hanmer's emendation; the Folio had *mock* not *make*.

Warburton chose mock, understanding it to mean loath; Johnson ruled that a wrong definition and 'received Hanmer's emendation'; Farmer contributed the obscure comment that 'In this place, and some others, to *mock* seems the same with to *mammock*'. A very long necessary evil from Steevens preferred *mock*, as meaning amuse or play with. It was not a satisfactory or well argued note, but ended sympathetically: 'To produce Sir Thomas Hanmer's meaning, a change in the text is necessary. I am counsel for the old reading'. Mason declared for Hanmer's reading, and Henley joining issue in support of Steevens raised the temperature of argument:

> To have been consistent with himself he should have charged Mr. Stee-vens with maintaining, that it was the property of a jealous husband, first to *mock* his *wife*, and afterwards to *eat* her.

Steevens expressed himself 'particularly indebted to Mr. Henley for the support he has given to my sentiments concerning this difficult passage', after which Malone occupied almost two pages beginning 'I have not the smallest doubt that Shakespeare wrote *make*, and have therefore inserted it in my text'. Make and mocke, the old spelling, 'are often confounded in these plays' he adds rather airily. Malone had not the smallest doubt, but the new Oxford editors choose *mock*.

So it went on, as sensibility withdrew before scholarship. On the whole it is easy in that example to accept Steevens, who found literary parallels to support his definition of mock as amuse, having in mind Iago's lines which followed:

> That cuckold lives in bliss,
> Who, certain of his fate, loves not his wronger;
> But, O, what damned minutes tells he o'er,
> Who dotes, yet doubts; suspects, yet strongly loves!

That argument is not settled by any editor's decision and this is no place to prolong it, but the temptation exists! Nor can any attempt be made to summarize Steevens and Malone, who need to be known at length and in context.

One crotchety figure, also beyond reach, Edward Capell, stands aside from them. His eccentricity in printing *Edward the Third* as 'a Play, thought to be writ by Shakespeare' was no more sensible than Theobald's claim for *Double Falshood;* his separately published volumes of notes to accompany the Shakespeare edition, failures in their day, remain difficult to read as hard to find. His manuscripts at Trinity College, Cambridge, in the incredible neatness of a slightly spidery hand, show the obsessional nature of the man; the printer, Dryden Leach, must have received instructions to follow precisely the design of that work as he wrote it. * Johnson found his style impossible. As a *bonne bouche* in editorial prose this chapter can end with his third-person statement of intention, which I copied from Capell's manuscript one summer afternoon in the Wren Library. After 1768, Capell wrote,

> his first business was – to compleat a work that was then in some forwardness, call'd – the 'School;' it is finish'd and will appear in due time. The work proceeded to next, was – the '*Notes*'; but was hardly begun upon, before evident tokens appear'd of a necessity for it's present suspension, to make way for another work, which should facilitate the business of note-writing, abridge it, and make it's process more regular; with this work, – a '*Glossary*', – which took up no little time, nor little labour, is usher'd-in to-day's publication. What the labour of his next business was, – the resum'd business of *Note-writing;* and, after that, of digesting and scrutinizing, purging too of it's trifles a collected body of *Readings* that were to go with these plays, – the bulk of both those articles shew, and ('tis hoped) their exactness: the former you will of course augment further . . .

---

* His earlier book, *Prolusions*, was designed similarly

5   The Growth of Apparatus

I   INDEXES, GLOSSARIES, BEAUTIES

The first Shakespeare Index occurred in Gildon's additional volume
to the Rowe editions of 1709, throwing its shadow across a subject
which would occupy much time and space: *References to the Classic
Authors, &c.* This brief work of reference settled no argument; it
pointed an 18th-century reader towards classical treatment of similar
themes, filling four leaves of paper and running out of steam in the
final list called 'The other Topics of Shakespear for which I have not
met with Parallels among the Latins'. It was perhaps a well planned
system but one wonders if anyone ever used it. Among unparalleled
topics were Imagination, Fall'n Greatness, Lowliness or Humility,
Slander, Melancholy. Gildon was examining poems, not plays.

Pope's edition offered the first attempt towards a systematic index,
of a complexity which must have baffled those who turned to it. The
title was *Index of the Characters, Sentiments, Speeches and
Descriptions in Shakespear;* close-set in several columns, its six
sections and sub-divisions filled almost 15 quarto leaves. Pope had no
hand in its preparation, though his instructions survive in a letter to
Jacob Tonson:

> Whoever you set upon ye Index, may proceed upon ye Plan of mine to
> Homer, & whoever has Sense & Judgement enough to draw up this Index,
> will find that a sufficient direction. He must begin in order as ye Plays lye,
> ranging whatever occurs under those heads; (but not upon one particular
> Play in an Index by itself), referring each Character, Speech, Simile, Descrip-
> tion, &c. to such a play, such an Act, such a Scene, such a Speaker.[1]

---

[1] *Correspondence*, ed. Sherburn, vol. 2, p.213

And that is roughly how it came: *Characters of Historical Persons; Index of Manners, Passions, and their external Effects: Index of fictitious Persons, with the Characters ascrib'd to them; Index of Thoughts or Sentiments; Speeches. A Table of the most considerable in Shakespear; Index of Descriptions, or Images; Index of some Similies and Allusions.* The Speeches were subdivided into Exhortatory, Vituperative, Execrative, Deliberative, Narrative, Pathetic and Soliloquies; Descriptions were split into Places, Persons, Things, Times and Seasons. Not a simple document for anyone to use. If you wanted to look up 'Gratitude in an Old Servant', for instance, you would find it under Descriptions, or Images, section III, Descriptions of Things, after wasting a little time among the Index of Thoughts, or Sentiments. This serious advance towards system reappeared in Theobald's second edition, 1740, and again in Warburton.

The only other Index with comparable column references may be found in each volume of the second large-quarto Hanmer edition, 1770, listing 'Various Readings of Mr. Theobald and Mr. Capell', the two literal critics Oxford chose to take seriously. This considerable editorial chore was a nuisance to use, relegated to the back of each volume with page and line references under each play and columns for T or C, Oxford unwilling to confuse a fine production by the distraction of more footnotes.

Glossaries grew from the first Hanmer edition to such large works as lie outside the scope of this book, as Mrs Cowden Clarke's *Complete Concordance to Shakspere: being A Verbal Index to All the Passages in the Dramatic Works of the Poet*, 1845, 860 pages of very small type in three columns (printed for subscribers, signed by the author); or *Shakespeare-Lexicon. A complete Dictionary of All the English Words, Phrases and Constructions in the Works of the Poet* by Alexander Schmidt, of which the second edition, two large volumes, was published in 1886 with a combined Berlin and London title page. Mrs. Cowden Clarke was not the pioneer: The Revd. Samuel Ayscough, F.S.A., on the Library staff at the British Museum, had produced in 1790, as Volume III of the new edition of Stockdale's *Shakspeare* which had first appeared in one volume, *An Index to the Remarkable Passages and Words; made use of by Shakspeare; calculated to point out the different meanings to which the words are applied.* The separately published Dublin edition, 1791, ran to 670 pages. Ayscough had another purpose than mere definition, providing quotations to show varied usage in Shakespeare. Schmidt gave definitions. These two streams, with their 18th-century names Glossary and Glossarial Index, may be traced back to source.

The first Glossary came at the end of Hanmer's edition, 'Explaining the obsolete and difficult Words in the Plays of Shakespear'. We know from Warburton's letter[2] that the work was farmed out to a friend for 'one hundred guineas, or some such sum', a generous fee for eight printed leaves in which many words needed no explanation. One page opened at random provides definitions of Besmirch or Smirch, a Bilberry, to Blench, a Brake, a Broch or Brooch or Browch, a Brock (badger), Brogues, Busky or Bosky, all comprehensible without help, but the Glossary marked a new departure. In the 1770 Hanmer edition, with Warton's assistance and ample reference to Johnson, it was extended to twice the length. The original Hanmer glossary had been reprinted in Tonson's anonymous piracy of 1745, and in his duodecimo edition two years later, and made a surprise appearance in Harding's edition, 1800.

Without mention of line, scene or act, the glossary definition was only another form of footnote; as a dictionary, with such reference, it could at least settle an argument or correct a quotation. Hanmer offered only limited help of this sort: 'when a word is used but once, or in a sense which is singular, the Volume and the Page are noted down, where the same is to be found'.

Johnson and the successive editions with his name had no such apparatus, but Malone in 1790 provided the first Glossarial Index, entirely a reference system, not concerned with definition; it was one possible solution where an editor felt no constraint in writing footnotes to clarify obscurities. Hanmer would never have wanted his text to be so cluttered; Malone's list gave references to words and phrases 'which have been explained or illustrated in the preceding Notes, and in the Appendix'. The five great note-writers, Theobald, Warburton, Johnson, Steevens and Malone, needed no glossary to explain terms.

Malone's 'Alphabetical Index, to serve the purposes of A Glossary', 16 leaves of small type in two columns, baffling and inadequate, cut a new channel. It is not helpful to find single references for such words as Quick, Power, Piece, Owls, Plates, Blot, Buxom, Bug – taking only two page-openings for example; but he pointed the way for Mrs. Cowden Clarke, and Schmidt's two large volumes combined both kinds of information. Malone's system was expanded in the 1803 variorum, where Reed first produced the unpleasant phrase 'Glossarial Index' for *Words, Phrases, Customs, and Persons, Explained or Mentioned in the Notes*. This fills 35 leaves, 70 double-column pages. The additions may strike us as equally unhelpful, giving single references on the opening page to abhor, abide, able, abroad, abstract,

---

[2] See p. 90

abuse, abysm, accommodation, accost, account, accuse, achieve, act, adamant.

Chalmers in 1805 had a somewhat different Glossarial Index, perhaps for reasons of copyright; Boswell in the 1821 variorum, considering again from first principles the uses and purpose of an index, arrived at sub-divisions which recall Pope's edition from a century earlier:

> As there are some who take little interest in discussions which are merely verbal, I have divided the Index into three distinct branches. The first contains only words and phrases: the second relates to manners, customs, and allusions, among which I have inserted the songs and proverbs to which Shakspeare is supposed to have referred ... In the third place, I have set down those names which have suggested historical illustrations in the notes, as far as they seemed important.

This was more useful than earlier efforts, with brief definitions before most of the references, as for instance 'stale, a stalking horse', 'stands upon, is important', 'sneaping, checking', 'ruddock, red-breast'. Though Pope had an Index of Manners, Passions, and their external Effects, it was not a model for the Manners, Customs, Super-stitions which interested Boswell whose entries included 'aldermen distinguished by thumb-rings', 'cakes made in honour of saints' days', 'fading, an old Irish dance, described' – curiosities which had begun to interest such antiquaries of his day as Brand and Grose and Strutt.

In this and other ways the 1821 variorum improved upon earlier editions, but no index could carry the heavy burden of reference; separate volumes with a life of labour were needed, and later in the century they came.

The concept had not matured, for publications of this kind, though the Index, familiar in editions of the classics, became an aspect of respectable publishing then and since. Looking for random ex-amples, the splendid Horace published by Payne and Edwards in 1793 was furnished with nearly 200 pages of index; the two-volume Lactantius published by De Bure in 1748 had its Index Auctorum Librorumque, followed by an Index Rerum Verborumque Notabi-lium; the great edition of Plutarch which came from the Imprimerie Royale in 1624 printed a long index of variant readings. Such were editorial routines, but an English classic author did not yield to quite the same treatment.

For instance, to look up the word *Index* provides a substantial exercise. Hanmer's glossary made no mention, the fine quarto edition of 1771 referred back to a footnote which gave the only help one needs: 'The *Index* was usually placed at the beginning of a book'. I have in mind of course the Queen in Hamlet:

> Ah me! what act,
> That roars so loud, and thunders in the index.

Other glossaries ignored the word; Malone 1790 had it in his Glossarial Index, four references, repeated in the long variorum editions of 1803 and 1813; Boswell in 1821 chose to delete them. These references were to volume and page, not play or scene, but that is easily resolved; and when we arrive, travelling back also among the earlier editors, *Index* provides appropriately an abstract and brief chronicle of this work.

Nobody questioned the matter before Warburton, whose predictably lunatic note and text started a doubt. 'Ay me! what act?' the Queen asks, and in Warburton's version Hamlet replies

> That roars so loud, it thunders to the Indies.

His footnote opened with the Folio reading, and continued:

> This is a strange answer. But the old quarto brings us nearer to the poet's sense by dividing the lines thus:
>
> > *Queen.* Ah me, what act?
> > *Ham.*　That roars so loud, and thunders in the Index.
>
> Here we find the Queen's answer very natural. He had said the Sun was *thought-sick at the act.* She says,
>
> > *Ah me! what act?*
>
> He replies (as we should read it)
>
> > *That roars so loud,* IT *thunders to the* INDIES.
>
> He had before said Heav'n was shocked at it; he now tells her, it resounded all the world over. This gives us a very good sense where all sense was wanting.

Johnson quoted Warburton and dismissed him, as usual, restoring the lines and their meaning, but failed to pick up the particular sense of Index:

> The meaning is, *what* is this act, of which the *discovery* or *mention*, cannot be made, but with this violence of clamour?

Canon IX in Edwards's *Canons of Criticism*, the irrefutable reply to Warburton, reads:

> He may interpret his Author so; as to make him mean directly contrary to what He says.

And these few words from the Queen in *Hamlet* provided his 12th Example. 'This is a strange answer,' Warburton had written, and Edwards added in parenthesis, 'I thought it had been a *question*'. His footnote gave the excellent point about an Index, which 'used formerly to be placed at the beginning of a book; not at the end, as now,' – and proceeded to murder Warburton no less thoroughly than Claudius had killed the King:

> Here Mr. Warburton takes occasion, from what seems a mistaken division of the passage in the old Quarto, to represent an act as *thundering to the Indies;* that is, *making a noise all over the world,* as he explains it; which was probably known only to the murderer himself, and to Hamlet; to whom his father's ghost had revealed it. And, when he has made the mistake, he contrives, as he frequently does, to commend himself; by commending Shakespear for what he never wrote, or thought of; 'This, says he, gives us a very good sense; where all sense was wanting'. Modest enough for a Professed Critic!

Even Jennens, supposed to choose most wrong readings, got this one right. Steevens in 1773 ignored Warburton but retained Johnson, adding his own airy comment:

> Mr. Edwards, I think, says, that the *Indexes* of many old books were at that time inserted at the beginning, instead of the end, as is now the custom. This observation I have often seen confirmed.

A characteristic entry from Steevens, who could have reached for his *Canons of Criticism* instead of thinking Edwards made that comment; and it is unlikely he had 'often seen' the observation confirmed, except in Edwards who gave three instances from *Richard the Third* and one from *Othello*, the last cribbed later without acknowledgement by Steevens and by Malone who provided his own useless example: 'Bullokar in his *Expositor*, 8vo 1616, defines an *Index* by "A *table* in a booke" ', adding nothing to the argument but continuing, as if to a deduction, with a paraphrase of Edwards:

> The *table* was almost always *prefixed* to the books of our poet's age. Indexes, in the sense in which we now understand the word, were very uncommon.

And thus the notes reappeared in each long variorum edition. Steevens had taken Malone's Bullokar gloss on board in 1793; Chalmers without acknowledgement repeated it verbatim as his single note on the passage in 1805. After all it is odd to find so much effort wasted upon Schmidt,[3] who defined Index as 'an explaining preface or prologue to a book or play'. We should now call it List of Contents.

*   *   *

Gildon inspired an editorial taste for isolating Shakespeare's 'Beau-

---

[3] Second edition, 1886

ties', in his appreciative *Remarks on the Plays* added at the end of 'Volume the Seventh' in 1710 as counterbalance to the prefatory *Essay on the Art, Rise and Progress of the Stage* which was perhaps too aggressive.

> I have in my Essay prefixt to this Volume, laid down the Rules, by which the Reader may judge of the Mistakes of our Poet so far, as by his Authority not to be drawn into an Imitation of his Errors, by mistaking them for Beauties. I shall now in these Remarks point out the Beauties of this Author, which are worthy the Observation of all the Ingenious Lovers of this Art, and those who desire to arrive at any Perfection in it.

Anthologies and Miscellanies were especially common in days when poetry often circulated in manuscript, but this theme of Beauties, in the sense of Extracts, was more difficult; comparable now perhaps with tapes of musical favourites offered in restaurants or to the returning motorist. Drawing attention to passages in the plays by the use of quotation marks became, as Johnson found, an intrusive nuisance; yet the habit reappeared occasionally and Dodd's scrupulous publication from 1752, *The Beauties of Shakespear*, laid a more formal path which others followed.

Gildon had provided a summary of each play's plot as the prelude to quoted passages, moral comment, classical parallel. Attention was sometimes directed in a rather offhand way to moments he admired:

> The Bastard's Speech, of the weakness of laying our Fate and Follies on the Stars, is worth reading – 'This is the excellent Foppery of the World, that when we are sick in Fortune, &c.'
> Lear's Passion, on the Ingratitude of his Daughter *Goneril*, is very well; and his Curses on her very naturally chose. Lear's Speech to *Regan*, is very well – 'No, *Regan*, thou shalt ne'er have my Curses, &c.' And his Passion in this whole Scene agreeable to the Manners.

Such brevity alternated with long scenes printed without comment, from Shakespeare or Euripides; Cleopatra in her barge, as described by Enobarbus in Shakespeare's play, was followed by comparable lines Dryden wrote for Antony in *All for Love*. Eccentric, casual and unexpected, Gildon was the pioneer of Shakespearean anthology.

If his perceptions survived as first-thoughts and marked passages from a reading of the plays, such was also the legacy of Pope's quarto volumes 14 years later. 'Some of the most shining passages are distinguish'd by comma's in the margin,' Pope wrote in the Preface; 'and where the beauty lay not in particulars but in the whole, a star is prefix'd to the scene.'

Nothing in 18th-century Shakespeare editions was more whimsical than the appearance or absence of Pope's commas in the margin, or his very rare award of a star to the scene. It would be false to find in these cavalier marks of approval any general understanding of his

9 Bellamy & Robarts, 'An Infant Shakespeare in the Realms of Fancy', 1791.
[Actual height of *image* 6½ inches]

10 *Merchant of Venice,* Bellamy and Robarts, 1791 (Jessica & Lorenzo).
[Actual height of *image* $6\frac{1}{4}$ inches]

W.N. Gardiner del. et sc.

Hamlet.

Page 96.

11 Ophelia in Harding's *Hamlet*, engraved 1797. [Actual height of *image* 3¾ inches]

Hamlet.

Page 106

Pub. 1 March 1797 by Edw. Harding, N° 98 Pall Mall.

12　Gravediggers in Harding's *Hamlet*, engraved 1797. [Actual height of *image* 3⅝ inches]

13 *Winter's Tale*, Boydell's *Shakespeare Gallery*, engraved 1793. [Actual height of *image* 17½ inches]

14   *As You Like It*, Boydell's *Shakespeare Gallery*, engraved 1801. [Actual height of *image* 15 inches]

15 *As You Like It* (from Alkin's send-up of the Seven Ages), 1824. [Actual height of *image* $7\frac{1}{4}$ inches]

16   *Romeo & Juliet*, Chalmers, engraved by Blake after Fuseli 1804. [Actual height of *image* $6\frac{3}{4}$ inches]

taste; they included or ignored indifferently passages which must always have shone, whoever read them; and minor moments which struck him as he read, of no special distinction, received the accolade.

Pope awarded stars to the two murder scenes in *Macbeth* (Act II, scenes 2 and 3 in his edition); to the brief scene in *The Tempest* when Caliban enters and Trinculo takes shelter beneath him; and to Act III scene 5 of *Othello*, in which Iago corrupts Othello's mind. No other stars were given, no more evidence provided than the perceptions of brief acquaintance discoverable from these which cannot be reckoned the distillation of judgement from a long period of study.

His commas in the margin revealed no finer balance of taste: Pope neither pointed to what might have been neglected, nor showed a preference for one quality above another; it is as if he had pencilmarked the margins at a single reading, and asked the printer to observe such signs. When *The Comedy of Errors* was by this system more admired than *Hamlet*, and *Timon of Athens* far above either, it is difficult now to declare what Pope intended. The advice of Polonius, and the King's penitence as he attempts to pray, nothing else, received margin commas in *Hamlet*. Helena's complaint to Hermia about loss of friendship is the only marked passage in *A Midsummer Night's Dream*. Through the whole of *King Lear* two pieces were chosen, the Fool's award of his own title to the King ('All thy other titles thou hast given away; that thou wast born with . . .') and Edgar's pretence in describing for blind Gloucester how Dover beach looked from the dizzy clifftop. Pope enjoyed harmless satire from the Clowns – Corin on courtiers in *As you Like It*, Launce in *The Two Gentlemen of Verona* – and he laughed with Falstaff.

This curious system was ignored by Theobald (1733) but taken up again in several of Tonson's separately published plays a year later, where many examples were imitated from Pope but others received this mark of recognition for the first time. *Hamlet*, in Tonson's unimportant edition, was well provided with commas in the margin.

Hanmer, next in line, having regard to the appearance of the page, ignored Pope's marks for merit while observing and wishing to increase his relegation of vulgar passages to footnotes in small type. Warburton, joining his name with Pope's on the title page, restored the scheme, 'the most beautiful passages distinguished, as in his book, with inverted commas', and added to it: 'In imitation of him, I have done the same by as many others as I thought most deserving of the Reader's attention, and have marked them with *double* commas'. This form of distinction in Warburton restored some balance, brought sense to the device; his *Hamlet*, for instance, has ample double commas.

Later editors agreed with Johnson in avoiding commas or stars which distracted readers and disturbed the rhythm of a scene – except for Francis Gentleman in Bell's first Shakespeare edition, 1774, where double commas plentifully reappeared. It was after all a simple way to suggest editorial labour where little had been given, but a more telling reason may have been the successful publication of Dodd's *Beauties of Shakespear* in two volumes, 1752.

'Dodd, William (1729–1777), forger ...' So began Leslie Stephens's wretched notice in the *Dictionary of National Biography*. The Shakespeare work, a youthful enthusiasm stuffed with educated comparison and classical translation, was succeeded by his Callimachus translation, a variety of religious works – and *Thoughts In Prison*, 1777, written while he waited sentence of execution. His plan to be rescued after an uncompleted hanging failed, though it was said 'that the body was carried to a surgeon, who tried to restore life; but the delay caused by the enormous crowd made the attempts hopeless'. Poor Dodd, tutor to Chesterfield's distant cousin, godson and heir, Philip Stanhope, forged the signature of his former pupil to pay urgent debts. In prison he could not believe that the unspeakable Fifth Earl

> whose filial ear
> Drank pleas'd the love of wisdom from my tongue

would fail to rescue him from this disaster. He wrote a brave poem, from the heart.

> Why then, mysterious Providence! pursued
> With such unfeeling ardour? why pursued
> To death's dread bourn, by men to me unknown!
> Why – Stop the deep question; it o'erwhelms my soul;
> It reels, it staggers! ... Earth turns round! ... my brain
> Whirls in confusion! my impetuous heart
> Throbs with pulsations not be restrain'd:
> Why? – where? – Oh Chesterfield! my son, my son!

Rising in the Church, a chaplain to the King, commended to old Lord Chesterfield by the Bishop of St. David's, with his wife's £1000 prize from a lottery ticket the Reverend William Dodd bought a Chapel in Pimlico where he preached to fashionable congregations and named it after Queen Charlotte. Chesterfield was forever telling Philip Stanhope to study his tutor's example:

> I am sure you are convinced that Dr. Dodd and I love you, and I really believe that you love us; what then is the natural inference, which your

THE
BEAUTIES
OF
SHAKESPEAR:

Regularly felected from each PLAY.

WITH A
GENERAL INDEX,

Digeſting them under Proper HEADS.

Illuſtrated with

EXPLANATORY NOTES, and Similar Paſſages
from Ancient and Modern AUTHORS.

By *WILLIAM DODD*, B. A.
Late of *Clare-Hall, Cambridge.*

The poet's eye, in a fine frenzy rowling,
Doth glance from heav'n to earth, from earth to heav'n,
And, as imagination bodies forth
The forms of things unknown, the poet's pen
Turns them to ſhape, and gives to airy nothing
A local habitation and a name.
See *Midſummer Night's Dream*, p. 87.

IN TWO VOLUMES.

VOL. I.

LONDON:
Printed for T. WALLER, at the *Mitre* and *Crown*,
oppoſite *Fetter-Lane, Fleet-Street.*
M.DCC.LII.

20 Title page of the first edition of Dodd, 1752. [Actual height of
type $5\frac{3}{4}$ inches]

own good sense must draw from these premises? Why, that we are more capable of advising you well, than you can be at your age, of conducting yourself.[4]

A more prophetic request, next year:

Pray desire the Doctor to have his account ready next time we meet, for I shall go to the Bath tomorrow, sevenight, and shall not be easy if I go there in debt.

On another ironic occasion he congratulated his godson upon making a distinction between *sentare* and *cogitare*, suggesting he discuss that with his tutor who might not yet have considered it. The letters were edited by a descendant, the Earl of Carnarvon, for whom Dodd was 'that unfortunate and much-to-be-lamented victim to dissipation and extravagance'.

Against this ageless background of opinion, the two small octavo volumes from 1752 have been unjustly ignored. Dodd's Preface, an essay written after Warburton's edition but before Johnson's, was a serious work. He had hoped to complete critical notes for all the plays – 'It was my first intention to have consider'd each play critically and regularly thro' all its parts' – but that proved too large a task; and he asked forgiveness for 'this juvenile performance' which 'was begun and finish'd, before I enter'd upon the sacred function, in which I am now happily employ'd ...'

He regretted those editorial disagreements which marred Shakespeare scholarship through the first half of the century:

For my own part, I cannot but read with regret the constant jarring and triumphant insults, one over another, found amidst the commentators on *Shakespear*: this is one of the reasons that has impeded our arrival at a thorough knowledge of his works: for some of the editors have not so much labour'd to elucidate their author, as to expose the follies of their brethren.

Theobald he regarded as the best editor, Hanmer the worst ('proceeds in the most unjustifiable method, foisting into his text a thousand idle alterations, without ever advertising his readers which are, and which are not *Shakespear's* genuine words') and Warburton not much better ('tho' he has for the most part preferred his own criticisms to the author's words, yet he hath always too given us the author's words, and his own reasons for those criticisms').

Dodd, surrendering his first ambition to write critical notes for all the plays, provided a critical edition of chosen passages. The Beauties were not high-flown excerpts but thematic descriptions or episodes, sometimes across several pages, through any mood from tragedy to

---

[4] Dated *Tuesday*, probably 1767. Philip was then eleven years old.

farce. Each was titled, indexed, footnoted with full apparatus of literary parallel and classical translation. For this concession to popular ignorance he apologized in the Preface:

> It would have been no hard task for me to have multiplied quotations from *Greek, Latin,* and *English* writers, and to have made no small display of what is commonly called, *learning;* but that I have industriously avoided; and never perplex'd the reader (or at least as little as possible) with the learned languages, always preferring the most plain and literal translations, much to his ease, tho' (according to the manner in which some judge) less to my own reputation.

Whatever the loss to Dodd's reputation through providing translations from Greek and Latin, it suffered more seriously 25 years later and has not recovered. It was outrageous of Stephens to call him 'forger'. That Goethe came to Shakespeare through Dodd is not a major point, but this considerable achievement from a scholar just down from Cambridge was not the lightweight work its title could now suggest.

In detail it is easy to find fault, of course. 'Love, the Nobleness of Life' was an inept heading for Antony's moment of decadent embrace at the start of *Antony and Cleopatra;* yet Pope's commas in the margin, commending Iago's profession of honesty in *Othello,* were equally foolish – as if one should admire Goneril on the nature of filial love. Dodd's ample verbal fencing with Warburton, less amusing but no less valid than Johnson's, would read tediously if quoted at length here. He himself quoted from Edwards on Warburton, showing small respect for his elders – as for instance in this first sentence of a note to *Love's Labour's Lost:*

> *Theobald* and *Warburton* have so much confus'd this passage, by endeavouring to explain what they did not understand, that almost every one who reads their comment on it, will be equally perplex'd with themselves.

Dodd, like Johnson who remained a loyal friend, avoided emendation more scrupulously than had his predecessors. An editor 'should not presume to alter ... any passages, which are not really flat nonsense and contradiction, but only such to his apprehension, and unintelligible solely to his unenliven'd imagination'.

He chose to travel through all the plays, rather than rearrange his extracts by group and subject: the Index, far from adequate (no entry under Music for instance) was supposed to do that. How were these two volumes used, in their day? His notoriety ensured plentiful reprints later. Educated readers could take on board a whole play; the uneducated would never have coped with his notes, or desired them. Dodd provided something which fell between laziness and learning.

II PROLEGOMENA

The 1778 Johnson and Steevens edition opened a new era with 350 pages of Prolegomena.[5] Johnson's Dictionary defined the word as 'previous discourse, introductory observations'. Bell's second edition, 1788, included two volumes called Prolegomena, so did the next Johnson and Steevens five years later; in 1803, 1813 and 1821 Prolegomena filled three volumes out of 21.

This apparatus increased through the whole period as it became usual after Johnson to print the growing numbers of Prefaces and Advertisements, followed by such documents as Shakespeare's Will, bibliographical lists, family history, commendatory poems. Bell took it all to great length, leading Steevens and Malone into another form of competition.

This second Johnson and Steevens edition, 1778, had been a pioneer in ascending these steeper slopes by including such essays as Malone's *Attempt to Ascertain the Order in which the Plays attributed to Shakspeare were written.* Bell printed an anonymous essay *On the Origin of the English Stage;* Malone's very much larger *Historical Account of the Rise and Progress of the English Stage* appeared in his own edition two years later. Malone's three volumes of *Supplement,* 1780 and 1783, introduced a new freedom to expand; the more formal arrangement of Prolegomena two decades later completed this period of editorial empire.

Its nature is clear from the start of Malone's *Life of William Shakspeare,* a new addition to the Prolegomena for 1821, which began the second volume, where after a couple of lines the flow of narrative is interrupted by a footnote occupying most of three pages, on the spelling of the name. It happens to be among the more interesting passages in this least distinguished of Malone's writings. He argued in favour of *Shakspeare* as a modernized spelling (consistent with most later 18th-century edited versions of the plays).

> That the pronunciation of his own time was *Shakspere,* is proved decisively, by illiterate persons, who spelt by the ear, writing the name either *Shaxpere,* or *Shackspere;* of which, instances from authentick documents will be given hereafter: and that he himself wrote his name without the middle *e,* appears from his autograph, of which a fac-simile will be found in a subsequent page. With respect to the last syllable of his name, the people of Stratford appear to have generally written the name *Shakspere,* or *Shackspere:* and I have now great doubts whether he did not frequently write the final syllable so himself; for I suspect that what was formerly supposed to be the letter *a* over his autograph above-

---

[5] So called by Malone in his Supplement, 1780

mentioned, was only a coarse and broad mark of a contraction; and in the signatures of his name subscribed to his will (as a very ingenious anonymous correspondent observes to me), certainly the letter *a* is not to be found in the second syllable ... But as *spere* was a misspelling of the word *speare*, from the cause already assigned; and as it is not so properly old spelling, as false spelling; in my opinion it ought not to be adopted in exhibiting our author's name at this day; and therefore I write *Shakspeare*, and not *Shakspere*.

As Pope's shaft aimed at Theobald in the *Dunciad* was caught gracefully by Malone, and our different habit of spelling has become rather dull, one may look back to a variety of 18th-century decisions. They provide witness, if more were needed, of wayward independence and the curiosities of emendation; for if one historic fact of Shakespeare can be accepted generally, it is the spelling of his name which appeared thus in the Folios, the separately published volumes of poems, and almost every quarto where the title page named him as author. Against this, they argued the evidence of his signature. Changed pronunciation could not seriously justify new spelling of a name, for Shakespeare or anyone else.

The first 18th-century editors used *Shakespear*, inheriting that version from Rymer and Winstanley though other critics in the 17th century had been more conventional. Among those who chose this form were Rowe, Pope, Hanmer and Warburton. Tonson's small acting editions, 1734, used it, so did the anonymous editors in 1745. Among mid-century critics he was *Shakespear* for Thomas Edwards, William Dodd, Charlotte Lennox and Elizabeth Montagu.

Theobald reverted to the old spelling which is also ours; for Johnson, as might be expected, Shakespeare was Shakespeare. The 1773, first Johnson and Steevens edition spelt him thus, but there was a difference: Johnson in 1765 had scrupulously observed the orthography chosen by the previous editors in the Prefaces he printed; Steevens in 1773 did not; yet it was Steevens, influenced by Malone no doubt, who instigated a change, for the 1778 Johnson and Steevens text had Shakespeare but the titles and half titles dropped his first e. Other editors following the conventional spelling include Capell, Jennens, Gentleman in the first Bell edition, and Chalmers; among the critics, Mason used it.

Shakspeare assumed authority through the next half century among such scholars as Steevens, Malone and Reed; Johnson's decision to follow early orthography was abandoned. As most publishers were pleased to name their texts 'Johnson and Steevens' in that prolific time it is not surprising to find *Shakspeare* on the title pages of Rann, Bellamy and Robarts, Harding, Boydell, Stockdale, Bowdler and Singer. As critic, Mrs. Griffith toed that line.

Just to be different perhaps, the second Bell edition, followed in Queen Victoria's reign by Knight and Mrs. Cowden Clarke, called him *Shakspere.*

The only early spelling without the first e had come in a 1608 quarto of *Lear*, when the name was hyphened as *Shak-speare;* but as the e was restored in another version surviving from the same year, no significance could be attached to that. Apart from three hyphened conventional spellings, the only other quarto variant was in *Love's Labour's Lost*, 1598, where he was *Shakespere*, a version followed by nobody.

Of the three Prolegomena volumes in 1821, altogether just over 1900 pages, three essays by Malone occupied 900: his *Essay on Phraseology and Metre* 80, *Life of Shakspeare, comprehending an Essay on the Chronological Order of his Plays* 528 and *History of the Stage* 292. They are not of equal merit.

Boswell had a lot of trouble putting together the *Essay on Phraseology and Metre*, left unfinished by Malone, from barely decipherable notes; as a connected argument it appeared in his own words, with plentiful reference in the third person to Malone. This essay formed a reply to the editorial style adopted by Steevens in reaction to the publication of Malone's 1790 edition. Boswell found in the 15-volume Johnson and Steevens edition a perverse withdrawal of the scruples Steevens had observed until then, with regard to emendation of phrases and correction of metre. These tendencies, condemned in Pope, Hanmer and Warburton, had reappeared from Steevens of all people.

> From this moment the whole system of Mr. Steevens was changed. That faithful adherence to the old copies, which he had represented as the principal recommendation of his former labours, was at once laid aside; and those unauthorised sophistications of the text, which in his first Advertisement he informed us he had left to some more daring commentator were, without scruple, introduced into this new edition in 1793, and still more unsparingly adopted in that which was posthumously published by Mr. Reed.

Steevens had so thoroughly left the path of righteousness that Malone's last message as set out by Boswell attacked the 'rage of emendation, and the wish to reduce every thing to a modern standard, which Mr. Steevens at one time so successfully opposed, and which he afterwards sanctioned by his example'. His point of view quite changed, Steevens in his last years opposed the habit of defending, by quotation from obscure parallels, what he came to regard as the heritage of inaccuracy. Boswell quotes:

> To assemble parallels in support of all these deformities, is no insuperable labour . . . we may aver that every casual combination of syllables may be

tortured into meaning, and every species of corruption exemplified by corresponding depravities of language: but not of such language as Shakspeare, if compared with himself, where he is perfect, can be supposed to have written.

Little progress had been made in three-quarters of a century since Pope had blamed 'the Players' for irregularity and vulgarity; Steevens and Reed were busy again making the crooked straight and rough places plain, Boswell in churning over familiar argument that Shakespeare wrote for the theatre using diction and syntax common in his time.

'The posture of your blows are yet unknown,' Cassius said to Antony in *Julius Caesar*. Footnote dialogue took place, Malone asserting 'the error was certainly Shakspeare's'. 'Rather the mistake of his transcriber or printer,' Steevens added, 'which therefor ought, in my opinion, to be corrected.' It would not do. 'What transcriber or printer,' Malone replied, 'finding the sentence right, would industriously construct it wrong' – and we are referred to a note on *Love's Labour's Lost*, with comparable examples.

Steevens stood upon dangerous ground in questioning whether greater metrical deviation existed anywhere in Shakespeare, than an occasional half-line:

> Though I once expressed a different opinion, I am now well convinced that the metre of Shakespeare's plays had originally no other irregularity than was occasioned by an accidental use of hemistichs. When we find the smoothest series of lines among our earliest dramatick writers (who could fairly boast of no other requisites for poetry) are we to expect less polished versification from Shakspeare?

Most of the rest of the Malone–Boswell essay expounded and defended irregularity in metre, Shakespeare's use of Alexandrines – as Hopkins and Bridges almost a century later discovered the art of similar irregularities in Milton, which inspired their theory of sprung rhythm or the habit of natural speech. Steadfast in accepting the irregular, Boswell concluded that 'the inexhaustible variety of his modulation never palls upon the ear'.

The much longer *Life of Shakspeare*, to which Boswell joined Malone's essay on the Chronology of the Plays, is an uneven and unsatisfying performance. Some replacement for Rowe was overdue, but the truth remained that few facts had come to light; so, minor matters were explored with exactness to spin out the story, from the defensive stance that in such a theme any charting of points distantly related was desirable. In Rowe's *Life*, he wrote, 'there are not more than *eleven* facts mentioned', in Malone's there may be 12 and a half. From background detail a general emphasis emerged, a focus upon Shakespeare's respectability, as for instance that deer-stealing was no crime but a common prank. After varied suppositions about 'our poet' we read minutiae concerning Sir Thomas Lucy's life, and under the same microscope examine the range of Spenser's cultural equipment, prompted by a phrase in *Tears of the Muses*, 'our pleasant Willy', identified with credible elaboration by Malone as Lyly rather than Shakespeare. It pleased him also to reflect that the father of our poet was no butcher but a glove maker.

Malone was much better on the chronology of the plays, able to offer just such relevant instances as the *Life* lacked, while modestly writing that in this 'attempt to trace the progress of his dramatick art, probability alone is pretended to'. Pope's contempt for all such reading as was never read was cast back with the conviction that such toil 'has been cheerfully endured, because no labour was thought too great, that might enable us to add one new laurel to the father of our drama'. Yet it was not the laurel, but artistic commonsense which grew from Malone's methodical patience. To quote a characteristic example, he brought back the likely date for *Comedy of Errors* four years from 1596 to 1592, by noticing a quibble to which his ear was attuned. Antonio of Syracuse in that play asks Dromio of Syracuse, 'In what part of her body stands – *France?*' The answer comes, 'In her forehead, arm'd and reverted, making war against the *hair*'. Malone wrote:

> I have no doubt that an equivoque was here intended, and that, beside the obvious sense, an allusion was intended to King Henry IV. the *heir* of France, concerning whose succession to the throne there was a civil war in that country, from August 1589, when his father was assassinated, for several years.

Against his earlier assumption that *Comedy of Errors* could not have been written until after 1595 when a translation of the *Menaechmi* of Plautus, the model for Shakespeare's plot, was printed, he believed 'that Shakspeare might have seen it before publication; for from the printer's advertisement to the reader, it appears that, for some time before, it had been handed about in MS. among the translator's friends'.

In such criticism based on small verbal perception Malone is excellent, as also in historic background. Thus *Henry VIII* was identified with what Sir Henry Wotton described in 1613 as 'a *new* play, called All is True'. Malone concluded there was nothing new about it in 1613 but 'its title, decorations, and perhaps the prologue and epilogue'. Here is his evidence:

> The Elector Palatine was in London in that year; and it appears from the MS. register of Lord Harrington, treasurer of the chambers to King James I that many of our author's plays were then exhibited for the entertainment of him and the princess Elizabeth. By the same register we learn,

that the titles of many of them were changed in that year. Princes are fond of opportunities to display their magnificence before strangers of distinction; and James, who on his arrival here must have been dazzled by a splendour foreign to the poverty of his native Kingdom, might have been peculiarly ambitious to exhibit before his son-in-law the mimick pomp of an English coronation. King Henry VIII therefore, after having lain by for some years unacted, on account of the costliness of the exhibition, might have been revived in 1613, under the title of All is True, with new decorations, and a new prologue and epilogue.[6]

The method could lead astray, following strands of evidence to dubious places. For instance, arguing that Middleton's play *The Witch* was written after *Macbeth*, not before as had earlier been thought and written, Malone quoted a line spoken by one of Middleton's characters called Florida:

> They talk of gentlemen, *performers*, and such things.

Innocuous and leading nowhere, one would think; but Malone scented a clue in finding that in 1603 'Don Juan de Taxis, the Spanish Ambassador, brought in his train to London a *performer*, which he scarcely would have done, had such a trade been established in London'. Why not? Kings and courtiers have travelled with their physicians, though doctors existed in the capitals they visited. Had Malone lived in the 20th century it would have intrigued him to learn that a Duchess of Gloucester, when her husband became Governor-General of Australia, took her hairdresser to that country which possessed already an adequate number of hairdressers.

After the essay on chronology Boswell completed the *Life*, concluding with 38 pages bracketed 'because I am by no means satisfied that what I am going to add would have met with the concurrence of Mr. Malone', and preceded by 15 pages put together from Malone's notes, not subject to the same doubt. Both showed a regard, not now fashionable among biographers, for the moral reputation of their subject. Boswell felt satisfied that Malone

> has shown, by an examination of the legendary tales which have so long been current respecting Shakspeare's early years, that they are wholly groundless; and that the greatest genius which his country has produced, maintained, from his youth upwards, that respectability of character which unquestionably belonged to him in after life.

Mr. Malone's Historical Account of the Rise and Progress of the English Stage, and of the Economy and Usages of our Ancient

---

[6] Malone thought the play was written in 1601 and printed four years later. This is not now believed, but the identification with *All is True* is so thoroughly accepted that the new Oxford editors prefer and use that title.

Theatres, filling about half the third Prolegomena volume, surveyed an old disagreement with Steevens as to whether scenery was used on Shakespeare's stage; Malone believed it was not, Steevens had replied with instances of device, pulleys and trap-doors. Long quotations from opposing views below three or four lines of the essay across several double page openings created vintage editorial discourse. Steevens was quoted in the confidence that he had blundered; a distinction was made between two terms, scenery and machinery:

> I subjoin the sentiments of Mr. Steevens, who differs with me in opinion on this subject; observing only that in general the passages to which he alludes, prove only that our author's plays were not exhibited without the aid of *machinery*, which is not denied; and that not a single passage is quoted, which proves that a moveable painted scene was employed in any of his plays in his theatre.

Malone's argument shrivelled to a distinction, between moveable scenes and moveable painted scenes.

His essay ended with fascinating statistics of Shakespeare production in the 18th century and late 17th from which readers learned that between 1678 and 1759 Dryden's *All for Love* was performed instead of *Antony and Cleopatra*, and that D'Avenant's version of *Macbeth* held the stage for eight years after 1663. When Macklin revived *The Merchant of Venice* at Drury Lane in 1741 it had not been acted, Malone believed, in the previous hundred years. It is curious that while the editors struggled and argued their way towards an authentic text, many of the plays were acted only in altered versions; yet the publication of domestic editions had its immediate effect. 'From 1709, when Mr. Rowe published his edition of Shakspeare, the exhibition of his plays became much more frequent than before.'

This contrast between editorial combing of old literature for any small parallel to establish accuracy, and adaptation for current taste in the theatre, had a parallel in the argument about Shakespeare's 'learning' by which was always meant classical education, and Nature; it crossed the boundary between fact and taste. Another comparable inconsistency in that same realm affected the attitude of these collector-editors to old books. Some unknown, therefore rare, Elizabethan pamphlet was coveted for the off-chance of a curious phrase, a parallel with Shakespeare's usage – or so they all supposed, though one suspects no more than a collector's point was scored; and Steevens contemptuously rejected the Third and Fourth Folios, as textually useless. It surprises now, because two centuries later they are of course coveted by collectors, less for absolute rarity than a sense that these were among the early appearances and are therefore objects of veneration. 'As to the third and fourth impressions, (which include the seven rejected plays),' Steevens wrote, 'they are little better than waste paper, for they differ only from the preceding ones by a larger accumulation of errors.' Rowe had based his text on the 1684 Folio, as the most recent edition; for Steevens it was merely inaccurate, a poor affair, not yet attractive as an historic treasure. Reed, most enthusiastic of collectors, never troubled to own the Third or Fourth Folios.

*　*　*

Farmer of Emmanuel, respected by them all, had settled the problem of Shakespeare's learning by his essay first published in 1767, reprinted by Steevens in the second volume of Prolegomena, 1793, reappearing in the three long variorum editions.[7]

Much of the critical discussion in each new 18th-century edition hinged upon a concern as to Shakespeare's learning, and apologia for the lack of it, the latter always following one line of argument: his natural genius did not need to be modelled from example or rule of Greece and Rome. Johnson's development of this theme gave new strength and application to the argument, but he was not first in solving the problem of small Latin and less Greek by calling him poet of nature. Readers of the Prolegomena were enabled to understand both branches of this heritage which provided material for the fundamental debate.

Jonson's graceful poem in the 1623 Folio deserved better than to be remembered by one line which was often understood as derogatory, rather than by another line,

> Nature herself was proud of his designs.

Moreover Jonson expanded the notion in asserting with no hint of irony that Shakespeare's own qualities had pushed the classics out of fashion – not only Nature in him, Jonson added, but also his art.

Digges, in lines which appeared in the small volume of Shakespeare's Poems, 1640, reversed the order of the same two thoughts, putting art first:

> Next Nature only help'd him, for look thorough
> This whole book, thou shalt find he doth not borrow
> One phrase from Greeks, nor Latins imitate . . .

Another poet (anonymous) in the same volume referred to the loss of 'Nature's self' in Shakespeare's death.

---

[7] More recently it has been unsettled again, but the 18th century was satisfied.

Dryden, who well understood the other side of the argument, assuming the shade of Shakespeare's ghost, wrote four epigrammatic lines to similar effect:

> And if I drain'd no Greek or Latin store,
> 'Twas, that my own abundance gave me more:
> On foreign trade I needed not rely,
> Like fruitful Britain rich without supply.

Even more concisely, in a passage less admirable because it denigrates Fletcher and Jonson, comes the forceful comment that Shakespeare 'is that nature which they paint and draw'. The same is said now of Mozart, that his music was often nature itself rather than translation, that he possessed some direct connection to heaven.

These 17th-century instances were the editorial heritage. Rowe as first editor wrote lines which changed the emphasis, though probably by 'art' he meant classical example:

> In such an age immortal Shakespeare wrote,
> By no quaint rules nor hamp'ring criticks taught;
> With rough majestick force he mov'd the heart,
> And strength and nature made amends for art.

He was assuming that lack of 'art' or education needed the counterbalance of strength and nature. Earlier writers (Jonson included) had rather excused their own dependence upon example, compared with Shakespeare's self-sufficient genius.

A similar theme developed during the 18th century, of comparison between English natural instinct and French contrivance. Elizabeth Montagu's book, published in 1769, was called *An Essay on the Writings and Genius of Shakespear, compared with the Greek and French Dramatic Poets. With Some Remarks Upon the Misrepresentations of Mons. de Voltaire.* The argument crystallized, but long before that Young had written with similar emotion:

> To claim attention and the heart invade,
> Shakspeare but *wrote* the play th' Almighty *made.*
> Our neighbour's stage-art too bare-fac'd betrays,
> 'Tis great Corneille at every scene we praise;
> On Nature's surer aid Britannia calls,
> Nor think of Shakspeare till the curtain falls . . .

Shakespeare's inspiration from Nature, so far from needing apology, was summoned by Young to personify Britannia herself.

Thus was the concept accepted, a common background before Johnson began to compose his Preface. Each editor received it, as has been seen in an earlier chapter on their Prefaces. For Thomson,

> Is not wild Shakspeare thine and nature's best?

For Mallet,

> Great above rule, and imitating none;
> Rich without borrowing, Nature was his own.

For Akenside, Shakespeare

> Doth now, will ever, that experience yield,
> Which his own genius only could acquire.

The adverse comparisons, mentioned above in Dryden, also re-appeared. Collins wrote a long *Epistle to Sir Thomas Hanmer on his Edition of Shakspeare's Works*, including a gently poisonous coup-let on Jonson:

> Too nicely Jonson knew the critick's part;
> Nature in him was almost lost in art.

Nearer to recent company and current debate, Joseph Warton asked

> What are the lays of artful Addison,
> Coldly correct, to Shakspeare's warblings wild?

and to Gray he was 'Nature's darling'.

Just as the editorial endeavours towards textual accuracy pro-ceeded alongside free adaptation in the theatre, so this new accep-tance of Nature as perfection ran ahead of contemporary practice in those very poets who expressed it. Through the Augustan century a theoretic ideal of Nature gained ground, became dogmatic, until its expression – not suddenly but with conscious enlightenment – in *Lyrical Ballads* towards its close. In this realm there is good ground for suggesting that the steady appreciation of Nature above Learn-ing[8] in 18th-century Shakespeare criticism, and its critical accep-tance by the poets, opened an avenue to romantic poetry in England.

Farmer's essay on Shakespeare's Learning became a permanent presence in the serious editions from 1793 to 1821, and the half-neglected Bell Prolegomena of 1788 included a large part of that essay, which had first appeared by itself in 1767. He was the friend to them all, classics tutor at Emmanuel College, Cambridge since 1760 and elected Master in 1775; above the editorial passions of London but often residing there, with Reynolds a member of the Eumelean Club, with Reed of the Unincreasable Club, with Johnson of the Literary Club.

Richard Farmer, an able classicist but bored with those other aspects of his duties which involved theology and mathematics, felt at ease in all such reading as was never read and would have liked to

---

[8] or Art or Example

complete a whole Commentary on Shakespeare. A Leicester man, he announced a *History and Antiquities of the Town of Leicester* but never advanced far into that and returned the subscriptions. As a tutor, parents of pupils occasionally complained of his unpunctuality. He owed the pleasures of London life to an appointment in 1767 as one of the Preachers of the Chapel Royal, 'a situation', as Nichols put it, 'favourable to one now becoming a collector of books'. Even more favourable was that of *Proto-Bibliothecarius* in Cambridge, in general responsibility for the University Library, 11 years later. An untidy man, he might have become a bishop had not 'the delights of the pipe and the bottle' prevented that form of advancement. He also enjoyed the stage, and bishops were not then seen in theatres. Farmer was a lovable eccentric and by any modern standard a formidably learned man. Johnson, when Steevens undertook a new edition of his Shakespeare in 1770, appealed to Farmer for comment and advice. Nichols left an intimate account of him:

> Indolence and the love of ease were, indeed, the Doctor's chief characteristics; and to them, with the disappointment already mentioned,[9] may be attributed a want of attention to his external appearance, and to the usual forms of behaviour belonging to his station. In the company of strangers, the eccentricity of his appearance and of his manners made him sometimes be taken for a person half crazed. The Writer of this sketch saw him one morning at Canterbury, dressed in stockings of unbleached thread, brown breeches, and a wig not worth a shilling; and when a Brother Prebendary of his, remarkable for elegance of manners and propriety of dress, put him in mind that they were to attend on the Archbishop, Dr. Farmer replied, that it had totally escaped him; but he went home, and dressed himself like a Clergyman.

Farmer's pupils in Cambridge often borrowed money, which by convenient absence of mind was not returned.

Though Nichols called him 'the friend of order' his life lacked it, and the Shakespeare essay was his one completed achievement; but, as Warton wrote, by that 'an end is put for ever to the dispute concerning the Learning of Shakspeare'. Farmer in his Advertisement before the third edition described this subject as one 'which had for a long time pretty warmly divided the cricks upon *Shakspeare*'. In the Preface to the second edition he had expressed some satisfaction with his achievement:

> Upon the whole, I may consider myself as the *pioneer* of the *commentators:* I have removed a deal of *learned rubbish*, and pointed out to them *Shakspeare's* track in the ever-pleasing *paths of nature*.

---

[9] Long and unhappy love for the daughter of Sir Thomas Hatton

In that sense, and appearing two years after Johnson's edition, he provided the final poet-of-nature definition.

Farmer's magnum opus, occupying less than 90 pages of generous type-setting, set out to prove that Shakespeare used his sources in English translation. This may strike a 20th-century reader as less important than it seemed to critics and editors in the 18th century.

He laid out the examples.

In the third Act of *Antony and Cleopatra*, Octavius represents to his courtiers the imperial pomp of those illustrious lovers, and arrangement of their dominion.

> Unto her
> He gave the 'stablishment of Egypt, made her
> Of lower Syria, Cyprus, *Lydia*,
> Absolute queen.

Read *Libya*, says the critick *authoritatively*, as is plain from *Plutarch* . . .

So Johnson changed the text to Libya. Warburton was the authoritative critic. But Farmer looked up North's Plutarch, 1579, to find what Shakespeare saw:

'First of all he did establish Cleopatra queene of Aegypt, of Cyprus, of *Lydia*, and the lower Syria.'

He provided ample instances of this sort, enough to satisfy Warton and all comers. 'I could furnish you with many more instances, but these are as good as a thousand.' It is only surprising that such a lively argument waited for Farmer in the third quarter of the century to settle it.

His general conclusion about Shakespeare's equipment in the classics was less generous than that of the recent Oxford editors who recognize that a pupil who went some distance in the grammar school at Stratford emerged with knowledge which could now seem formidable. To Farmer it looked derisory. 'He remembered perhaps enough of his *school-boy* learning to put the *Hig, hag, hog*, into the mouth of Sir Hugh Evans.'

Farmer also ranged across a few less controversial matters of taste, dismissing from the canon *A Yorkshire Tragedy*, which could not have been written before 1604 because the incident which inspired it occurred then, as 'much too late for so mean a performance from the hand of Shakspeare'. Theobald had shown no such perception in his claims for *Double Falshood*, content to accept for that wretched play a date after 1611 when its source story was published. Farmer's detective work on *Double Falshood* focused upon one very minor point, the too recent pronunciation of *aspect*:

The word *aspect*, you perceive, is here accented on the *first* syllable, which, I am confident, in *any* sense of it, was never the case in the time of Shakspeare; though it may sometimes appear to be so, when we do not observe a preceding *elision*.

Edward Capell, described rather vaguely by Farmer as a 'very curious and intelligent gentleman, to whom the lovers of Shakspeare will some time or other owe great obligations', has his place in the essay. Denying that Shakespeare wrote *Edward the Third*,[10] he was grateful to Capell for perfecting his argument by revealing an English source for *Hamlet*:

> 'Dr Grey and Mr. Whalley assure us, that for *this* Shakspeare *must* have read *Saxo Grammaticus* in Latin, for no translation hath been made into any modern language. But the truth is, he did not take it from *Saxo* at all; a novel called *The Historie of Hamblet*, was his original: a fragment of which in *black letter*, I have been favoured with by a very curious and intelligent gentleman . . .'

No part of the apparatus surrounding these editions looks now more peculiar than this restless debate about Shakespeare's acquaintance with Latin and Greek, settled after 150 years by Farmer's essay which everyone accepted as the last word. Only Pope among earlier editors had taken the commonsense view that it really didn't matter. They wanted some heavy counterbalance to his peculiarity, to the puns, coarseness, irreverence. If he knew no better but could then be seen as poet of nature, natural genius, in direct touch with the gods, a way of acceptance was opened without more need of excuse.

---

[10] 'I have no doubt but *Henry the Sixth* had the same author with *Edward the Third*, which hath been recovered to the world in Mr. Capell's *Prolusions*.'

6   Illustration

All original 18th-century editions of the plays except Rowe's and Hanmer's appeared first without illustration. They often had portraits, as the volumes multiplied accumulating plans of the Globe, engravings of Shakespeare's house, facsimiles of his signature, but no attempt to illustrate scenes from the plays was thought appropriate for Pope, Theobald (1733), Warburton, Johnson or the successive editions from Steevens, Capell, Malone.

Every illustrated edition from that time has some charm now, size and illustration ranging from diminutive to colossal. Through those decades one passes from French and Dutch influence in engraving to Boydell's patronage of English historical art as a turn away from portrait painting. Towards the end of the century another stream entered with the publication of Grainger's *Biographical History of England*, 1769, based on Ames's catalogue of portrait heads. It became fashionable to remove portrait engravings from published books to 'extra-illustrate' Grainger's *History* and many other books, a practice taken to absurd lengths. Picture research for publishers in the late 20th century means asking libraries or galleries to provide photographs; in the late 18th century the need was supplied by booksellers from published work.

This makes for confusion if one wants to know the published state of a Shakespeare edition, when binders and booksellers constructed sets swollen by engravings which had no business to be there, a nuisance compounded by the issue of plates without text for plundering in this way. The practice did not start with Grainger's *History*. The bibliographer, Jaggard, must have seen a set of Theobald's first edition with plates from the second. Engravings for both Bell editions are likely to turn up anywhere else, and Boydell's large (not his largest) series, published separately without text in 1805, was

ILLUSTRATION   199

snapped up by Stockdale to illustrate Bensley's text. Just as editorial notes and prefaces suffered no copyright restriction, the published work of artists and engravers was sold for general distribution. It is therefore difficult to collate, declaring one version perfect and another incomplete. There is enough evidence to suggest that in the late 18th century the publishers offered sets extra-illustrated, fully and partially illustrated, or without illustration.

A more interesting point is what they chose to interpret. Static emotion seldom transfers satisfactorily to literal art. In a different subject, nothing has been more thoroughly and foolishly illustrated through the last hundred years than Elizabeth Barrett's love poems to Robert Browning, *Sonnets from the Portuguese;* nothing happened there, except his visits to her in Wimpole Street. The Shakespeare artists often chose scenes of action, rather than attempt a translation of emotional stress, and 'Once more unto the breach' was a simpler matter than 'To be or not to be'. It is fortunate that among these 18th-century editions one travels in a period of renaissance for English book illustration, through great charm to maximal splendour. From Tonson to Boydell the plays and poems were interpreted with etchings and engravings of considerable merit.

Artists and print-makers seldom signed their names below the Shakespeare plates done for Tonson: Michael van der Gucht worked on Rowe's 1709 edition, Louis du Guernier re-engraved many of those designs and prepared 16 of his own for the Rowe duodecimos of 1714. Elisha Kirkall signed several of the 1714 designs, and others in both versions have been attributed to him. Print artists from the continent were finding work at that time in England. Fourdrinier was engaged by Tonson to re-make similar illustrations for Pope's 1728 octavo edition. A note by Boase in his Warburg Institute article, saying that Pope's edition of 1736 was the first to be illustrated, is perhaps explained by the tiresome habit among booksellers then, and later, of selling some sets with plates and others without, and of stripping the engravings from one set to adorn another. Fourdrinier, engraving again the designs from 1714, page-numbered them for binding where they belonged in Pope's edition; and as they appear also (wrongly page-numbered) in Tonson's little 1734 set, printed for sale in the theatres, they could not have appeared first in 1736.

For 35 years, from Rowe to Hanmer, most of the original designs commissioned for Rowe's first edition held their place. It was a remarkable achievement for Tonson who conceived an illustrated Shakespeare for the first time.

These were not eminent artists but they produced varied and delightful work which makes it still a pleasure to handle their books. Critical attention has focused on evidence they provide of contemporary production or scene or dress in the theatre, but simply as book decoration they were often excellent. The style varies, leaving no doubt that several hands were responsible; beyond that, taste and sense are free to choose but I do not detect the improvement Merchant mentions, as the first Rowe edition advanced, finding rather that comedies received better treatment than histories or tragedies. I may be expressing preference for pastoral above neo-classical stance and architectural background, and viewed thus none of the six volumes from 1709 is so successful as the first, no engraving more remarkable than that for *The Tempest* which began it.[1]

As to technique, the anonymous 1709 plates show heavier use of engraving, compared with their re-making five years later by Du Guernier who often chose to etch and so gave his figures and drapery the freedom of a lighter line. Du Guernier had come to England in 1712 as assistant to Nicholas Dorigny in engraving the Raphael cartoons; he must have set to work at once on the duo-decimo Shakespeare plays, sometimes without understanding the job very well. Steevens observed a detail, that when the ghost of Banquo following the line of Kings held up a *glass* to reflect their future heritage, the French artist showed him holding a small wine glass. The 1709 *Merry Wives of Windsor* has a delightful plate of the comic duel arranged between Ford and Slender, against a pastoral background of the slopes towards Windsor; Du Guernier changed this to an elegant young Falstaff stepping into the laundry basket, under guidance from two pretty girls (Mistress Ford and Mistress Quickly). *Cymbeline* in 1709 is illustrated with the sinister moment when Iachimo, climbing from his chest in Imogen's bedroom, was about to observe the mole on her breast as she slept. Du Guernier, missing that point, chose to show a solicitous and rather charming Iachimo approaching like a family doctor to feel the pulse of languishing but wakeful Imogen, her bosom well covered by bed-clothes, who looks relieved by his presence however unusual the means of transport by which he came. That may have puzzled Du Guernier, for we only see half the back of the open-lidded chest.

More surprising than faults of literal detail is the commonly undramatic illustration of drama in both editions. Limited to one frontispiece for each play, the choice of subject is often surprising. *The Merchant of Venice* has a court of law which displays perhaps some historical interest but fails to convey the least hint of tension: Shylock's knife is displayed to the two well-dressed young men with

---

[1] Shakespeare's medallion portrait engraved by Van der Gucht, with its derivative baroque surround, appears opposite the title page of each volume

ILLUSTRATION   201

their proffered money-bag, as an exhibit not a threat. A little more excitement was managed in 1714.

An elderly Juliet's dagger at her breast in the tomb, 1709, became more attractive with better figure drawing and grouping five years later but it was not the memorable moment we would now choose as characterizing that play. *Much Ado* was surely illustrated in 1709 by the artist of *The Merchant,* but in that merry play he chose to engrave Hero fainting when she is publicly denounced by Claudio, a stiff and formal composition; Du Guernier treated the same scene quite differently, a good instance of his light figure-etching but unhelpful as a guide to the piece. Hamlet with his mother has been quoted in such details as the kicked-over chair (1709), a piece of business for which Betterton was remembered, not repeated in 1714, but both were poor interpretations of tension. Feste in a room with straw like a pigeon's nest gives little notion of Shakespeare's play, where Toby and Andrew watching Malvolio would have been a characteristic and entertaining subject. When high moments were attempted those artists and engravers generally failed to produce anything better than formal compositions in neo-classical or modern dress, which may or may not offer evidence of performance but make dull viewing as book illustration now. Hermione coming to life in *The Winter's Tale* looks like an apprentice conductor of classical dance; strange to have chosen this scene, almost impossible to act or illustrate, rather than Autolycus and Perdita or, if drama were wanted, the jealousy of Leontes. Isabella's tears as she pleaded for her brother's life in *Measure for Measure* present a scene of ludicrous formality, greatly improved by Du Guernier's lightly etched grouping of the same scene in 1714, though he made Angelo into such a romantic young figure that one imagines a different event from Shakespeare's.

If these were the semi-failures they are balanced by delightful successes. Parolles, blindfold, the victim of a trick, begging for his life in *All's Well that Ends Well,* shows surprisingly the most amusing moment in that play and conveys enjoyment. Copied reversed and de-fused in 1714 it was still an adequate plate. Rare and welcome excursions towards comedy include Doll Tearsheet on the lap of an expressive Falstaff in 1709, too fugitive to repeat successfully in the duodecimo.

It would be wrong to declare that the engravings in these Rowe editions lacked drama. Elisha Kirkall managed it with Cleopatra and the asp in 1714, making her less ethereal in a more enclosed space than the earlier artist had shown. Volumnia pleads with understandable effect to Coriolanus in both editions; again the light etching of Du Guernier's group was effective. Timon in the forest with gold looks truly mad, as the prostitutes enjoyed their transparently silly promises.

These are arguments of drama, but pastoral or nature was the crowning pleasure of the frontispieces in 1709. None was finer than the stormy sea, black sky, hobgoblins, wild lightning and half-crazed seamen of *The Tempest*, admirable in composition and engraving, better expressing the text than any stage production I recall and no doubt beyond imitation; Du Guernier provided a competent flat elderly unromantic grouping in which the dim background couple are Ferdinand and Miranda at chess. 'Look at the young people, idling when they should be busy,' Prospero seems to say.

For pure pastoral *As You Like It* and *The Two Gentlemen of Verona* have much charm as indeed they should in both versions; Falstaff on Gadshill, an amusing success in 1709 and grey failure in the later copy, was shown in a strong night-time leafy scene; the 1709 storm in *Lear* has a powerful country setting equal to the staging of that episode, and a wild sky which demonstrates that the engraver of *The Tempest* frontispiece was responsible. Du Guernier, adding the Fool as every observer has pointed out, was not able to create a storm.

The anonymous, mannered and very charming engraving for *Venus and Adonis* in Gildon's additional volume of 1710 was changed but not improved by Michael van der Gucht in the ninth volume, 1714, where he also created a good rhythmic plate for a seductive Lucrece whose face looks rather more distracted than terrified by the prospect of rape.

Tonson provided in 1709 a series of illustrations interesting historically or attractive artistically, often both, never negligible; with their help he exchanged uncompromising folios for small books of charm and visual merit. Every play became more approachable through their presence, and such engravings as illustrate *The Tempest* or *The Two Gentlemen of Verona* remain memorable by comparison with any publication of their day.

Du Guernier and his associates seldom brought improvement by their reductions and alterations for the smaller format, though a lighter style of etching for groups of foreground figures was used effectively. Fourdrinier, last and least of them, copied or re-worked most of the plates for Pope's octavo edition of 1728 and Tonson used these again for the plays separately issued in 1734, not troubling to change volume and page numbers below, which referred to Pope. After a careful look it is difficult to decide whether Fourdrinier re-worked *all* the plates, putting his name below those which engaged him most, or left some alone and closely copied others. He produced no new composition. Assuming none had been lost, it appears prob-

ILLUSTRATION   203

able that he was responsible for re-working them all, as many were lightly etched and worn. The imitation is too exact to suggest fresh plates; in the vague days of copyright it was generous to let him sign his name below for hack work.

*   *   *

Theobald's first edition was only illustrated by a portrait but the smaller eight-volume edition of 1740 had a notable series of etchings by or after Gravelot. These were delicate in the style of French books at that time as one would expect, not always suited to Shakespeare and generally unequal to tragic climax. They changed Tonson's humble production into a work of some elegance.

Gravelot's manner appeared in all the books illustrated by him, whether his hand or another etched the plates. Tonson produced two volumes of *Gay's Fables* in 1737 and 1738; the second volume had charming illustrations after Gravelot, faithfully in his style. In the Shakespeares two years later he etched many of his own designs, but others done by Gerard van der Gucht are indistinguishable in manner. Gerard, eldest son of Michael van der Gucht (who had worked for Tonson since the beginning of the century), was father of more than 30 children by the same wife;[2] one of them, Benjamin, is remembered as a fashionable print seller at the end of the 18th century. Gravelot had come to England in 1732 to work upon engravings for the new edition of a major work, Picart's *Cérémonies Religieuses*, and stayed 13 years, time enough to leave his mark upon the Shakespeare scene by illustrating Theobald's edition and taking an important share of responsibility for Hanmer's.

His strength lay in lightness but he achieved some success in tragic scenes. Caesar's murder in 1740 was an improvement upon the undramatic revelation of his corpse in 1709. Juliet in the tomb was chosen again, puzzled as she wakes beside Romeo dead. A credible Othello murders Desdemona in a composition which balanced his black face with a tall sinister twisty candelabra at her bed head. More often his light treatment was unequal to the tension: 'By heaven I'll make a ghost of him that lets me' showed a man in armour politely conducting a few argumentative visitors round the castle at Elsinore; Lear is any old fellow dying peacefully in his chair surrounded by friends; Timon burying gold looks like an elderly gardener employed by Apemantus who suggests that shrub might thrive better in another place; hand-chopping in *Titus Andronicus* appears to be a

---

[2] My source is not the *Guinness Book of Records* but Lionel Cust in the *Dictionary of National Biography*

routine affair; Macbeth rises with pleasure to greet Banquo to his feast while Lady Macbeth seems distressed that he should accept so ill-dressed a visitor at her table.

In the elegance of happier episodes Gravelot's art was most at ease. Instead of Hero's collapse in a scene which never approached tragedy, *Much Ado* is illustrated by Benedict smiling to himself as he urges Claudio to read the epitaph on her supposed tomb – not the natural choice but nearer the spirit of that play. Portia's Moroccan visitor reading his message from the casket as she and Nerissa watch from behind suited Gravelot well, a great improvement over the trial scenes in Rowe; the old shepherd finding Perdita is a good composition in itself, as her ship sinks, far better than the 1709 attempt to express Hermione returning to life. Hubert resolving to save Arthur's eyes was a fine moment to choose for the frontispiece to *King John;* in *Henry the Fifth* Gravelot failed to convey such characterization as was needed for his choice of deathbed scene with prince and King and the crown.

On the whole Gravelot's series was a triumph for his time, reaching further than mere elegance and showing a wiser choice of scene, as it now seems, to illustrate, though the etching never achieved those wonderful effects of pastoral foliage and sky found in Rowe. The simplest approach suited him well, as in *Troilus* where we see two blissful lovers, nothing more ambitious, in front of Pandarus; and it is not surprising to find him well at home in *The Tempest,* where Ferdinand lightly enjoys his stint of shifting a few tree trunks, delighted by Miranda's concern for him and watched by Prospero from the shadows. This design, recalling Watteau, was in maximal contrast to the storm fantasy of 1709.

*　　*　　*

In 1838 Sir Henry Bunbury, a descendant, published the correspondence and memoir of Sir Thomas Hanmer. Only a small part of that book is relevant to the 1744 Shakespeare, but Bunbury owned and quoted from the formal agreement by which Hanmer commissioned a series of illustrations. It is an interesting document, especially the first clause, leaving no doubt as to who was in command:

> 1st. The said Francis Hayman is to design and delineate a drawing to be prefix'd to each play of Shakespeare, taking the subject of such scenes as the said Sir Thomas Hanmer shall direct; and that he shall finish the same with Indian ink in such manner as shall be fit for an engraver to work after them, and approved by the said Sir Thomas Hanmer.

If Hayman had lived at the end of the century he would have been a

ILLUSTRATION 205

prominent contributor to Boydell's *Shakespeare Gallery*, as a pioneer in English 'historical' art qualified by his years of scene-painting at Drury Lane. This experience made theatrical sense of the 1744 designs which he shared with Gravelot. As several of the history plays were illustrated by Gravelot without his help, explained perhaps by Hanmer's strict deadline after which Hayman 'shall not be entitled to receive any payment or consideration whatsoever for any part of the said work', and those Gravelot plates are in no way inferior to the others, it is difficult to assess Hayman's particular qualities in this work. His original drawings survive and have of course been the subject of study. Viewing them as translated by Gravelot one is led to suggest that the artist, who understood Shakespeare better than any immigrant French engraver, and had worked in the theatre, excelled in facial expression. This and the size of the plates, the first set of quarto illustrations to Shakespeare, and Hanmer's perception of the right scene to choose, distinguished them above others until Boydell's visionary scheme stole the show.

The choice of subject was more literate and better understood than before. Instead of Hermione in the final act, at last in *The Winter's Tale* we have Perdita and Florizel as their idyll is interrupted by Polixenes and Camillo, a delightful etching which suited the skills of both artists. In *Julius Caesar*, rather than view his corpse we see the poignant moment when Brutus quarrels with Cassius, under strain before revealing that Portia is dead. Cleopatra's wretched asp is chosen again, but in *Titus Andronicus* the one human opportunity is seized, Aaron ready to fight for the life of his infant. Cressida delivered over to Diomedes was a better moment than others chosen before, but fails as illustration. *Romeo and Juliet* is represented by the corpse of Paris, as Romeo discovers Juliet's tomb, far from obvious in scene or interpretation but carefully plotted and needing attention as a poem does. Hamlet, squatting beside a melancholy slim Ophelia, watches as Claudius rises frighted with false fire; behind, a pleasant young man empties his bottle into the ear of the player King who dozes in his chair, while musicians play from the gallery above. If this 18th-century scene looks at first far from our notion of *Hamlet* or the play within it, tension is there if one stops to look, and this of all subjects, with curtain above, must derive straight from a production on stage. Hayman's figures and Hanmer's subjects come through, though Gravelot filtered each scene into elegant French. Eighteenth-century dress in these illustrated editions was as natural as modern spelling of the text.

As Tonson brought Shakespeare into the library, so Hayman and Gravelot domesticated him. 'Ladies, or fair Ladies,' they seem to say with Bottom, 'I would wish you, or I would request you, not to fear, not to tremble.' Within that scope there are scaled-down successes, even among the tragedies. Othello looks like a footman politely requesting that Desdemona wait a moment, and then one notices his thick black left fist clenched and about to strike her. Hayman's four people in *Lear* are perhaps more understandable than before or since: on the heath again, the old King upright and powerful, bare-headed, intellectual; the Fool bent, sheltering against his gown like a beaten dog; 'poor Tom' a crazy youth outside his cottage, Kent alone sane and therefore bewildered. The stormy sky was more than Gravelot could manage.

Hanmer's fine understanding of the plays raised the intelligence of most illustrations to his edition. If evidence for this is too easy in the comedies one might turn to Shakespeare's most tedious plays, all three parts of *Henry the Sixth*. Joan of Arc appeared without distinction in 1709, but Hanmer chose more wisely the plucking of a white rose and a red, start of all the trouble,

> Now by this maiden blossom in my hand,
> I scorn thee and thy faction, peevish boy.

– for a charming plate drawn and etched, as were all these three, by Gravelot. The death of Beaufort in Part Two is no better than adequate, but it opened a succession of attempts to record that scene. Part Three again shows excellent perception in this impoverished text, by choosing a tableau of the 'Son bearing his Father' and 'Father bearing his Son', abstract and brief chronicles of war, appropriate for Gravelot's formal art.

It is very strange that in *Henry the Eighth* we still see nothing of Catherine, whose presence and action alone (plus one set piece from Wolsey) make that play worth reading.

The comedies provided predictably excellent designs, from which one must take as obvious example Bottom's entry as an ass on two legs, 'Why do they run away? this is a knavery of them to make me afeard'; a charming group with expressive faces, before the pastoral and Athenian distance. *As You Like It*, in similar vein, shows a focal action but not the most prominent one, Charles the wrestler laid flat by a slim and puzzled Orlando. *The Taming of the Shrew* had been illustrated previously by the supper episode, Petruchio rejecting food as inadequate for his hungry bride; but Hanmer brought charm without losing truth, by showing their arrival before that event, on bony horses, a perfect composition.

The reputation of this Oxford Shakespeare in both editions as a handsome work was partly due to large format, rather little owing to its typography, but much on account of the frontispieces which displayed a fine combination of art, skill and intelligence. If Hanmer's

ILLUSTRATION   207

text troubles those who know Shakespeare intimately, his illustrations deserve attentive understanding.

*   *   *

Warburton, Johnson and the successive editions called Johnson and Steevens, Reed, Capell, Malone all appeared with no illustration except for the Prolegomena; after Hanmer no new set of Shakespeare illustrations was made for 30 years.

In the last quarter of the 18th century a sudden cascade of small engravings, often attractive artistically and precious as stage history, decorated several popular editions, in contrast to Boydell's great venture of the 1790s. John Bell began it. The *Dictionary of National Biography* has a condescending note about him as 'the pioneer of that kind of publication so much in vogue in later days, by which the multitude is taught to feel an interest in the best literature by means of prints and illustrations executed by good artists'. His nine-volume Shakespeare, 1773–4, was an early work; Bell's edition of the British Poets, 1782, in 109 small slim volumes, established his reputation.

One can understand the success of the nine-volume publication, however faithless its text. Though Bowdler was then in his nursery, these censored theatre versions were the first family Shakespeare, each play illustrated with an engraving; portraits of Shakespeare and Garrick face the title and dedication. It becomes difficult to sort out the several series of illustrations issued by Bell after 1774, but these for his first edition remain coherent. Edward Edwards designed most of them, ably and with some originality. Hamlet handles Yorick's skull, instead of quarrelling with his mother or following his father's ghost; in *The Tempest* we see Stephano Trinculo and Caliban, not Prospero or Ferdinand and Miranda; *Henry the Fifth* is represented by a comic scene with Fluellen, rather than the King roaming through his army's tents at night. *Midsummer Night's Dream* has Bottom as an ass, as one would expect of any popular production, and a charming plate for *Love's Labour's Lost* shows Biron exposed as a sonneteer. *Taming of the Shrew* portrays the secondary comedy of Bianca learning music and love from Lucentio; for *Romeo and Juliet* a strange scene was chosen, 'I sell thee poison thou hast sold me none', as Romeo buys his lethal dose from the apothecary. One of the best engravings comes in volume nine, the Poems, where Lucrece is ignored in favour of some pastoral lament to illustrate two lines from *A Lover's Complaint.*

After this, the deluge. Plates from Bell's 1773–4 volumes were issued separately, evidence of their popularity, and used as additional illustration for later texts. A set of engravings dated 1776 offered another innovation, showing particular actors in Shakespearean parts, 'Publish'd for Bells Edition of Shakespeare' though no new edition came from him until nine years later; so these too must have been intended as extra-illustration for the existing nine volumes, binders no doubt using them thus, especially in large-paper sets for which 134 subscriptions were received. These excellent plates were portraits of moments in performance, framed above the spoken line. Always in modern dress, they have the look of accuracy: 'Mr Baddeley in the Character of Trinculo', melancholy and expressive; 'Mrs Yates in the Character of Isabella', passionate and eloquent without quoted lines; 'Mrs Barry in the Character of Constance' (*King John*), as if in a storm at sea, one arm stretched out and ripping off her headdress with the right hand,

> I will not keep this form upon my head,
> When there is such disorder in my wit.

None of the book illustrations before this series had offered such close report of stage performance, and the scenes from 1773–4 were faithfully done. As had been shown long before by Aldus, and in the Elzevir series, cheap need not mean nasty. Bell hoped to emulate the French engravers in his books, or rise to their standard, writing in the Advertisement of 1773:

> When it is considered that the Artists of this Kingdom, seldom or never have been employed in Miniature Engraving, beyond the scanty Encouragement of a Sixpenny Magazine, it need not be wondered that the French, at present, boast so much of their superior Excellence in this delicate Art.

He intended to redress the balance:

> If he should by any Means fail, in his future attempts, he still will have the Satisfaction of having evinced that this Species of Art, by proper Encouragement, may soon be brought to as great Perfection in this, as in any other Country.

This species of art was well served by Bell's edition in 20 volumes, 1786–8, a pioneer of popularization to high standards of text, type and engraving. 'He took great pains over its copper-plates and letterpress,' Stanley Morison wrote in his book on Bell, which relates in some detail the printing of the Shakespeare. Bell's researches into type took him to Paris, where he engaged several artists to help with illustration under the general guidance of Bartolozzi.

But the two most active artists for this scheme were German by birth, Philip James De Loutherbourgh and Johann Heinrich Ramberg, both successful in their contrasting careers. Ramberg, coming to England at the age of 18 from Hanover where his father held high

ILLUSTRATION   209

government office, exhibited at the Academy the following year (1782). After making a reputation with portraits and scenes from history he returned to Hanover in 1792 to become painter to the electoral court. De Loutherbourgh, remembered now for topographical paintings and several charming books with aquatint illustrations, had served under Garrick as scene designer at Drury Lane. Both were very well suited to work for Bell's Shakespeare, one from his skill in portraits and the other through intimate knowledge of stage production.

The general plan was to have one 'vignette' and one actor-portrait for each play, and it worked very well. Drawn by De Loutherbourgh and engraved by Bartolozzi, as most of the vignettes were, with such excellent variants as Moreau le Jeune and Hamilton, the result was a fine mixture of elegance with truth. Each scene, circular with ornament above, rests on a pediment where the relevant quotation serves for caption. Ramberg's portraits in ovals, opposite, identified actors in their roles ('Miss Farron in the Character of Hermia') above lines they were speaking.

This admirable scheme was not always carried out scrupulously by binders, who could behave rather casually so long as 20 elegant volumes in calf with coloured title labels adorned the bookshelf; indifferent to the position of notes and text, sometimes misplacing the engravings, or adding to them, or leaving out vignettes which might have been used as extra-illustration for another set. One result of such comparison shows two different subjects engraved as vignettes for *Lear* and for *Timon*, and two alternative actor-portraits for *Richard the Third, Cymbeline* and *Othello*. Bell was prolific in his organization.

The subjects illustrated included a handsome stipple of the young Prince of Wales by Burk after Cosway – and 'Mr. Lewin in the Prince of Wales', *Henry IV Part I*, looking amusingly Hanoverian; several Shakespeare portraits, and others showing most of the 18th century editors; such curious details as 'Specimens of Fans' appropriate for *The Merry Wives of Windsor*, and a folding plate of Morris Dancers from a window in Stratford, to assist in understanding *Henry IV Part 2*.

A few of the figures strike strangely now: *Henry the Eighth* was represented by 'Mrs. Barnes in Anne Bullen' – still no thought for Catherine; Romeo and Juliet were once again in their tomb; 'Mrs. Wells in the Character of Lavinia' could lead anyone to think of *Titus Andronicus* as pastoral comedy; but generally the portraits and roundels provide a survey of theatre Shakespeare of the 1780s in delightful engravings. As lively acting portraits one might look at such instances as 'Mrs. Siddons in Lady Macbeth', Mrs. Siddons with passions in full flow as Isabella in *Measure for Measure*, the virtuous pose of 'Mrs. Warren in the Character of Helena', explaining in *All's Well that Ends Well*

> You must know
> I am supposed dead,

an admirably villainous Macklin as Shylock and charming 'Mr Edwin in Autolicus'. Other examples of equal merit could be given; the vignettes are not less enchanting than the portraits. Stage, text, editors and printers were brought together by Bell's taste and energy in a remarkable publication which seems to receive less recognition from modern critics than it deserves. Apart from the qualities of production in small format, this should have its place among mainstream variorum editions.

The eight octavo volumes published by Bellamy and Robarts in 1791 imitated Bell's in its scheme of illustration, but not in editorial equipment. As in both Bell issues, talented young artists were engaged. The Bellamy and Robarts edition has much interest as advancing into a romantic gothic manner which reappears on a different scale in Boydell. These engravings interpreted the text by decorative imagination or allegorical fantasy rather than local habitation and a name. Oval illustrations within gothic arches halfway to ruin from untamed foliage create a different atmosphere from Bell's near-classical vignettes; they became, perhaps for the first time, book illustration and not actual or imagined stage reproduction.

Two allegories in the same scheme of design begin each volume, a generous innovation again observed by Boydell, having such titles as 'The Comic Muse Surrounded by the Visions of Fancy', 'Youth Attending the Dictates of Shakspeare', and 'Fairies Adorning Shakspeare's Grave'. The publishers chose young artists (not yet expensive) or students who had just begun to exhibit at the Academy, such as Henry James Richter who had shown two landscapes there in 1788 when he was only 16 years old. A few months after that, Richter must have been working on these allegorical and dramatic ovals for Bellamy and Robarts. Richter in his maturity became 'a student of metaphysical philosophy, a devoted disciple of Kant, and an intimate friend of William Blake'.[3] Another active contributor was Charles Reuben Ryley, of less robust constitution, who won an Academy gold medal in his twenties for a painting of 'Orestes on the point of being sacrificed by Iphigenia'. Such minor but excellent artists pooled their styles to illustrate this half-forgotten edition of Shakespeare.

Occasionally their treatment looks silly now, as when Richter

---

[3] Lionel Cust in the *Dictionary of National Biography*

ILLUSTRATION   211

represented *Twelfth Night* by an all-too-literal Patience sitting on her monument, smiling at grief in the form of a funeral urn. Allegory may be out of taste, but the compositions are delightful: 'An Infant Shakespeare in the Realms of Fancy' is shown by Ryley as some well-groomed child danced by a bride along avenues of classical sculpture; Richard Corbould, another prolific illustrator, made light work of 'The Comic Muse Dictating to Shakspeare, and Fancy Strewing Flowers over his Productions'; 'Shakspeare Holding up the Mirror to Dignified Guilt' was a more complex matter for Richter to express. He was, after all, the son of a Prussian artist, engraver, scagliolist.

These allegories led into more romantic scenes from the plays than had been attempted before. The young princes, sleeping before their murder in the Tower, look like sepulchral marble angels by Landseer; Ophelia climbs into her willow aslant the brook; at last we view Romeo below the balcony of a living Juliet, instead of both together in their tomb.

And there were several very palpable hits, in the freer flow of imagination. Corbould conveyed a farcical gaiety for the mock-trial when Falstaff changed roles with the Prince; and we see with pleasure the poetic moment when Jessica and Lorenzo at Belmont discuss the nature of music,

> In such a night as this,
> When the sweet wind did gently kiss the trees,
> And they did make no noise.

The several Bell Shakespeares revealed a taste for prolific small illustration, ranging from allegory to portrait; in Bellamy and Robarts it was more gothic and romantic. At the turn of the century Harding's edition again showed a bias towards book illustration, away from theatre portraits, often using stipple as suitable for fantasy. Stothard's design as frontispiece to *The Tempest*, for instance, shows Ariel's ability 'to ride / On the curl'd clouds', far above the devices of a producer. It was a period of large plates influenced by the Boydell Gallery and a proliferation of such minor works as in these ten volumes of Harding's Shakespeare.

'Accurately Printed from the Text of Mr. Steevens's Last Edition' by Bensley, called 'Harding's Edition' on the title page of each play, it was an attractive production. Harding chose the text of Steevens rather than Malone's, though both were in circulation during the 1790s. The plays are dated 1798, the general title 1800. Among his artists was Stothard, equally in demand for large-scale work, and Thurston who found Shakespeare a useful source of commissions over the next decades.

These and others established a Shakespeare tradition of decorative book illustration in which the artist became free to invent from his experience of reading. After almost a century of pleasant small volumes, domestic Shakespeare veered away from stage appearance. If facial expression, especially in tragedy, still caused problems, a readiness to depart from realism offered some answer for the future. Gardiner's frontispiece of Lear in the storm shows it, not too distant from Fuseli and Blake. 'When the rain came to wet me once, and the wind to make me chatter; when the thunder would not peace at my bidding; there I found them, there I smelt them out.' Thurston's interpretation of Richard III's dream before battle, in similar style, for that reason improved upon earlier attempts at the same subject. Singleton, remembered like Stothard for both large-scale and small compositions, and Rivers contributed as minor artists delicate work to an edition which leads into the next century, when minor illustration became habitual.

This edition was published by Edward Harding who had previously worked in partnership with his brother Silvester. Both were talented engravers, competent artists; after 1803 Edward enjoyed a comfortable form of patronage as librarian to Queen Charlotte, living at Frogmore and later in Buckingham Palace. As they produced a mass of good small plates, useful in the current fad for extra-illustration, it is not surprising to learn that Edward 'became a great favourite with the queen, and "grangerised" many historical works for her amusement'.[4]

Their relevance here is that in 1793 the partnership produced a work called *Shakespeare illustrated by an assemblage of portraits and views appropriated to the whole series of that author's historical dramas. To which are added portraits of actors, editors, etc.* Its success was no doubt due to the high convenience of ripping out so many suitable engravings to grangerize the more earnest sets which stopped short at a portrait or two, a picture of the birthplace and facsimile of the poet's signature. Here suddenly was every imaginable person and scene to catch the flagging attention, even in special copies 'an additional plate of Jane Shore in low cut dress'. A variant version issued in the same year gave the show away by announcing the plates were arranged 'with directions for their insertion in any edition'. Booksellers loved it. I have the 1811 edition published for six guineas by Edward Jeffrey who added plates of places from his own store, relevant but unhelpful. A pretty colour-printed engraving of Florence, for example, is not likely to have

---

[4] Edward Harding also published several fine and famous folios, such as the edition of Dryden's Fables (1797) 'ornamented with engravings from the pencil of Lady Diana Beauclerc', which Bensley printed

ILLUSTRATION   213

eased anyone's journey through *All's Well that Ends Well*, but such was the nature of extra-illustration. The versatile brothers, Edward and Silvester Harding, and Silvester's son Edward who died very young, turn up as publishers, artists and engravers equally. The Duke of Aumerle's portrait, as an instance at random, 'from a Limning in the British Museum', was drawn by Silvester, engraved by Edward Junior and published by the partnership in 1793. Though so many potted biographies and histories are unlikely to gain attention now, and perhaps received little then, the notes on 18th-century editors and critics, with their portraits, still make this an attractive book.

A study of Victorian illustrated editions may provide the theme for another volume; it lies outside the scope of this chapter, but two or three examples from the early 19th century catch one's eye, each separated from the next by about 14 years and suggesting a line of development. Shakespeare's works 'from the text of Isaac Reed' were issued by Thomas Tegg in 12 octavo volumes from 1812–15, with a few sets on large paper, illustrated by engravings after designs by Thurston. They look like wood engravings, which Thurston as a follower of Bewick could well have managed. A volume of proofs on china paper, mounted on large paper, shows the fine character of such work, and the engraved title pages with charming vignettes are models of neo-classical taste as greater freedom of interpretation marked a move from the 18th century. Decorative lettering learned from the writing masters, Thurston's art with Tegg's eye for page design made flawless unity, and book illustration had taken leave of the theatre.

The first appearance of Singer's edition of Shakespeare, printed by Charles Whittingham at the Chiswick Press in 1826, had 'Sixty Engravings on Wood, by John Thompson; from Drawings by Stothard, Corbould, Harvey, etc'. This delightful publication in ten volumes, showing the work of another of Bewick's disciples, still came from the age of discretion in book design. Thompson's wood engravings give little evidence that he ever saw the plays in a theatre. Apart from thumbnail sketches here and there, the number rises to 60 by his homely 'Seven Ages of Man' series not printed in *As You Like It* but with Jaques's speech as part of the preliminary pages, following the 'Life of Shakespeare' by Charles Symmons. They are far from Smirke's treatment of that theme in the Shakespeare Gallery (and from Alken's updated version, hand-coloured lithographs published by McLean in 1824).

Charles Knight's 'Pictorial Edition' heralded the new age, his advertisement dated 18 May, 1839, printed in two columns on character-less paper, employing a crowd of draughtsmen and wood engravers; ably edited, like some early experiment towards the *Illustrated*

London News. This archetype of Victorian industry, many times reprinted, closed the door upon those old books with copper engravings from 1709 to Thomas Tegg.

*   *   *

It is difficult to begin to assess Boydell's colossal *Collection of Prints from Pictures Painted for the Purpose of Illustrating the Dramatic Works of Shakspeare, by the Artists of Great-Britain*, completed in 1805 and published in two volumes for the high price of 60 guineas. George Nicol had aired his dream 'to celebrate genius, or cultivate the fine Arts' during a memorable dinner at the Hampstead home of Josiah Boydell in 1787, but uncle and nephew[5] changed it as the scheme developed, their first purpose the creation of a great tradition of 'Historical Painting' in England where the focus had been upon portraits and sport and family scenes. Shakespeare became for the Boydells instrumental to their design, their main purpose the commissioning of historical painting by the best artists, their unifying theme to be episodes from Shakespeare's plays. All would be exhibited in a Shakespeare Gallery, its great expense recovered by the sale of glorious engravings from so much art; and a spin-off or by-product would be Nicol's first idea, the folio edition with Martin's types.

It happened, we have the printed result, yet by the misfortune of war Boydell's resources were not multiplied but greatly depleted, the paintings not presented to the nation but wretchedly sold off by lottery and auction; for he had relied upon the continental trade, until 'a Vandalick Revolution . . . which, in convulsing all Europe, has entirely extinguished except in this happy Island, all those who had the taste or the power to promote the fine Arts'.[6]

His monument is neither wealth nor ruin but this magnificent work. When I first visited the Humanities Research Center in Austin, Texas, the large prints were exhibited round four walls of a gallery; if most people associate Texas with size, these impressed as sympathetic to the place. Average dimensions of about 23 by 17 inches for almost all of a work extending to 100 plates impresses by immensity. From that inartistic approach one may rise through admiration for a brilliant group of engravers to some understanding of how the artists viewed Shakespeare. Leafing through this now, bound as a book which is best kept flat, interpretation of the plays

---

[5] John Boydell died in 1804, Josiah (who completed this great work) died in 1817
[6] From John Boydell's letter to Sir William Anderson 1804

ILLUSTRATION   215

takes second place to their dramatic excellence of concept and engraving within the immense scope provided.

The merit of these large-scale prints is very clear by comparison with others which illustrate the Boydell edition in nine 'atlas-folio' volumes, where an image measures upon average about ten and a half inches by six and a half – often after the same artists, sometimes repeating the same subject, almost always of less interest, darker, with less contrast, crowded. It is my experience that the large prints do not lose their quality of surprise; the smaller become book illustration, of a fairly undistinguished sort. For such great moments in a play, tragic or comic or in some way dramatic, as were naturally chosen by publisher and artists, the scope of vast copper-plates offered opportunities in which the engravers time and again rejoiced. A sight of original paintings which survive – in the museum of the Royal Shakespeare Theatre at Stratford for example – exposes this work as the triumph of that secondary group, engravers, rather than for the famous painters whom they interpreted. We are most fortunate to receive it thus: a decade or two later the medium would have been aquatint, or lithograph on poorish paper brown-spotted across one-and-a-half centuries. For strong definition on excellent paper at the summit of skill, their performance has our grateful applause.

As the ink chosen by Bulmer in book illustration generally transferred to the opposite page, and for it he used paper which browned unpredictably, the nine-volume edition with admirable types is a far less satisfactory story. His Milton illustrations in a comparable production are often no better. In several examples of the Shakespeare Gallery which have over the years been in my possession there was no evidence of such faults; the prints are on stronger paper and of ink undimmed across nearly two centuries.

Nicol's spark at that Hampstead dinner started a fire he could not have imagined – the outbreak of historical painting which Alderman Boydell created with even more enthusiasm than an edition of Shakespeare. Northcote's comments on this were recorded to the life by an artist friend, James Ward.[7] 'Ah! but it didn't answer!' he said. 'With the exception of a few pictures by Sir Joshua and Opie, and – I hope I may add – myself, it was such a collection of slip-slop imbecility as was dreadful to look at, and turned out, as I had expected it would, in the ruin of poor Boydell's affairs.' No doubt they were transformed by the process of engraving, which does not

[7] *Conversations of James Northcote R.A. with James Ward on Art and Artists,* 1901

lend itself to slip-slop imbecility; for among the great talents engaged by Boydell it turns out that each artist produced outstanding work, and one cannot assume the reputations which now stand highest were always responsible for the finest. Northcote himself went to town on the murder of the two young princes in *Richard the Third*, producing three paintings which were all reproduced in large engravings, and has an interesting comment on this:

> Painters should always try to tell their story well ... My *Murder of the Princes in the Tower* has never been mistaken for anything else; it was clearly the murder of two innocent children, and that was the essence of it.

That he sentimentalized the scene was neither here nor there, for him; his two angelic infants on whom heaven's light shone would never have spoken the pert and street-wise lines provided for them by Shakespeare. Historical painting was a false phrase, he thought. 'Now it ought to be called *poetical painting*, for its object is not to give information, but to make an impression, precisely the same as poetry does, only by different means.'

That may not have been the view of other artists, but it led away from theatre scenes, tempted further by the scale of painting and print. The splendid chiaroscuro effects in Middiman's engraving after the painting by Smirke and Farington, of Falstaff on Gadshill, the figures relatively small against a night scene of forest trees, is almost unconnected with stage production; paintings offered, of course, the chance to improve upon it.

The Gallery of paintings is beyond recall, its sculptured pediment of 'Shakspeare seated between the Dramatic Muse and the Genius of Painting' may be visited in the garden of Shakespeare's house at Stratford and the engraver's drawing for that, with a misquotation from Hamlet on the base, [*] is in my possession. The great book opens with Romney's allegory of a stolid little 'Infant Shakspeare attended by Nature and the Passions', and closes (almost) with a smaller engraving after Romney, of the poet 'Nursed by Tragedy and Comedy'. Between those two is the finest set of Shakespeare illustrations ever made. The phrase 'Shakespeare Gallery' will refer to this work which goes by that little, rather than to the collection of paintings which is irrecoverable.

Criticism of the large plates must be to some extent subjective, as one responds to the qualities of a print and another to the story explained. My own surprise, going through them all, has been in finding excellence fairly evenly distributed among the many artists. I

---

[*] In remarkably early sans-serif capitals it reads: 'A man. Take him for all in all we never shall look on his like again'.

ILLUSTRATION   217

cannot report the inevitable superiority of engravings after Fuseli, for instance, over others which interpret paintings by such minor artists as Smirke, Hamilton, Westall or even the younger Boydell himself who seems to have claimed some of the more popular scenes. Though Westall's imagination was not exciting, the print from his painting of Brutus and the Ghost of Caesar is among the most brilliant and immediate. Josiah Boydell's heartbroken Othello by Desdemona's bed offers for this scene a stronger representation than the earlier illustrators had managed, the large black Moor a credible figure stooping away from his sleeping wife on whom the light falls – more successful than the alternative plate which follows it, of the same moment, by Leney after another minor artist.

Thew's engraving after Hamilton achieves the impossible for *Winter's Tale*, in an acceptably stately statuesque Hermione coming to life. It is the simple fact of size that on such a scale classical stillness has space for drama. Hamilton's static Coriolanus with Volumnia and family pleading, in a superb engraving by Caldwell, succeeds by expressive gesture where all others before him had failed, because of the space available without crowding.

Reynolds, best paid and the biggest catch, excelled in this work once; his Death of Cardinal Beaufort in *Henry the Sixth*, engraved by Caroline Watson, became famous and popular. No doubt the subject chosen, not now especially memorable or moving, a wicked dying Cardinal refusing to show the King his penitence, was partly responsible. Caroline Watson performed with conspicuous brilliance. Reynolds's *Macbeth* scene of Banquo's ghostly succession, watched by the highlit witch looking like a dotty queen on her throne, fails to convey more than a muddled impression.

Fuseli, who illustrated scenes from Shakespeare for several publishers and contributed to six of the plays here, was happiest in fantasy. His Hamlet following the Ghost ('Still am I call'd. – unhand me, gentlemen') is not among the great engravings of this book; his contribution to *Lear*, the King dismissing Cordelia ('Thy truth then be thy dower') even in such ample space is too crowded a composition. Bottom with Titania, engraved by Simon, a freely sensuous idea recalling Blake's monoprint from *Macbeth* ('Pity like a naked new-born babe') rises far above the trivial fun, and his magnificent plate for *The Tempest*, again engraved by Simon, of Prospero addressing Caliban across a gulf both visual and moral, excels them all: Miranda, safe and stately in the protection of his command, looks back to an impotent but frightful monster, while Ariel whizzes through the sky like a falling angel and plant-life beside Prospero's foot takes the form of humanity damned. Fuseli created an island of magic, emblematic, halfway between heaven and hell, a composition perhaps more Miltonic than Shakespearean but the peak of illustration in this work. From it he descends, by way of Macbeth's witches, to Doll Tearsheet on Falstaff's lap in *Henry the Fourth*. One would like to have heard Fuseli, before his painting of Prospero: according to Northcote, who was against such talk, he 'used to palaver before his pictures . . . and did himself much harm by it'. Not an easy man, he 'has a manner with him that never appears to me like that of a gentleman, but more like that of a Swiss valet'. His style would be acceptable, palavering about *The Tempest*.

John Boydell's observation in the 1789 Prospectus was perhaps overcome in this painting by Fuseli – that Shakespeare 'possessed powers which no pencil can reach; for such was the force of his creative imagination, that though he frequently goes beyond nature, he still continues to be natural, and seems only to do that which nature would have done, had she o'erstep'd her usual limits – It must not, then, be expected, that the art of the Painter can ever equal the sublimity of our Poet'.

This touches any artist's difficulty in illustrating poetry which transcends mere narrative, but a delight of the Shakespeare Gallery – as of the plays – is in tragi-comedy, the crossing of borders between poetry, high tension and farce, demonstrated by Fuseli's passage from Prospero to Doll.

Most of this had little to do with any recollection of performance on stage. A wonderful night scene by Hodges shows Jessica and Lorenzo by the lake –

> Sit, Jessica: Look how the floor of heaven
> Is thick inlay'd with patines of bright gold

– a fine engraving in which the smallish poorish figures are best ignored; the scene, which belonged to no theatre, was more Shakespearean than actors' faces. Hodges had another admirable representation of darkness, of melancholy this time not ecstasy, Jaques by the brook, sharing his mood with an equally gloomy stag,

> Today my Lord of Amiens, and myself,
> Did steal behind him, as he lay along
> Under an oak, whose antique root peeps out
> Upon the brook that brawls along this wood.

It is a curiosity of illustration, compared with literature, that good seems to have presented less difficulty than evil. Milton's Satan makes better reading than his Abdiel, it is generally agreed, but the real malice of Fuseli's Caliban was a rare success among such pantomime-dame wickedness as, for instance, Northcote's Richard of Gloucester ushering his innocent little nephews to the Tower. It would be false to suggest overtones of sentiment, where strength of engraved

ILLUSTRATION 219

design prevails, yet one cannot always distinguish evil (Queen Margaret and the Duke of Suffolk in Hamilton's painting from *Henry the Sixth* could equally be Jessica and Lorenzo) from laughter (Wheatley's Petruchio travelling away with Kate could credibly illustrate a tragedy). Reynolds managed evil in Cardinal Beaufort.

The subject chosen for illustration seems occasionally inadequate, as in *Love's Labours' Lost,* a play which held little attraction for some 18th-century critics. Theobald's edition showed the entertaining scene when one after another the votaries of chastity are exposed as authors of love-sick sonnets; the Shakespeare Gallery makes do with only one engraving, a spiritless pastoral by Ryder after Hamilton, in which the Princess of France and her women learn where they are to hunt.

More surprising often is the distribution of engravings through the plays, whether comedy, history or tragedy. *Measure for Measure* is represented by a characteristic piece of whimsy from Smirke (Elbow and Froth before the Justice) and the Friar's self-revelation as spying Duke – nothing of Isabella or Claudio, who so captivated the 19th century; *Twelfth Night* has two subjects, *Richard the Second* two, *Henry the Fifth* only one as against three for the first part of *Henry the Sixth* and four for the third part. *Antony and Cleopatra* is rationed to one, by a forgotten painter, Henry Tresham, who also provided two for the text: inadequate in theme and treatment, an implausible Cleopatra fainting as Antony, muscular and unclothed, resolves to depart again for his duty and the wars. *Hamlet* has two subjects (Fuseli's mentioned above, and Benjamin West's mad Ophelia, too crowded with dull figures of the others, moderately successful in Ophelia herself) and *Othello* also has only two (Boydell's dramatic scene before Desdemona's death, and an unremarkable composition by Stothard of the two lovers in happier days). Such were the oddities of distribution: one questions whether the Boydells dictated it, for some consistency is detectable, where one after another the Roman plays received only a single large engraving – *Coriolanus, Caesar, Antony and Cleopatra, Timon, Titus* – in no way reflecting a play's general popularity.

Perhaps Boydell's taste gave the most generous allowance to *As You Like It*, with Smirke's 'Seven Ages' in addition to two excellent engravings including an amusingly romantic design by Downman of Orlando receiving Rosalind's 'chain' in Act One, framing the background withdrawal of a groggy Charles the Wrestler. Alken's later parody testifies to the popular success of Smirke's series.

Accepting a strange distribution and unexpected emphasis, as is natural after two centuries, it would be false to choose one artist above others in this vast enterprise; all produced surprising successes, and a measure of commonplace. Northcote leaned towards sentimental infants but achieved impressive drama for Juliet in the tomb; Hamilton and Westall, not the most distinguished painters, provided fine moments for Coriolanus and Caesar. Boydell's comment from his 1789 Prospectus remains true:

> I believe there never was a perfect Picture, in all the three great requisites of Composition, Colouring, and Design – It must not therefore be expected that such a phenomenon will be found here. – This much, however, I will venture to say, that in every Picture in the Gallery there is something to be praised . . .

Let us now praise those *less* famous men, and one woman, whose incomparable skill produced the Shakespeare Gallery we may still enjoy.

Viewing the 'small' engravings after these is like walking down after a wonderful day on the hills. Callot's art was best when smallest, Moreau le Jeune needed large margins and few inches; in the Shakespeare Gallery, size produced inspiration, sadly reduced in the different scope of Boydell's books. Though paper and wrong ink were partly responsible, these smaller prints in satisfactory state of survival remain inferior. A few statistics were given in the *Dictionary of National Biography* notice of John Boydell:

> In 1789 the Shakespeare Gallery contained thirty-four pictures, in 1791 sixty-five, in 1802 one hundred and sixty-two, of which eighty-four were of large size. The total number of works executed was 170, three of which were pieces of sculpture, and the artists employed were thirty-three painters and two sculptors, Thomas Banks and the Hon. Mrs. Damer.

So in 1802 about half the paintings were large, and half small, a point which had little to do with their large reproduction as engravings in the Shakespeare Gallery or, smaller, to illustrate Boydell's nine volumes. Most of them cannot now be traced, but the truth becomes apparent by examining both forms of publication; it is not clear from Boydell's heading to the list of Shakespeare Gallery plates: 'A List of the Large Plates to Illustrate the Shakspeare' – which seems to mean, the edition itself, not generally Shakespeare's plays; and three supplementary plates were 'not engraved from the large Pictures, but may be added to Vol.II'.

Now it is not impossible that some besotted bibliophile may have dismembered the edition, mounted every text leaf on huge paper and so produced a flamboyant set of library furniture, but that was never the publisher's purpose. Anyone who bought the set of large engravings to supplement his Boydell Shakespeare could have felt disappointed by the extent of duplication, for many of the text

ILLUSTRATION   221

illustrations had been reduced, sometimes by different engravers, from the same paintings. There was no simple division of large paintings for the large plates, small paintings to illustrate Boydell's nine volumes.

All this is worth hammering home, because Jaggard's bibliography quite wrongly describes the great volume of engravings as 'reprinted from Boydell's edition of Shakespeare's works, 1802'. Boase[8] was concerned with such paintings as survive, noting simply that in 1802 a 'folio edition of the poet's works appeared in nine volumes with 100 plates, and a Royal folio of plates only, with few exceptions different from those in the collected works, had also been published'. The true title of the large series was *A Collection of Prints from Pictures Painted for the Purpose of Illustrating the Dramatic Works of Shakspeare, by the Artists of Great-Britain* in both volumes (often bound together); both title pages were dated 1803, and both Dedications (to the King and the Queen) 1805. These two publishing enterprises followed their different courses; there is no suggestion that subscribers were expected to buy both, and I have never seen them together as one work. The collection of large plates is less commonly found.

Jaggard's 1802 entry probably refers to a separate issue of the text illustrations, bought on their merits by a few collectors or by binders and booksellers as suitable adornment for other editions. In its second issue, with different paper or more suitable ink, one is better able to judge this set of engravings, which emerge generally, by comparison with the major work, dim, crowded and static in the shadowy valley of average performance. Whether a painting is reproduced in the nine-volume set by the same or a different engraver, the result is almost always less interesting and the same may be said of the original subjects – as for instance, in *The Merry Wives* where Smirke's painting of Falstaff in Windsor Forest, engraved large, is superior to his different painting of the same scene reproduced in the text.

Midsummer Night's Dream, popular and therefore often illustrated, offers a fair example. Fuseli's two large plates in the Shakespeare Gallery were among his best works of crowded fantasy; neither of the illustrations for Boydell's edition succeeds in becoming airborne, though every effort was made – one was again from a Fuseli painting, the other by Schiavonetti after Reynolds, which should have provided a fine combination, but Reynolds's Robin

---

[8] *Illustrations of Shakespeare's Plays in the Seventeenth and Eighteenth Centuries*

Goodfellow looks no better than a backward infant with some deformity. There are exceptions: Josiah Boydell's pleasant design for the
plucking of red and white roses in *Henry the Sixth* reduces well, and
Middiman's smaller engraving after Hodges, of Jaques looking melancholy by the wooded stream in *As You Like It*, is almost as fine as the
same splendid work, also engraved by Middiman, in the Shakespeare
Gallery.

If Nicol during that Hampstead evening suggested to the Boydells
his ambitious scheme for illustrating Shakespeare, in their imagination it became divided into the gallery of historical paintings, a
partial failure in itself and by the bad fortune of European War; the
Shakespeare Gallery, a magnificent success in both Shakespeare
interpretation and the history of copper engraving; and, typographically splendid but as illustration disappointing, those nine volumes
which gained wide circulation – for they may still be found without
much difficulty – known always as the Boydell Shakespeare, which I
choose to view in my hybrid set of Stockdale's six large-paper quarto
volumes printed by Bensley, 'Heath's Edition', where the re-issued
Boydell plates were used as extra-illustration; for there the paper
remains unspotted, the impressions clear, with ample margins
though the original Boydell page was about three inches taller.

Apart from a general impression of narrative merit leading towards
Victorian book illustration, one detail deserves mention: Opie's
painting of Juliet discovered in her bed apparently dead, Lady Capu-
let receiving cold comfort from the Friar, engraved by Simon, appears
here and in the published text – but in this assembly is also a
'Variation', so called, engraved by Blake who chose to add several
distraught figures and make a few alterations. Simon's plate was
published in 1792, Blake's seven years later. Simon used stipple for
Juliet and her bedclothes; her hair rests on the hand of Paris; Blake,
using no stipple, hides the hand as part of Juliet's hair. He also ignores
a large foreground urn which Opie painted, and there are other
changes. Blake engraved several of Fuseli's designs for Chalmers'
1805 octavo edition, but his name is not generally associated with
Boydell's Shakespeare.

Among those who emulated the Boydell project, lacking his scale
or flair, were Heath (publisher and engraver) and Woodmason.
Heath's pleasant series, issued between 1802 and 1804, plundered
rather than commissioned by Stockdale, included oval title designs in
ornamental settings and full-page illustrations after Stothard, Hamilton and Fuseli. His style of engraving gave them all a placid unexcep-
tionable manner. Woodmason was quicker off the mark, publishing
Shakespeare plates in 1794 after bold but ineffectual compositions
by Fuseli, Hamilton, Peters and Opie. It became an established indus-

ILLUSTRATION   223

try. John Murray published a comparable series in 1817, after such artists as Wheatley, Northcote, Peters, Opie, Fuseli: nothing in any of this touched the miraculous Shakespeare Gallery prints.

The only remarkable set after that but within this period, advertised on the nine title pages as having 'a Series of Engravings, from Original Designs of Henry Fuseli, Esq. R.A. Professor of Painting', was the first Chalmers edition published by Rivington and others in 1805. Fuseli showed more interest in Shakespeare than other painters of the period, several publishers commissioned his work, but in these Chalmers volumes the illustrations were translated into poorish plates and one looks back with regret to elegant competence in such earlier engravers as Gravelot and the Van der Guchts. Fuseli's rhythmic interpretations, unsentimental and visionary, lack life in the routine performances of Cromeck, Bromley, Neagle and others; Walker's use of stipple in the plate for *All's Well* suggests on Helena's bare arms a serious case of measles; it is unfortunate that nothing better came from a fine idea. Two engravings by Blake, for *Henry the Eighth* and *Romeo and Juliet,* broke through routine to a sympathetic texture. Fuseli's courage in choosing the dramatic moment succeeds well in Blake's interpretation of the strange apothecary, to whom Romeo offers gold for deadly poison:

> Come hither, Man I see that thou art poor:
> Hold, there's forty ducats.

Fuseli's fantasies needed more than competence; Blake's excellence shows what might have been. One illustration was provided for each play.

7 The Fable and the Moral

Three women of contrasting backgrounds, all born in 1720, living through very different fortunes to old age, each produced in middle life formidable books of Shakespeare criticism. Charlotte Ramsay, daughter of an army officer serving in America, was sent back to England at the age of 15, escaped from insane and impossible conditions by marriage to an unremarkable man called Lennox, and made her way by sprightly writing. At the end of the century a few wretched grants from the Royal Literary Fund kept her alive. Elizabeth Robinson, inheriting a variety of estates, became doubly wealthy by marrying Edward Montagu, much older than herself, is remembered as the archetypal blue-stocking and died blind but still glorious. Elizabeth Griffith, Irish with a Welsh name, married into another Irish family called Griffith; the sentimental letters she and her fiancé exchanged during a long engagement were published and achieved popularity in their day.

Charlotte Lennox seems now perhaps the most impressive among the three, a brilliant and neglected woman of the 18th century. Her satirical novel *The Female Quixote* should be reprinted. Johnson befriended her, wrote the dedication for her Shakespeare book and celebrated publication of another novel by holding an all-night party, memorable from the weary account of it in the *Life* by Sir John Hawkins, during which bay leaves were used to decorate both the authoress and a large apple pie. Johnson in a fit of gaiety still takes us by surprise.

Her Shakespeare book in three small elegant volumes, 1753–4, appeared more than a decade before his edition. The long title is *Shakespear Illustrated: or the Novels and Histories, On which the Plays of Shakespear Are Founded, collected and translated from the Original Authors. With Critical Remarks*. Announced as a two-volume work in 1753, 'By the Author of the Female Quixote', a third followed the next year. This labour of learning and originality owed much to her tutor in Italian, Johnson's friend Baretti.

Elizabeth Montagu, best known of the three, brought out her *Essay on the Writings and Genius of Shakespear* in 1769, as an attack on Voltaire who had dared compare him with Corneille to the advantage of the latter. Mrs Montagu's title page mentions 'Greek and French Dramatic Poets' but the burden of her book lies in *Some Remarks Upon the Misrepresentations of Mons. de Voltaire*. One wonders how he dared face her again but she cheerfully attended his Shakespeare lecture in Paris many years later. Apart from the infant death of her only son, and a tumble downstairs in blind old age, it seems unlikely that Mrs. Montagu ever suffered misfortune. Her early-summer parties for chimney-sweep boys, in the garden of her palace in Portland Place, were evidence of a kind heart.

Mrs. Griffith hacked her way through a difficult life of literature and the stage, achieving some success as playwright with Garrick, hard at work and devoted to an ineffectual husband who withdrew at last to his family home in Ireland. Her Shakespeare book, dedicated to Garrick and published in 1775, is called *The Morality of Shakespeare's Drama Illustrated*. Though this substantial octavo runs to 528 pages, many of them were filled by Shakespeare rather than Mrs. Griffith.

Nicol Smith in his 1903 essay identified four themes which occupied 18th-century critics of Shakespeare:

> The first deals with his neglect of the so-called rules of the drama; the second determines what was the extent of his learning; the third considers the treatment of his text; and the fourth, more purely aesthetic, shows his value as a delineator of character.

From somewhere along this range he would perhaps have agreed that Shakespeare's treatment of his plots ('fables') and the presence or absence of moral purpose rose up as very visible peaks. 'The effecting certain moral purposes,' wrote Mrs. Montagu in her Introduction, 'by the representation of a fable, seems to have been the universal intention, from the first institution of the drama to this time.'

Johnson's worry about 'instruction' in the plays may be found in direct statement or in such concern as was expressed by his assessment of Iago's character: 'There is always danger lest wickedness conjoined with abilities should steal upon esteem, though it misses of approbation'; fortunately he could hate and despise Iago from first to last.

This stream of criticism, concerned with fable and moral, descended from the admirable and intemperate Thomas Rymer who wrote two short books with long titles, published as one in the last decade of the 17th century: *The Tragedies of the Last Age, Consider'd and Examin'd by the Practice of the Ancients, And by the Common sense of All Ages in a Letter to Fleetwood Shepheard Esq;* and *A Short View of Tragedy: It's Original, Excellency, and Corruption. With Some Reflections on Shakespear, and other Practitioners for the Stage.* Rymer's style was censorious and he had reason to be angry, for his father was hanged as a traitor and the family fortunes had disappeared. Though he is remembered as a defender of classical rules, both books express a reverence for dramatic tragedy as close to religion, and from that position he found modern examples trivial. The two themes, moral value and Shakespeare's treatment of a received plot, were Rymer's concern; but Johnson in mid-century took them over, dominating the three women who produced books on both.

Morality of one sort or another occupied Mrs. Griffith, though the word has different overtones now; one might think of her as searching for Shakespeare's perceptions, rather than his precepts. Morality also inspired Mrs. Montagu, together with an aggressive response to Voltaire which took the form of attack upon Corneille. Charlotte Lennox, too racy and rapid to be bothered with morals, provided impressive analysis of Shakespeare's treatment of his sources in fable and chronicle.

Rymer as a younger man had advocated Aristotle's rules for drama, in publishing an English translation of a work by Rapin, *Reflections on Aristotle's Treatise of Poesie;* his *Tragedies of the Last Age* came soon after that, and its second edition in 1692 formed the first part of a single work, with *A Short View of Tragedy* (1693) as its second part. The heart of the man is there, rather than in his Aristotelian defence which accompanied a translation. A charming literary device opened the first essay: as his friend could not come to town, Rymer resolved to console himself by reading a few recent English Tragedies, 'those *Master-pieces* of Wit, so renown'd every-where, and so edifying to the *Stage.* I mean the choicest and most applauded *English Tragedies* of this last age'. And it was not the presence or absence of classical unities which disappointed him:

> I had heard that the *Theater* was wont to be call'd the *School* of *Vertue;* and *Tragedy* a *Poem* for *Kings:* That they who first brought Tragedy to perfection, were made *Vice-Roys* and Governors of *Islands;* were honoured every-where with Statues of Marble, and Statues of Brass; were stil'd the *Wise Sophocles,* the *Wise Euripides* by God and Man, by Oracles and Philosophers.

Rymer's two essays embraced two opinions which Johnson later

A
Short View
OF
TRAGEDY;

It's *Original, Excellency,* and
Corruption.

WITH SOME

Reflections on *Shakespear*,
and other Practitioners for
the S T A G E.

By Mr. *Rymer*, Servant to their Majesties.
£55.

— *Hodieque manent vestigia ruris.* Hor.

L O N D O N,
Printed and are to be sold by *Richard Baldwin*, near
the Oxford *Arms* in *Warwick Lane*, and at
the *Black Lyon* in *Fleetstreet*, between
the two Temple-Gates. 1 6 9 3.

21 Title page for Rymer, 1693. [Actual height of *type* $5\frac{15}{16}$ inches]

demolished: on Tragi-comedy, accepted by Johnson as the poet of nature's rendering of life itself, and on theatrical improbability, as no more absurd than other aspects of dramatic experience. Johnson was not arguing against moral instruction in the theatre, but Rymer went back to strictest standards of the good old days:

> Tragedy was originally, with the Ancients, a piece of *Religious* worship, a part of their *Liturgy*. The Priests sung an Anthem to their god *Dionysus*, whilst the *Goat* stood at his Altar to be *sacrific'd:* And this was call'd the *Goat-song* or *Tragedy*.

And he failed to find that, in those plays he had chosen to console himself for the absence of Fleetwood Shepheard.

I could today be guilty of making similar objections against opera. Rymer, and Charlotte Lennox after him, were distracted by trivialities and improbabilities which shattered serious drama. The shallow audience was satisfied by *action*, he complained, no matter how silly. Where Shakespeare had changed the received story of Othello, it was 'always for the worse'. So much fuss about a handkerchief! In Act II the bantering talk struck him as intolerable,

> ...Jack-pudden farce between Iago and Desdemona, that runs on with all the little plays, jingle, and trash below the patience of any Countrey Kitchin-maid with her Sweet-heart. The Venetian *Donna* is hard put to't for pastime! And this is all, when they are newly got on shoar, from a dismal Tempest, and when every moment she might expect to hear her Lord (as she calls him) that she runs so mad after, is arriv'd or lost.

Fable, parable, allegory, these were serious matters with a mandate from highest history: Greece, Rome, the Bible. 'The wisest part of the World were always taken with the *Fables*, as the most delightful means to convey Instruction, and leave the strongest Impression on our Mind.' 'The Old Prophets could devise nothing higher for the future *Messiah*, than that every thing he should say would be a *Parable*.' Othello and Caesar he chose merely as examples of triviality in tragedy:

> Nothing is more odious in Nature than an improbable lye; And, certainly, never was any Play fraught, like this of *Othello*, with improbabilities.

One can only be grateful for Rymer's style in presenting his case for the prosecution. That Shakespeare lacked education was a familiar argument by the 1690s; that he also wrecked his fables by converting them to nonsense, and destroyed the religious character of tragedy, formed the foundation of critical debate for a hundred years. Rymer made his own contribution to the argument from Aristotle.

Charlotte Lennox, though perversely rejecting his strictures against *Othello*, went further than Rymer in criticizing Shakespeare's

treatment of the sources. It was highly original of her to have produced such a learned work as *Shakespear Illustrated* in the early
1750s. With Baretti's help she was able to translate from Cinthio,
Bandello, Boccaccio, Ariosto – the impression is given, at least, that
she translated from the Italian, rather than adapted from English
versions which had also been available to Shakespeare. 'How much
the Translation of the following Novels will add to the Reputation of
Shakespear,' we read in the Dedication written for her by Johnson,
'or take away from it, You, my Lord . . . must now determine.' The
title page describes these *Novels and Histories* as *Collected and
Translated from the Original Authors*.

How far the original plays and tales were used is not always clear
from her book. The *Menaechmi* of Plautus had been translated or
adapted and published in English in 1593, 'but not being able to
procure a copy of it, and being wholly unacquainted with the *Latin*
Tongue, I have turned Monsieur *Gueudiville's French* Translation of
the *Menaechmi* into *English* . . .'. That was clear, but when it came to
Hamlet no explanation for her English text of Saxo-Grammaticus
was offered. Chaucer and the old Chronicles gave no problem.

Whether she used cribs or received help sometimes or always or
often, this was a daring work to undertake; nobody had attempted
anything of the sort before; none except Rymer took such an uncompromising stance in opposition. Johnson is supposed to have suggested the task, as a form of research assistance when he planned his
own edition, but referred to it only three times in notes to those
volumes. The cheerful irreverence of her approach was out of tune
with mid-century editing.

Even in his anonymous contribution Johnson distanced himself a
little from the argument, declaring 'that a very small Part of the
Reputation of this mighty Genius depends upon the naked Plot, or
Story of his Plays'. That was a strange way to commend the book.
Again, '*Shakespear's* Excellence is not the Fiction of a Tale, but the
Representation of Life'. It reads more like his critical notice than her
Dedication.

Her arrangement with Baretti, who had brought the Johnson connection, was for mutual teaching of languages. It seems probable that
Charlotte Lennox could manage Italian after these lessons, that she
was a fast-learning pupil. Shakespeare also read Italian and French, it
is now believed; no Elizabethan translation of Cinthio existed. He and
his 18th-century critic held roughly the same position as to languages, except that she quite lacked Latin and Greek. Her translations which produced a little income in later life were always from
the French.

Mrs. Lennox occasionally mentioned a moral – events in Cinthio's

Shakeſpear Illuſtrated :

OR THE

NOVELS and HISTORIES,

On which the

PLAYS of SHAKESPEAR
Are Founded,

COLLECTED and TRANSLATED from the

ORIGINAL AUTHORS.

WITH

CRITICAL REMARKS.

In TWO VOLUMES.

BY THE

Author of the FEMALE QUIXOTE.

LONDON:

Printed for A. MILLAR in the Strand.
MDCCLIII.

22 Title page of Charlotte Lennox, 1753. A third volume appeared
in the next year. [Actual height of *type* $5\frac{1}{8}$ inches]

story (distorted by Shakespeare when he wrote *Measure for Measure*) 'convey Instruction equally useful and just'; but light satirical criticism of his treatment of a fable better suited her style. Cressida has 'the Character of a compleat Jilt'. In *Richard the Second*, when the Duke of York reports his son Aumerle's treason to the King, 'because there is something truly ludicrous in this very tragical Passage, I shall transcribe it'. *Twelfth Night* she found full of absurdities 'which might have been avoided, had the Characters as well as the Action been the same with the Novel'. Like Rymer, Charlotte Lennox could not accept the operatic improbabilities of Shakespeare, puzzled that in the *Comedy of Errors* he 'presents us with two Pairs of Twins instead of one'. 'One good beheading' was required in *Measure for Measure* rather than several weddings.

It is impossible now to judge these wayward responses to familiar scenes. Often her comment was sensible and just. *Hamlet* ends volume two; nobody would reject her final sentence, shrewd in its day:

> He stabs the King immediately upon the Information of his Treachery to himself! thus the Revenge becomes interested, and he seems to punish his Uncle rather for his own Death, than the murder of the King, his father.

This footnote perception was at the same time moral criticism. As *Shakespear Illustrated* descended from Rymer's two essays, it was characteristic of the author to defend sympathetically the one play, *Othello*, he had most attacked. Shakespeare made that fable *more* plausible, she suggests, by Iago's jealousy of Emilia; his changes to the character of Othello himself improved it; she takes issue with Rymer, who saw no human reason for Desdemona's love:

> Such Affections are not very common indeed; but a very few Instances of them prove that they are not impossible; and even in *England* we see some very handsome Women married to Blacks, where their Colour is less familiar than at *Venice:* besides the *Italian* Ladies are remarkable for such Sallies of irregular Passions.

Like any good debater, she was able with equal ease to take either side. More commonly, with a vigorous literal mind, the improbabilities are analysed. Shakespeare's rapid arrival at a dilemma in *Twelfth Night* is described thus:

> The Passion of *Olivia*, the Duke's Mistress, for the disguised Lady, is attended with Circumstances that make it appear highly improbable and ridiculous: She is represented as a noble and virtuous Lady, overwhelmed with Grief for the Death of a beloved Brother; her Grief indeed is of a very extraordinary Nature, and inspired her with strange Resolutions according to the Report of *Valentine*, the Duke's Servant . . .

> This sorrowful Lady, however makes her first Appearance in the Company of a Jester, with whom she is extremely diverted; and notwithstanding her Vow which we are told of in another Place, not to admit the Sight or Company of Men, she permits the Duke's Page to approach her, shews him her Face, and bandies Jests and smart Sentences with all the lively Wit of an airy Coquet.

In the late 20th century, most absurdities in Shakespeare accepted in the scheme and taught as holy logic to puzzled children, there is some relief in listening to this clear soprano voice above hymns of praise which became in her day conventional. *Shakespear Illustrated* is best when most destructive; among plots which struck the author as ridiculous one turns naturally to *The Winter's Tale* for her account of Hermione's return to life from statuary, the last act:

> The Novel makes the Wife of the jealous King die through Affliction for the Loss of her Son; *Shakespear* seems to have preserved her alive for the sake of her representing her own Statue in the last Scene; a mean and absurd Contrivance; for how can it be imagined that *Hermione*, a virtuous and affectionate Wife, would conceal herself during sixteen Years in a solitary House, though she was sensible that her repentant Husband was all that Time consuming away with Grief and Remorse for her Death; and what Reason could she have for chusing to live in such a miserable Confinement, when she might have been happy in the Possession of her Husband's Affection and have shared his Throne: how ridiculous also in a great Queen, on so interesting an Occasion, to submit to such Buffoonery as standing on a Pedestal, motionless, her Eyes fixed, and at last to be conjured down by this magical Command of *Paulina* . . .
>
> To bring about this Scene, ridiculous as it is, *Shakespear* has been guilty of many Absurdities, which would be too tedious to mention, and which are too glaring to escape the Observation of the most careless Reader.
>
> The Novel has nothing in it half so low and improbable as this Contrivance of the Statue; and indeed wherever *Shakespear* has altered or invented, his *Winter's Tale* is greatly inferior to the old paltry Story that furnished him with the Subject of it.

Such fearless heresy still reads well. Had there been laws of critical blasphemy Charlotte Lennox would have been guilty without right of appeal. Though there is now no way of measuring the help she received from Baretti, he surely provided a little specialized knowledge about the precise meaning of *Cittadina* in Cinthio, which Rymer had taken to be a simple Citizen;

> but the *Italians* by that Phrase mean a Woman of Quality. If they were, for Example, to speak of a Woman of the middle Rank in *Rome*, they would say, *Una Romana;* if of a noble Lady, *Una Cittadina Romana:* So in *Venice* they call a simple Citizen *Una Venitiana;* but a Woman of Quality, *Una Cittadina Venitiana.* That Simplicity in the Manners of

Desdemona, which Mr. *Rymer* calls Folly and Meanness of Spirit is the Characteristic of Virtue and Innocence.

Mrs. Lennox found correction irresistible, whether attending to Shakespeare or Rymer; in this instance a short session with Baretti remains almost audible.

The method had its defects. She had no ear for great passages as justifying incredible situations, only for story and character. The inadequacy of all three *Henry the Sixth* plays, and splendours within imperfection of *Troilus* or *Measure for Measure*, seem alike to have passed unnoticed through her brain which searched chiefly for folly in narrative. Long parallel passages from the Chronicles are printed with minimal comment. Her comprehension of *Hamlet* was quite off the rails, in seeing Laertes as a mirror image of the Prince:

> Thus has *Shakespear*, undesignedly, no doubt given us two Heroes instead of one in this Play; the only Difference between them is that one of them is a Prince, the other a Nobleman, and but for this slight Distinction the Play might have been as well called the *Tragedy of Laertes* as *Hamlet*.

Her summaries of the plays were perfectly lucid, her style so informal as to seem like conversation; occasionally a critical comment shows perception which confirms that her work should not be ignored. Here is an instance from her judgement of *Henry the Eighth* as a work of art, considering Catherine and the Cardinal:

> The Fate of this Queen, or that of Cardinal *Wolsey*, each singly afforded a Subject for Tragedy. *Shakespear*, by blending them in the same Piece, has destroyed the Unity of his Fable, divided our Attention between them; and, by adding many other inconnected Incidents, all foreign to his Design, has given us an irregular historical Drama, instead of a finished Tragedy.

But searching for absurdity is the exercise of a literal mind. If *Macbeth* was a play about certainty built upon prophetic fantasy, Mrs. Lennox dived into the shallow end by complaining that after Dunsinane woods had moved the King should have known the witches' final forecast would also fail him. Her writing lacked cross-reference to tension in performance, but students needing a break from Theobald and Warburton will find it in these three lively volumes by Mrs. Lennox.

*   *   *

Elizabeth Montagu's Shakespeare book shows a different sort of eccentricity, in mingling many fine observations and instances with aggressive distaste for Voltaire, Corneille and any notions of French merit which could compare with her idol. Apart from francophobia, inherited from the argument about Aristotle's rules for drama, her focus searched for that other part of Rymer's criticism concerned with morality in Shakespeare. She appears as witness for the defence, agreeing with Pope that genius inhabits a higher sphere than rules, being 'of a bold enterprizing nature, ill adapted to the formal restraints of critic institutions'; that 'a dramatic poet, whose chief interest it is to please the people, should, more than any other writer, conform himself to their humour; and appear most strongly infected with the faults of the times, where they be such as belong to unpolished, or corrupted taste'.

She could laugh at Falstaff – they all did, perhaps more than we do now – but held a moral opinion quite alien to modern playwrights, that evil makes poor entertainment:

> It is strange that a dramatic writer should not have studied human nature enough to perceive [she wrote of Corneille] that the only character which cannot interest upon the stage, is that which is mean, low and contemptible.

It was beyond reproach to declare, though one wonders if the leader of salon life believed, that 'only graceful nature and decent customs give proper subject for imitation'.

Perhaps an advocate is best in passing beyond his brief, throwing out some perception he had never intended to express, as someone starting a novel or letter may find his pen takes charge. There is such a moment in her chapter on Dramatic Poetry, when Mrs. Montagu gave three instances (from *Lear, King John, Macbeth*) of moments which penetrated and moved her more than would have been possible through mere narrative. Lear hopes his daughter may feel

> How sharper than a serpent's tooth it is,
> To have a thankless child.

Constance cannot accept consolation from the legate after learning that Arthur her son was dead:

> He speaks to me that never had a son.

After murdering Duncan, Macbeth thinks of the grooms who lay guarding him:

> One cry'd, God bless us! and Amen! the other;
> As they had seen me with these hangman's hands,
> Listening their fear. I could not say, Amen,
> When they did say, God bless us!

After 200 years one is touched by her understanding of those moments, which inspired the discovery (transcending morality and

AN ESSAY

ON THE

WRITINGS AND GENIUS

OF

SHAKESPEAR,

COMPARED WITH THE

GREEK AND FRENCH DRAMATIC POETS.

WITH

SOME REMARKS

Upon the MISREPRESENTATIONS of

Monſ. de VOLTAIRE.

LONDON:

Printed for J. DODSLEY, Pall-mall ; Meſſ. BAKER and LEIGH, York-ſtreet, Covent-garden ; J. WALTER, Charing-croſs ; T. CADELL, in the Strand ; and J. WILKIE, Nº 71. St. Paul's Church-yard.

M.DCC.LXIX.

23 Title page for Elizabeth Montagu, 1769. [Actual height of *type* 6½ inches]

rules) that Shakespeare 'could throw his soul into the body of another man'.

From time to time and to fill a few pages Mrs. Montagu took to printing long passages and pointing out the beauties, but generally her concern rests with undefined moralities (when she is not chastising Voltaire or Corneille) which only occasionally discover obscenity as in *Henry the Fourth*:

> Every scene in which Doll Tearsheet appears is indecent, and therefore not only indefensible but inexcusable. There are delicacies of decorum in one age unknown to another age, but whatever is immoral is equally blamable in all ages, and every approach to obscenity is an offence for which wit cannot atone, nor the barbarity or corruption of the times excuse.

Morality was never an entertaining theme for literary criticism, but the 18th century commonly took a position which is often supposed to belong to the 19th. This classical stiff-lip descended through Rymer to Johnson and most others except Mrs. Lennox; they dealt with the convention in their own ways; Elizabeth Montagu balanced its boredom by wit at the expense of the French. Morality remained a fixture behind their comment, as religious faith could be assumed in theological debate. The kind of philosophical statement which supported her Shakespeare essay must strike anyone now as uninteresting, and generally false.

> The poet collects, as it were, into a focus those truths, which lie scattered in the diffuse volume of the historian, and kindles the flame of virtue, while he shews the miseries and calamities of vice.

It was because Lear showed the very opposite that Tate provided his different ending.

Falstaff was the puzzling one because they found him irresistible and the discussion continued from Maurice Morgann to C.S. Lewis. Gluttonous, corpulent, cowardly, he was 'ridiculous without folly', inspiring enough contempt to defeat the dangers of infection. It was a questionable argument.

> The admirable speech upon honour would have been both indecent and dangerous from any other person. We must every where allow his wit is just, his humour genuine, and his character perfectly original, and sustained through every scene, in every play, in which it appears.

Of these three intellectual women Mrs. Montagu was probably the most accomplished, assisted at every stage of her life by wealth and well-satisfied ambition. At the age of 18 she had defined the qualities of a husband: 'He should have a great deal of sense and prudence to direct me and instruct me, much wit to divert me, beauty to please me, good humour to indulge me in the right, and reprove me gently when I am in the wrong; money enough to afford me more than I can want, and as much as I can wish.'

It was not easy for a woman in her position to publish upon intellectual themes, 'especially if they invade those regions of litera-ture' (as she wrote in a letter to her father) 'which the men are desirous to reserve to themselves'. She apologized for telling him nothing of the book before it appeared upon an intimidating scene.

> Mr. Pope our great poet, the Bishop of Gloucester our great Critick, and Dr. Johnson our great Scholar, having already given their criticisms upon Shakespear, there was a degree of presumption in pretending to meddle with a subject they had already treated – sure to incur their envy if I succeeded tolerably well, their contempt if I did not.

She succeeded tolerably well, but it might have been a dull book without the critical passages on Voltaire as translator, and Corneille as playwright. Her own translations from Corneille were skilfully ridiculous, and her excellent French enabled her to point out a few howlers in Voltaire's rendering of Shakespeare. Here is Mrs. Montagu enjoying herself at the expense of Corneille:

> It is a common error in the plan of Corneille's tragedies, that the interest of the piece turns upon some unknown person, generally a haughty princess; so that instead of the representation of an important event, and the characters of illustrious persons, the business of the drama is the love-intrigue of a termagent lady, who, if she is a Roman, insults the Barbarians, if she is a Barbarian, braves the Romans, and even to her lover is insolent and fierce. Were such a person to be produced on our theatre, she would be taken for a mad poetess escaped from her keepers in Bedlam, who, fancying herself a queen, was ranting, and delivering her mandates in rhyme upon the stage.

The Reverend William Dodd is remembered (apart from forgery) as author or editor of the work which introduced Shakespeare to Goethe; it is equally worth recalling that in the view of her French biographer[1], Elizabeth Montagu 'opened the eyes of French critics to Voltaire's shortcomings as an English scholar, and that Shakespeare's cause profited by his adversary's partial loss of credit'.

*   *   *

By the last quarter of the 18th century it was difficult for any outsider to think up a new theme in appreciation of Shakespeare: Dodd had chosen his beauties, Mrs. Montagu written on his genius, and only the very learned could dare to edit. Mrs. Griffith showed ingenuity in

---

[1] R. Huchon, *Mrs. Montagu 1720–1800, An Essay*, London 1907

isolating or illustrating his morality for a public which tended or pretended to examine drama for instruction. Inspired by Johnson and Mrs. Montagu, she says, Shakespeare is her philosopher. Her book might have been called 'Moral Beauties' of Shakespeare.

As a possible publishing idea this was acceptable, though hardly amusing, and so it remains; and it would not be worth more than passing reference, but for her own escape from morality into wider appreciation of Shakespeare's perceptions, as Mrs. Montagu had also been moved by those moments when he could 'throw his soul into the body of another man'. When these several abstracts meet (genius, beauty, perception) Elizabeth Griffith can focus on some small comment missed in rapid reading. Perhaps no other critic found occasion to quote what was said by Orlando's bullying brother Oliver in the first act of *As You Like It*, but Mrs. Griffith observed him in Scene III:

> The last speech, here, though it presents us with no moral, I cannot pass by without remarking, that it seems to be a perfect description of our author's own character. Oliver, speaking of Orlando, his younger brother, says, 'Yet he's gentle; ne⸴er schooled, and yet learned; full of noble device; and of all sorts enchantingly beloved'.

She was particularly good in this play, which supplies ample fuel for her theme; and if Jaques reflecting upon 'that poor and broken bankrupt' the

> sequestered stag,
> That from the hunter's aim had ta'en a hurt,

caused her to wonder how anyone 'could read the above description, and *eat venison*, on the same day', she made a meal of its country-against-court moralities.

Other plays proved less tractable for her purpose; not much moral beauty to be ferreted from *Midsummer Night's Dream* for instance, and *Merchant of Venice* brought her to the brink of despair in such voyages of discovery:

> I shall take no further notice of the want of a moral fable, in the rest of these Plays; but shall proceed to observe upon the characters and dialogue, without interruption, for the future.

In *Measure for Measure*, on the other hand, her approach was impeded by no such embarrassment as has upset more recent editors; severe upon Claudio for his fear of death, well able to accept Isabella's outraged response. 'More than our brother is our chastity' offered no problem to Mrs. Griffith, and her cleaning of old varnish from that picture seems now to have been good criticism.

In *Twelfth Night* 'all the moral that I have been able to extract from

THE

MORALITY

OF

SHAKESPEARE's DRAMA

ILLUSTRATED.

By Mrs. GRIFFITH.

Ille per extentum funem mihi poſſe videtur
Ire poëta, meum qui pectus inaniter angit ;
Irritat, mulcet, falſis terroribus implet,
Ut magus ; et modò me Thebis, modò ponit Athenis.
Epiſt. Lib. 2. E. 1. l 210.   Hor.

LONDON:

Printed for T. CADELL, in the Strand.

MDCCLXXV.

24 Title page for Mrs Griffith, 1775. [Actual height of *type* $6\frac{7}{8}$ inches]

this Piece' ends with Act III; and she quite missed the point of *Love's Labour's Lost*, fastening upon the high sentiments which open that play, and which it was Shakespeare's excellent purpose to explode:

> A Laudable ambition for fame [she says] which inspires every person whose character is above contempt, is beautifully described and distinguished from false heroism, in this place.

As for *The Taming of the Shrew*, 'the business of this Play, declared by the title of it, is, I fear, a work rather of *discipline* than of *precept'*, so 'we are to expect but few helps from it toward the enrichment of this collection'.

The trouble with such a wide field of prairie farming (528 pages include whole scenes quoted) is that profundities were often levelled with the commonplace, for impeccable morality may be carried in boring verse. Elizabeth Griffith was not less likely to praise dullness than to ignore magnificence, when both were relevant to her earnest theme. Quoting three unremarkable lines from Titus,

> My faction if thou strengthen with thy friends,
> I will most thankful be – And thanks, to men
> Of noble minds, is honourable meed.

she offered the excessive comment:

> There is something truly great in the above sentiment, and shews the speaker of it worthy of being an emperor.

Yet, for example, that marvellous and most directly moral passage in *Troilus* beginning

> Time hath my lord a wallet at his back
> Wherein to place alms for oblivion

passed her by.

It would be wrong to ignore Mrs. Griffith of the long engagement, whose book was not adequately described in its title but remains memorable for private and surprising perceptions which make one ask who would have paused at *that*, had she not pointed it out. *The Morality of Shakespeare's Drama Illustrated* becomes almost a manual for illustrators, a succession of vignettes which she observed. Once in *The Merchant of Venice* her thought suggested it:

> The description here given of the parting of two friends, would make a beautiful and affecting subject for the pencil:
> *Salamio*   And even there, his eye being big with tears,
>   Turning his face, he put his hand behind him,
>   And, with affection wond'rous sensible,
>   He wrung Bassanio's hand: and so they parted.

'The death of Cardinal Beaufort' painted by Reynolds was not far distant, a better known instance of Shakespeare's morality illustrated.

Index

241